178

SUNDAY SCHOOL
CHANGES
EVERYTHING

Your Church's **Best Opportunity** to Reach the Next Generation for Christ

HENRIETTA C. MEARS

Published by Gospel Light
Ventura, California, U.S.A.
www.gospellight.com
Printed in the U.S.A.

Library of Congress Cataloging-in-Publication Data
Mears, Henrietta C. (Henrietta Cornelia), 1890-1963.
Sunday school changes everything : your church's best opportunity
to reach the next generation for Christ / Henrietta C. Mears.
p. cm.
Includes bibliographical references and index.
ISBN 978-0-8307-6407-5 (alk. paper)
1. Sunday schools. I. Title.
BV1521.3.M43 2012
268—dc23
2012015010

Rights for publishing this book outside the U.S.A. or in non-English languages
are administered by Gospel Light Worldwide, an international not-for-profit
ministry. For additional information, please visit www.glww.org, email
info@glww.org, or write to Gospel Light Worldwide, 1957 Eastman Avenue,
Ventura, CA 93003, U.S.A.

To order copies of this book and other Gospel Light products in
bulk quantities, please contact us at 1-800-446-7735.

Contents

Foreword

BY DR. THOM S. RAINER

I met Henrietta Mears shortly after I became a Christian. Okay, I didn't meet her in person, but I was introduced to her book *What the Bible Is All About*. That resource became a constant companion to me, alongside my Bible.

Henrietta Mears became my heroine.

The story of Henrietta Mears as Christian Education Director at First Presbyterian Church in Hollywood, California, is nothing short of miraculous. She built one of the largest Sunday Schools in the world. She wrote a curriculum that was in such demand that she founded a publishing company. Among her students were Richard C. Halverson and Bill Bright. Among those she influenced profoundly is Billy Graham.

One of my favorite quotes comes from Henrietta Mears: "There is no magic in small plans. When I consider my ministry, I think of the world. Anything less than that would not be worthy of Christ nor of His will for my life." Now we have the opportunity to hear from Henrietta Mears again. In this never-before published book, *Sunday School Changes Everything*, she demonstrates her passion for and knowledge of Sunday School.

Somewhere in the midst of the conversation, confusion and debate, the value of Sunday School has been lost. Do you realize that a person in a Sunday School class is five times more likely to be assimilated and discipled in a church than a person who only attends worship? Did you know that Sunday School increases biblical literacy and encourages personal Bible study? Are you aware that churches with the healthiest Sunday School organizations are likely to be the healthiest churches evangelistically?

The evidence of the efficacy of Sunday School is clear, if not overwhelming. Yet for many church leaders, it's not edgy or cool. It therefore is devalued and minimized.

Henrietta Mears will bring back your passion for Sunday School. Although she has been with the Lord for a half a century, her words are fresh and powerful. Read this book and be inspired. Read this book and be educated. Read this book and be challenged. Read this book, implement the principles, and see how Sunday School can truly change the world.

Dr. Thom S. Rainer
President and CEO, LifeWay Christian Resources

THE CHALLENGE

Reconsider Your Sunday School's Potential

BY DAMON DELILLO

I don't spend a lot of time thinking about the way we used to do things. As anyone in ministry knows, every church has plenty of people who remind us of how it "has always been done." Instead, I spend most of my time thinking about where we are going and how we are going to get there. Things such as, *How are we going to reach the families who never consider church a relevant option? What can we do to prepare young people for what they will experience in college? How can we help families make Jesus the center of their homes?* When I ask myself these questions, I usually don't find the answer in *how it has always been done.*

While the original content of this book was written nearly 60 years ago (it has been updated to reflect current trends and changes in technology), you won't find a book about how things have always been done or how to re-create the Sunday School of the past. What you will find is a *challenge* to reconsider the purpose of what you do on Sunday morning. Whether you call what you do Sunday School, small groups, Bible fellowship or something else, *Sunday School Changes Everything* will provide you with a set of principles for building ministry that will change lives. It was written by someone who reinvented Sunday School when "how it was always done" was no longer working.

When Henrietta Mears began her ministry in Hollywood, California, in the 1930s, she was facing several very real challenges:

- Sixty percent of children were not attending a church of any sort.
- Fewer than 15 percent of children who attended Sunday School ever made a decision to follow Jesus.
- Youth in their early college years were walking away from faith at an unprecedented rate, never to return.

- Church attendance across the United States was experiencing decline instead of growth.

Today, the Church is facing similar challenges. Year after year, church attendance in mainline denominations is declining. It is well documented that young adults are walking away from the faith during the first few years of college; the question is whether it is 60 or 80 percent who are walking away and whether some of those come back or not. That 60 to 80 percent figure represents children who came to our churches; however, we know there are many thousands of kids in our own communities (nearly 45 million nationwide) who never come to our churches at all.

In the midst of these challenges, we seem to be experiencing an in-house debate among ministry leaders that Elmer Towns has summarized as a sort of "identity crisis." There is a great deal of discussion about who the constituency of our Sunday morning programs really is. Is it religious education for the children of the faithful? Or outreach to the unchurched? Or is it discipleship and evangelism?

The book you are holding in your hands is part of the answer to this debate. It is based on years of ministry best practices that have the potential to solve some of our more pressing issues, such as how we can reach the next generation and prepare kids for a life-long relationship with Jesus Christ. It represents a set of ideas that helped Henrietta Mears lead a Sunday School that grew from 450 to more than 4,000 in just three short years. In this book, you will find a fearless appraisal of the state of ministry and recommendations for what needs to be done to change it, but more importantly you will discover that the Church is *still* perfectly suited to carry out the mission that God has given it.

Sunday School has the potential to change everything because it introduces people to Jesus. However, as an institution it must always be changing to meet the changing needs of each generation. That is uncomfortable for some of us, because it means that what we've always done might not always work, and what is currently working now may not work in the future. We must look afresh at ways to engage the next generation. According to Henrietta Mears, we must be willing to "adopt and adapt every method we can discover to make [the next generation] feel that Christ is more necessary than life itself and that His claims are paramount!"

As you read this book, you will find several examples of what Henrietta Mears believed were unchanging ingredients of successful ministry. We believe those ingredients can be boiled down into five main categories: (1) Jesus, (2) the Bible, (3) relationships, (4) a comprehensive plan, and (5) life change. We have highlighted many of these ideas using the following icons:

 Meet Jesus: Life-changing ministry begins with a commitment to one thing: "winning people to Christ and a commitment of life to Him." Ministry must lead people to Jesus. That's what we are all about. We need to reaffirm this today just as much as we did in the past.

 The Bible: The Bible is one story—the story of Jesus. We believe that every story in the Bible points to Jesus, and so should Sunday School. Successful ministries teach people the Bible in ways that are relevant to each age and stage of life and in ways that are sensitive to the spiritual seasons God has hard-wired into all of us.

 Relationships: Successful ministries recognize that spiritual growth happens best in the context of close personal relationships. It's about people leading other people to Jesus.

 Complete Plan: Whatever you do, whether it is small groups, Sunday School or Bible fellowship, great things begin with great plans. Successful ministries have a plan from birth through adult.

 Life Change: The goal of ministry is changed lives. It is as much about the here and now as it is about the future and eternity.

Your church can have world-changing, life-transforming ministry. As Henrietta Mears wrote, "Hollywood is not the most ideal spot on earth in which to build a large and spiritual Sunday School, but God has seen fit to make it so. . . . If it can be done in Hollywood, it can be done anywhere."

Damon DeLillo
Family Ministry Director, Ventura, California

PREFACE

Build an Effective Sunday School

To myriads of outsiders, Hollywood is a synonym for "sinfulness"—it is the Mecca of mimics, the fane of follies. It is the city of make-believe, a place of unrealities, the capital of the world. But residents of this beautiful city know the mountains and the sea, heaven's blue-arched dome and eternal sunshine. Forests and flowering deserts have lured many saints as well as sinners here, and it is well to remember that church spires overshadow theaters and studios.

One of the mightiest powers for righteousness amid this blend of good and evil is the First Presbyterian Church of Hollywood, teeming with youth. The 1930s through the early 1950s saw a chapter from the romance of the modern Sunday School, which I will tell you about in this book. Many illustrations in this book will be taken from this school because I was at the heart of this work during all those years. This book is written for every pastor and Sunday School teacher, for every Director of Christian Education and for every Sunday School leader or youth worker. This book is for you, because the young are our greatest asset!

So many people feel that there is magic involved in building a large Sunday School. They beg you to divulge your tricks. They write and ask you to put down in a few words how it can be done. The answer can be summed up in one word: WORK! It is spelled as Webster spells it: W-O-R-K, and it means just what he says it does. Wishful longing will never take the place of hard work. There are certain things that are necessary if you wish to build a better Sunday School. If a church is really determined to increase its Sunday School, it will find ways and means to accomplish its purpose—and it will *work* to reach its goals.

Aside from work as a necessary ingredient to growing a Sunday School, a greater faith in a wonderful God is also of primary importance. Jesus said He could not do many things among the people in

His day, because of their unbelief. The building of a Sunday School is a long road, and there are many turns and bumps along the road, but it is worth it! Working out the plans that I present in the following chapters will, I believe, bring results both numerically and spiritually to any Sunday School. This book is a true story!

Start with a Plan

How do you start a Sunday School? The first thing you should do is sit down and make a plan. Dream of what you would want for your Sunday School. You must plan today for what you want your school to be five years from now. Write down the improvements you would like to make in your organization, in the teaching staff, in the lessons and in spirit. You cannot set an aim for your Sunday School today unless you know what you want it to be 10 years from now.

Every successful leader must plan the work and work the plan. And the plan must be sound. In fact, your achievement can be no greater than the boundaries of your plan. Christ left His disciples with a definite plan in Acts 1:8. A leader who moves by guesswork without practical, definite plans is like a ship without a rudder. Sooner or later he or she will land on the rocks.

Every successful leader must plan
the work and work the plan.
And the plan must be sound.

When I came into this field, I sat down one evening and wrote in a notebook all that I wished Sunday School to be. A closely graded program, teaching material that would present Christ and His claims in every lesson, a trained teaching staff, a new education building, choirs, clubs, a camp program, a missionary vision, youth trained for the hour—all these were among the desires expressed. All have come to fruition—and many more.

Draw a blueprint, as it were, by putting down in writing what you would like your Sunday School to be so that it can minister effectively to your community. A plan is essential for building. This is your first task!

To Reach People

The size of your Sunday School is not necessarily measured by the numbers on its roll but by all of the young people in your church that should belong to it, whether they be few or many. Some of us who have large Sunday Schools cannot boast of our numbers, but rather we must be sobered by the fact that we are not reaching the hundreds of still unreached in our communities. Your success depends on the percentage you are reaching, not on the numbers you have on your rolls.

Your success depends on the percentage you are reaching, not on the numbers you have on your rolls.

For a Common Goal

Do not be discouraged as you read this book and say, "Oh, these plans are for a large school. Ours is only small." All Sunday Schools—large and small—are alike and must be put to the same tests as to efficiency. All Sunday Schools have the same main constituency: the youth of today. All have the same goal and objective: winning people to Christ and a commitment of life to Him. All are maintained by voluntary financial support—there is no taxation that supports our efforts. All Sunday Schools must be graded, departmentalized and carefully administered. Remember, one teacher and one child can start a class, but you plan for expansion as you reach more and more of the unchurched. The Sunday School is a lay movement. For the most part it is the people's project.

All have the same goal and objective: winning people to Christ and a commitment of life to Him.

In Any Place

Hollywood is not the most ideal spot on earth in which to build a large and spiritual Sunday School, but God has seen fit to make it so. Here He has planted a mighty Sunday School whose motto is "Christ Supreme." We humbly believe that men and women will say, as they look upon this modern miracle of a great Sunday School in the heart of the city of make-believe, "If it can be done in Hollywood, it can be done anywhere." The greatest competition the world can offer is but a stone's throw from the doors of this edifice. The young are on the auction block, being sold to the highest bidder in this city, yet our Sunday School is filled with throngs of happy young people.

Evaluate Your School

Develop tests to prove the efficiency of your school. Be honest in your evaluation!

1. Do You Count Your Numbers?

Discover whether you are reaching every unchurched boy or girl in your community. Don't be afraid to count numbers, as long as they are the numbers of those you still plan to reach. Numbers were counted on the day of Pentecost, and the number saved that day was 3,000! Christ counted the 5,000 whom He fed. Numbers stand for people for whom Christ died. Let us believe that any church in any community in the United States can grow! We can grow bigger and better. The best way to reach the untold numbers of unchurched boys and girls in the country is to reach the ones in your community! This may mean that you will have to begin by making a canvass of your neighborhood.

2. Do You Teach the Word of God?

The Bible is the living seed that brings life. We are born, fed, enlightened, equipped for service, and kept by the Word of God. All young people must learn and practice how to use this Chart and Compass. Are you presenting the Word of God to each life and heart? Other things may be good, but this is the best. Always specialize in *the best!*

Are you presenting the Word of God to each life and heart?

3. Do You Win for Christ?

Are boys and girls introduced to a living Savior in your Sunday School? This is paramount. Childhood is the time that God has made hearts tender. Fill the hearts of children at an early age with the knowledge of a personal Savior who has a plan for their lives. Carry out every means of winning them to Christ. Every attempt to enlist youth in the service of the Lord and all programs that deepen the spiritual life and strengthen the faith of youth are necessary. Do this before a treacherous world enmeshes them in its soul-destroying standards of living.

Carry out every means of winning them to Christ. . . . If children are not brought to Christ while they are still young, the work of evangelizing them becomes more and more difficult.

If boys and girls are not won for Christ and built into the church life, they will leave Sunday School and likely be lost to the Church forever. If children are not brought to Christ while they are still

young, the work of evangelizing them becomes more and more difficult. Adolescents who are not won to Christ will likely turn from the
Church and enter a world filled with everything that will draw them
further and further away from Christ. They will build their lives without God and the Church. When young people who have not taken a
stand for Christ reach college, they are tremendously difficult to win
back to the Church, because they have learned to live without Christ.

It is good for us to remember that the high water mark of conversion comes before the age of 14. After people reach 20 years of age, the
likelihood of accepting Jesus approaches zero. Time is of the essence
in our Sunday Schools.

4. Do You Enlist Youth for Service?

Are you helping youngsters find God's plan for their lives? We let
them go out on an uncharted sea, but they must know that they are
each accountable to God for his or her life and that the Lord has a
plan for him or her in this world. What is more exciting than finding
God's plan in one's life? Several hundred young people from our college department have found God's call on their lives and are today
engaged in full-time church vocations, both at home and abroad.
Hundreds more have found that God's will has led them to profes-
sions and businesses and the ministry of teaching. Christ has all commissioned officers in His service.

5. Do You Have Adequate Room?

We must have a place for every child, and a child in his or her place if
we are to hold and build. Look over your facility. Are the rooms attractive to the young people in your community? Sometimes a can of
paint will work wonders. Curtains will divide a large room into individual classrooms. With a bit of carpentry work, basements can be
converted into department rooms. Look over what you have and be
daring in your thinking.

When our Sunday School grew from about 450 to 4,000 in the
space of three and a half years, we had to build screens in rooms; use
curtains for partitions; use every available space—under steps, in clos-
ets and in offices; buy adjoining apartments and houses. We grew our
Sunday School out of what was at hand. Eventually, we built an edu-

cational plant to meet our needs. This was a dream come true. Nothing is so thrilling as to have to knock down partitions, build on an annex, change a porch into a room, or pitch a tent! Anything that indicates growth thrills people!

6. Do You Have a Schedule for All that You Offer?
It is our duty to do all we can to introduce every generation to Christ. In order to do this when I was at First Presbyterian of Hollywood, teachers conducted a highly graded, carefully administered Sunday School in 18 departments every Sunday. During the church hour, a primary church, a junior church and two nursery groups for preschool children were in session. All the adult classes met at 11 o'clock. And our youth choir attended the 9:30 service and then enjoyed the privilege of a study hour during the 11 o'clock service.

It is our duty to do all we can to introduce every generation to Christ.

Many churches today are finding it necessary to have a double service on Sunday morning in order to schedule all that they offer. This enables them to stagger the components of their Sunday School program.

Study your program and then create a schedule that accommodates it.

7. Do You Have a Balanced Program?
As you study the program of your Sunday School, is it merely an assortment of ideas, or do you have a comprehensive, long-range plan? Master the art of program making. Your success will increase as you further define and balance your program. Listen to a radio broadcast and note how each minute counts. Balance your program. Don't run to extremes. See that you put the proper emphasis on attendance, worship, teaching, stewardship, missions, social life *and* evangelism.

Strive always for a successful balanced program, remembering that nothing succeeds like success. Everyone likes to belong to a growing concern.

 Strive always for a successful balanced program, remembering that nothing succeeds like success. Everyone likes to belong to a growing concern.

Improve All Areas

How can you build a better Sunday School? Few who read this book will feel as if their Sunday School is as good as they can make it. While it would be impossible to estimate the good that has been done for Sunday School through the years by the great army of faithful, unpaid and, for the most part, unappreciated workers, at the same time there is an enormous need to improve our methods and plans if we are to build a school that meets the needs of the youth of each succeeding generation.

Start with Responsibility

Too long we have blamed youth for not being interested in Christ and the Church when the fault is really ours. Too often, we have presented our glorious Christ in a drab, uninteresting way. The world constantly studies the psychology of the young in order to discover what will interest and hold them. The world has something to sell to this generation and does everything it can to make its offerings attractive. Let us, as Christian leaders, study the situation of our young in their relationship to the Church and look at that relationship from their viewpoint. Let us adopt and adapt every method we can discover to make the young feel that Christ is more necessary than life itself and that His claims are paramount!

Let us adopt and adapt every method we can discover to make the young feel that Christ is more necessary than life itself and that His claims are paramount!

Recognize the Needs

The following needs are some of the subjects that will be discussed in this book.

We need greater numbers in our Sunday Schools. The losses in the past years have been shocking. We are not reaching the young. And too many children in America receive no religious training at all. Go out into your neighborhood and ring doorbells. Go out into the housing developments and the apartment complexes, the main roads and the side roads, and compel the young to come in.

We need better equipment. "Just anything" is not sufficient to build a Sunday School. Enlarged quarters, separate classrooms and better equipment should be the goals. Modern school buildings offer youth everything today. The poorly equipped Sunday School is in sad contrast to it. Keep improving your equipment.

We need more time devoted to youth. One hour on Sunday is not sufficient. Add extracurricular activities for the days in the week.

We need better teaching, which means trained teachers. Ninety percent of the success of any Sunday School rests with the teachers. The Bible is the most poorly taught book in the world. If we do not make it attractive, the young person will leave Sunday School and be lost to the church forever.

We need better literature—a return to the teaching of the Word. This is the textbook that God has given us. The spiritual illiteracy of America is appalling. Our youth know little of God's Word.

We need organization. A Sunday School will not run itself. There must be goals set and aims established to accomplish what we desire. Are you building a chicken coop or a skyscraper? Anything will do in your Sunday School if a chicken coop is your goal. But dreams transformed into mighty plans are necessary before a skyscraper can be built.

We need more up-to-date methods to appeal to modern youth.

Think Positively

It is not our intention to deal with the theory of teaching psychology as such. The bookstores are filled with excellent texts along that line. This book will present some practical and workable plans that, when applied, have built one of America's largest Sunday Schools and have brought new life into literally hundreds of others. With every statement and every suggestion I offer, I say, "It can be done because it has been done." You can do it!

It is our duty to Christianize every generation. We can only save America by saving her children. It seems like an impossible task to reach those who are untouched by any church. But it can be done. Christ has commissioned us to do it. It is the task of the Church. There are enough churches over this great land of ours, not only to carry it out, but also to do the task successfully.

Christ told us where to begin: "Suffer the little children to come unto me" (Mark 10:14). Most of our time is spent in trying to urge men and women to come. Jesus began His movement with the young—yes, with *little* children. When we save a child, we not only save a soul, but we also gain a life. Do you realize that about two-thirds of the Church members become Christians in early childhood? And that a high percentage of our Church members come from children in the Sunday School? You may say, "This is not true in our church." Yes, it is. In some great downtown churches, the membership may not come through your Sunday School, but these same people who are coming in have been reached in other Sunday Schools in the past.

The winning of a child to Christ is our most important task today. Jesus said, "Despise not one of these little ones" (Matthew 18:10). The Bible says, in the words of the wisest of men, "Remember now thy Creator in the days of thy youth, while the evil days come not, nor the years draw nigh, when thou shalt say, I have no pleasure in them" (Ecclesiastes 12:1).

The winning of a child to Christ is our most important task today.

Plan Inclusively

In the Sunday School, we must have a place and plan for every man, woman and child. We must have an interest in all the diversified life of our young people if we would hold them. Why turn our young over to the world and allow agencies outside the Church to gain the hold on them when they should belong to Christ and the Church?

In the Sunday School, we must have a place and plan for every man, woman and child.

For All Ages of Both Sexes

Sunday School is for all ages of boys and girls, young men and women, adult men and women. Too many Sunday Schools are just for children preteen and younger. We must have people from the cradle to the grave. No one department should be stronger than another. Our aim is to prosper along every front.

How can we build a Sunday School for all? Too often there is a scarcity of boys and men. The high school department often is composed of two boys and twenty girls. This should not be! Boys will not come to a class if girls are running it. I have heard my young college girls say, "Oh, you are partial to the boys." My answer? "I know if we have a big group of good-looking fellows, we will have plenty of lovely girls." And this has been true. Every teacher ought to test the virility of his or her message by the boys and men it attracts. Don't lose the boys in the Sunday School! Hold on to the boys in the junior high and high school classes! Watch the men in the college and adult departments!

For Fellowship

When I was at First Presbyterian Church of Hollywood, clubs for all ages of boys and girls—from preteens to college men and women, young adults and young marrieds—filled the weekdays. Every Wednesday evening there were four prayer services, Junior High and Senior High Bible Club, college fellowship and the adult midweek service. Church athletic teams, composed of only those who attend the church, have carried away many a city trophy. "Sings" for high school, college and young business people, where only religious hymns and choruses are sung, were held after church on Sunday evenings at homes large enough to accommodate the crowd of young people. This sort of togetherness affords a wonderful time of Christian fellowship and camaraderie and a time when the talent of a group can be discovered and used.

You must use talented people or lose them. Our duty is to enlist lives for the Lord and Master, and every opportunity must be seized to accomplish this all-important task.

Create a spirit of fellowship and camaraderie in *your* church. This is of paramount importance. The young will go where their own friends are; hence, I believe the strongest instrument we may use in holding the young to Christ and the Church is Christian fellowship. This was the program of the Early Church (see Acts 2). Seek to have the Church as the center of every young person's life. If this is done, every young person will make every effort to be at your church when the doors open. One young pilot wrote concerning the church: "I love that pile of bricks there on that corner in Hollywood! It was there I found my God. It was there I found my friends. It was there I found my purpose for living." Yes, the Church and its Lord must mean everything to our young if it is to hold them today. Listen as each young person says, "Use me or lose me." Because we have not done the former, we have suffered the latter.

How many parents say, "I have lost my son! He is in the wrong crowd. I can't do anything with him." Let us see to it that our young are with the right crowd. Make it the church crowd! Christ understood the power of fellowship in a life. It is said of His relationship to His disciples, "He ordained twelve, that they should be *with* Him" (Mark 3:14, emphasis added). This was a great fraternity of the highest kind of fellowship.

Expressional Groups
On Sunday evenings at First Presbyterian Church of Hollywood, there were four expressional groups that met under the most careful supervision. These included the junior high, the senior high, collegians and Ambassadors (young business and professionals). Organized and trained deputation (or outreach) teams of youth went all over Southern California to hold meetings in other churches, at camps or at missions. Out of this grew a world deputation team. Young men and women went for a summer to Europe, Africa, Greece, Japan or South America; and this ministry of youth led our church to espouse a new missionary goal. Bible class groups gathered on many nights during the week in homes throughout the city. Many who will not attend church are drawn into it through this fellowship.

Social Occasions
Social occasions that meet Christian standards of excellence and entertainment as well as interest the different age groups brighten the life of every department at First Presbyterian Church of Hollywood. The president of the student body of one of our great universities in Southern California once said, "We don't have anything on campus that is as good as the social things our department puts on."

Service Programs
Drama groups present missionary programs, Christmas pageants and Mother's Day banquets, and serve in innumerable ways to beautify many functions held at First Presbyterian Church. Youth are anxious to serve. They just need motivation, and anything that makes them feel their talents are needed is most gratifying.

Camping Programs
Take your youth to summer conferences and camps as well as spring and winter retreats. Nothing brings greater returns. This ministers to the need of each age group. Here young and old can have real mountaintop experiences. At First Presbyterian Church, camps have helped in the spiritual growth of all ages during the years. Try these things with your youth. Such camps work miracles in drawing the young to Christ and the Church—and holding them there.

Mission Trips
Out of the fellowship at First Presbyterian Church of Hollywood, thousands of youth have gone abroad all over the world. In the last 20 years, they have gone out from the college department of this church into full-time service for the King—as pastors, missionaries, directors of education, boys' and girls' workers, evangelists, singers, camp directors, authors of Christian literature, church board secretaries, institute directors, chaplains, teachers in Christian schools and, last but not least, ministers' wives. A warm Christian fellowship is the atmosphere in which the Spirit works.

For Currency
We will discover that when we present the claims of Christ in new and challenging ways, young people will respond as quickly to that which is righteous as they will to that which is evil. Christ is the great attraction. Jesus said, "And I, if I be lifted up from the earth, will draw all men unto me" (John 12:32). Let us spend our time and genius in presenting Christ so that our young people will know the truth of the statement of Jesus when He said, "Seek ye first the kingdom of God, and His righteousness; and all these things shall be added unto you" (Matthew 6:33).

Let us spend our time and genius in presenting Christ so that our young people will know the truth of the statement of Jesus when He said, "Seek ye first the kingdom of God, and His righteousness; and all these things shall be added unto you" (Matthew 6:33).

Young people will not be enticed to ride in an old vintage Ford when they are invited to ride in the newest model. If Christianity only rides in outmoded vehicles, you cannot censor young people for finding it unattractive. The day of electronic technology is here. Young people wish to ride on the wings of the latest gadget! Let them know the Christ of heaven, who alone can lift them from the mundane things of life.

For Continuity

All the foregoing points to one thing: The present Sunday School must become a vastly more efficient institution that has continuity. Its sessions must be carried over to a weekday program, for no child can receive all the Christian instruction and training he or she needs in one hour on Sunday morning. The Church must be prepared to reach out and bring in the many millions of boys and girls who are *without religious instruction* of any sort.

Train Tomorrow's Leaders

The Church is being challenged to do a big work in order to train the kind of people needed in the world today. The Church must train its own leadership or die! Sam Walter Foss, in his poem "The Coming American," wrote:

> Bring me men to match my mountains,
> Bring me men to match my plains;
> Men with empires in their purpose
> And new eras in their brains.

The world needs Christian leadership today as never before—leadership of the highest type to meet the exigencies of the hour. The world is looking to America for leadership in every field. America must supply this demand. This means we must have strong training schools for all of our young people, which is just what the average Sunday School does *not* exemplify.

Youngsters today are willing to pay the price of leadership. And they are seeking a training school for life. If the Church fails to give the young what they are looking for, they will go elsewhere to find it.

What do we wish tomorrow's leadership to be? Train them today! Do *now* what you desire tomorrow. The German writer Emil Ludwig, in *The Moral Conquest of Germany*, stated a great truth when he wrote in regard to changing the attitude of the German people after World War II:

> Education should begin with the five-year-olds. No one can save the Hitler youth of today, the boys of fourteen. But starting with the five-year-olds an education period of fifteen years should be sufficient. . . . The spirit of any community follows the spirit of its younger generation. . . . Those who are five years today may live to see, as young men and women, their nation's free return to the world.

The British sociologist Benjamin Kidd said, "You can completely change civilization in one generation." What we want in the nation we must put into the school, the home and the Church. We will have to add current technology to the schoolroom. The addition of technological advancements will make a strong and lasting impression on our young people.

Make Sunday School the Priority

The Church should change her attitude toward the Christian education of her young people. The Church must win and educate and train its children and youth for Christ and Christian service if she is to survive. Christian education of the child must be as important in the Church as secular education of the child is in school.

A Rightful Place

The Church school, as the teaching arm of the Church, must be given its rightful place. When the Church fully believes that its finest opportunity is with its young people, then Sunday School and every other institution touching youth will receive due recognition and help. The Sunday School too often is merely tolerated. We must *know* that the Sunday School is the Church functioning in its educational task of teaching and training those who are to be its future members and leaders.

Too many churches have considered anything as good enough for the children. An old piano that will not stay in tune is deposited in the Elementary Department. Chairs whose backs are faded are good enough for the Preteen Department. Anything that cannot be used elsewhere is good enough for Sunday School. The equipment in many Sunday Schools looks like an assortment gleaned from the local Goodwill store.

Although the Sunday School is the "gold mine" of the Church, for too long it has been considered a side issue. It has been entrusted to a faithful few who were willing to invest their lives, week in and week out, working against all odds to bring Christ to the young and the young to Christ. They could do just what they wished just so long as they did not interfere with the program of the Church. (The young must never get in the way of the church services!)

Sunday School must be given its rightful place in the life of every church if every church is to continue to be a living entity!

A Trained Staff

It is too often the case that in Sunday School, the lesson from God's Word is taught by a teacher who has accepted the class because there was no one else willing to take it. In fact, Sunday School teaching is the only teaching a person will undertake without training. Imagine a pilot offering to fly a jet across the Atlantic without ever having had a lesson in flying! And yet men and women nonchalantly attempt to carry our wonderful young people in a Sunday School ship across the ocean of life without knowing a thing about the art of teaching!

The new Sunday School must have capable, worthy teachers, trained for their task. We need a determined effort to prepare teachers. Pastors must give themselves to this task. The purpose of this book is to help in this tremendous task.

Prioritize Christ and the Children

Christ First

But even with fine buildings, equipment and teachers, the new Sunday School will be no more successful than its predecessor unless it introduces its students to the Lord Jesus Christ as Savior and Lord of their lives. There has been too little emphasis on this vital message. Too often, the Church school has tried to teach the things the public school is commissioned to do. Unless the Sunday School makes *Christ* the center of its life and activity, it will never grip and hold young people. The young want reality not religion and Christ, not "Churchianity." Children are being given religious education but little Christian education.

Children Next

We have not put enough importance in our children. Have we realized the value and possibilities of childhood? Our churches have spent millions building large sanctuaries, installing stages and stained-glass windows and the latest technology, which are to be enjoyed once a week, but how much has the average church invested in its children, its little children? How much does your church spend yearly on its Sunday School? Have you considered these precious jewels to be of more worth than bricks and stones? We should have every Christian child in America in Sunday School. This is a colossal task, but it is ours! We can do it!

INTRODUCTION

Sunday School Is Big Business

Teaching is a business. Building a Sunday School may be classified as big business because it is God's business. We are dealing not only with problems of time but also of eternity. No board of directors in the world is carrying on a work as important as ours in the Sunday School. Those who run big businesses may be dealing with millions or billions of dollars, but time will bring that all to an end. What we are doing is of eternal significance. We are preparing lives not only for this world but also for the world that is to come. We must be impressed with the magnitude of our task.

If building a Sunday School is big business, let us consider how to carry it on, for no business in this world can be conducted successfully unless there is someone who understands how to do it. This is the reason for the tragic situation that exists today in our Sunday Schools—untrained leaders. We, as Christian educators, have undertaken the running of a big business, yet we remain novices in our field.

Put the "School" Back in Sunday School

Start out in your Sunday School with the idea that the boys and girls of your school should receive the best possible religious training. Put the "school" in Sunday School.

You know that a school must have teachers as well as students, that only good teachers produce a good Sunday School, and that good teachers must be trained. "As feathers are to the arrow, so training is to teachers," said Marion Laicrance; and Christian minister and author Dr. P. H. Welshimer said, "Every teacher can succeed if he is willing to pay the price—preparation."

The Need for Teacher Training

I have learned that to say teachers are born, not made, is about as far from the full truth as to say the same of doctors, lawyers, ministers and engineers. However, this much is true: Some people are born who are willing to pay the price of good teaching. Dr. Athearn, an American master teacher and a pioneer of religious education, wrote:

> Society . . . insists that justice be not thwarted by untrained jurists; it guards the bodies of its citizenship from the untrained "quack"; it excludes the charlatan from the school-room, that the *minds* of our children may not be maimed and crippled by unskilled workmen; but the souls of children have been left unprotected from malpractice at the hands of well-meaning but untrained workers in the field of religious education.

Strange, is it not, that those parents who rise up in righteous indignation because their children are being taught the three *R*s by incompetent public school teachers, sit back calmly and never raise a question about the ability of Sunday School teachers to instruct their children in the fourth *R*, a right knowledge of a God whom to know aright is life everlasting. We demand a diploma before a doctor can practice medicine, a public school teacher can educate and a nurse can tend to others, but we demand nothing from our Sunday School teachers. We would not think of sending missionaries to a foreign land without first training them in the language and ways of the other country, but we will let almost anyone teach our boys and girls.

The Need for a Method

There is no such thing as carrying on a business without a method. Everyone has a procedure that is followed in order to successfully complete a job. The method is simply the way to carry work on, the systematic plan followed in order to succeed at a task. No one ever builds a shed without a plan. The plan may be a poor one, but there *is* a plan.

Everyone running a Sunday School—whether it is one of 25 or 250 or 2,500—is running it by some method. Don't forget this! By what method are you conducting your school? Is it antiquated, outmoded or shiftless, or does it breathe of the new, the fresh and the well planned? We must be honest in considering our weaknesses, or we cannot improve no matter how many books on Christian education are studied. When you admit your problems and face them squarely, the battle is half won. Most people refuse to look their problems in the face. As they look at the obstacles that stare at them, they find excuses for themselves. They refuse to deal with existing situations that might be improved.

The Need for Endurance

Christian education is a very comprehensive field, indeed, and cannot be run by the weak or the totally inexperienced. It is a hard task because it is endless. This great evangelistic and educational process is one from which we can never rest. It means a marathon of physical endurance, of mental acumen, of moral courage and of spiritual strength. It is a task for strong individuals, not babes. There was a day when men like the great merchant prince John Wanamaker devoted much of his time outside of business obligations to his work in Sunday School. That kind of time investment made spiritual history. We need to make such history again.

The Need for the Holy Spirit

Workmen in our Sunday Schools need not be ashamed of their dependence on the Holy Spirit. Sunday School teachers must know their subject, observe their students, and then do something about it. The more teachers depend upon the Holy Spirit, the more they will wish to make themselves instruments fit for His use. They will wish to know how God made the human mind. They will want to probe the depths of the human heart. They will want to know the laws that govern their approach to their students who were created to be temples of the living God.

Operate According to the Laws of God

There are laws in the spiritual world, just as there are in the physical world. God established the laws for both. It is our failure to work according to God's laws that has characterized much of what has been done under the name of Sunday School teaching. A high-powered car is of no value to the owner unless the owner knows the laws that operate it. A five-year-old who attempts to drive it can end up dying, because the child does not understand the simple principles that govern its use. The need to operate a vehicle according to what we are told to do in the owner's manual is necessary.

Have you studied the way spiritual laws operate in the life of a child? We must obey them if we want to succeed. For example, there is the law of nourishment. A baby must be fed milk. And certain vitamins are needed if the little body is to grow. You cannot feed the baby meat, because a baby cannot digest it. So too a Christian must be built up by "the milk of the Word." If you try to feed a new believer the meat of doctrine, he or she will die; it means nothing to the new Christian. We cannot go contrary to the laws of nature and live; neither can we go against God's laws in the spiritual life and thrive. In Christian education, we must operate according to God's laws.

In Life

We may study the life of the child because, like all of God's creation, it is under His laws, and God's laws are unchangeable and universal. Certain causes will always produce certain results when the conditions are normal. The basic laws of life may be known. This means that we may have the right to expect certain results in a life where certain laws operate. It also reminds us that haphazard, ignorant work with a young life produces disastrous results. A mistake with a life cannot be wholly rectified. There is a best time in nature to sow and to reap. If the best time is passed, the results come with greater effort and with less success—if success is ever obtained. Measured on the dial, an hour a week to prepare a life for eternity is too brief a time to allow one wasted moment or one careless touch upon a soul.

In Growth

Only the Holy Spirit can make our work effective, but He always operates in accordance with God's laws. Between the teacher and God there are conditions that must be met before He can work. Equally important, there are conditions between the teacher and the student that must be considered. There is nothing mysterious in the way God works. The farmer may not thoroughly understand how God brings out from the tiny seeds that are sown, the fields of waving grain; but the farmer certainly knows that if the laws of planting in the spring and cultivating and watering in the summer are obeyed, a harvest in the fall can be expected. This is not a matter of chance; no chance is involved in it. Law is operating. A wise farmer works *with* God's laws, not *against* them.

In Training

God says, "Train up a child in the way he should go: and when he is old, he will not depart from it" (Proverbs 22:6). This is one of the laws of God. There is no mystery in this law either. What is wrong then? Children have departed from God by the thousands! It is obvious that we have not done what God has told us to do; hence, we are not gathering the harvest.

"Train up a child." Children have not had religious training in these last years. We have produced a generation of spiritual illiterates. A growing segment of the population of America is not in touch with any church, and millions of our children receive no instruction in our Sunday Schools. Statistics show that a large percent of the youth in our penitentiaries today come from families untouched by religion. J. Edgar Hoover, the first director of the Federal Bureau of Investigation, once said:

> The American home is still the basis of our social order, and the nation will never be any stronger than the home. The rising youth problem in crime stems directly from the home. The one thing that most juvenile criminals have in common is a lack of home training. There is no character building agency that can take the place of a good home. . . .
>
> The tragic condition is due to a lack of conscience, which in turn comes from a lack of religious training. There is a necessary connection between crime and the decline of faith and religious practice. When men do not know God or His justice, they do not respect His laws. The way to make America safe from crime, the way to make her people moral, is a return to religion.

In other words, Hoover reiterated God's law: "Train up a child in the way he should go."

We have trained our young people in everything except the things of God. The current generation can do exploits, but they do not know how to pray. They can navigate ships, but they have never been trained to chart courses for their lives. To *train* involves everything in the education processes. To *train* means *more than to tell*. We have *told* youth for centuries, and we have told them "off" too often. Our method of teaching has been a transmissive one. Let us begin to *train* youth!

To *train* involves everything in the education processes. To *train* means *more than to tell*. We have *told* youth for centuries, and we have told them "off" too often. Our method of teaching has been a transmissive one. Let us begin to *train* youth!

Learn About Teaching from Jesus' Example

One of the best ways to learn how to do anything is by following someone else's example. Who can teach us about teaching? Let us learn from the Lord Jesus. If we turn to Christ's parable of the sower in Matthew 13, we see that Jesus has thrown much light on the entire subject of teaching. There are three things to consider:

1. The sower: the teacher
2. The seed: the Word
3. The soil: the student

Each element has its place in the field of Christian teaching: The sower is necessary to perform the task; the seed is necessary if there is to be a harvest; and the soil makes a difference in the harvest. Let us examine in our study those three important factors in the planting process. The intelligent planter makes use of a knowledge of soils, seeds and seasons in planning for an abundant harvest. The wise planter does not carry orange trees from sunny California and try to plant them in frozen Alaska; neither is there an attempt to plant cotton in the cold, damp soil of Maine. So must the teacher consider the different needs of each individual child if the teacher is to succeed.

The Sower: The Teacher

Training

The sower is the teacher. Every teacher must understand the art of teaching. A Sunday School teacher must have knowledge of the material to be taught, of the children being taught and their vocabulary, and of the aim of the lesson. To teach a Sunday School class without any preparation and any training in the art of teaching a Sunday School class is inexcusable today, for Sunday School teacher-training information is easily and readily available. Aside from books and manuals available from Christian publishers, much information is accessible on the Internet. And some Sunday School curriculums also include teacher-training articles and tips.

Don't let training be lacking for your Sunday School staff, for it will mean too many casualties. No Sunday School can be directed and taught and carried to the port of success without experts. Set out to train your own leadership!

Tools

The sower must have tools that can be used to help get the soil ready for the planting. So must the teacher have books and other resources that can be used to help in preparing the hearts of the students to be receptive to the Word that will be planted. No one thinks of entering the field of medicine, engineering, dentistry or any other profession without textbooks of information on the chosen subject. One spends vast sums to acquire the facts of one's profession.

What books are in the library that your teachers will be using? If you cannot afford to buy many books, use the public library. Continual demand for certain books often means that the library will add them to its collection. Abraham Lincoln is said to have sacrificed everything else to buy a book. What about you? It is also now possible to access many teaching resources online, so if possible, have available for use by your teachers a computer with an Internet connection.

You must have some good books and other resources, for the most important word in a teacher's vocabulary is "preparation." The prepared teacher succeeds. The unprepared teacher fails.

The prepared teacher must, above all, have a knowledge of and own a copy of the *Bible*. Invest in a good Bible for each teacher, one that can be marked and written in. Too many teachers depend upon their lesson material, instead of the Book. Also have a good *concordance* for teachers to use. Word study and topical study will make teachers' presentations sparkle and glow. Also have a Bible *atlas* available for the teachers. Encourage the teachers to know the lands of the Bible. With this reference at hand, teachers will be better able to make the history of God's Word come alive. Add a *commentary* to the library. Reading a commentary on the lesson material will provide motivation for continual study.

Students

The Sunday School exists for the students, and everything about a successful Sunday School must revolve around the students. We must have teachers trained to teach them. We must have a building to house them. We must seek ways and means to hold their interest. In fact we must have plans to meet their needs from the day they are born until the day they die. This is our task as teachers.

We must have plans to meet their needs from the day they are born until the day they die.

Our students are also the way to test our teaching. Our teaching is to be tested by its effect on each student. Remember that the noisy, inattentive troublemaker needs the Sunday School as much as the class angel needs it. We want each to be taught. Yes, Christ said there was more rejoicing in heaven over the recovery of one of the lost sheep than over all the others who were safe in the fold, so we should plan our lessons from the standpoint of those who need the most help.

And yes, we would not have had the preacher of Pentecost if Christ had not worked with Peter when he was most unpromising. But we are to teach to all.

How can the Sunday School minister to all? Don't try to teach everyone alike. We are all different. The fact that each period of human life is marked by widely different traits compels a variation in treatment by the teacher. Just as a preschooler cannot be dealt with in the same way as a preteen; neither can a man or woman be treated in the same way as a preschooler.

Credentials

How seldom are Sunday School teachers asked for their credentials! Public school teachers are not questioned whether they *will* teach, but rather whether they *can* teach. Our request in securing Sunday School teachers is invariably, "Will you take a class?" The good-natured men and women, much against their wills, each answer, "I will keep the class going until you can find someone else." If the math teacher were absent, can you imagine the principal going out in the neighborhood and ringing doorbells and asking the stranger who answers the door, "Will you come over to the school and take a class in math because the regular teacher is sick?" Absurd! The principal notifies the superintendent's office of the need, and a trained person comes. The question to ask and have answered is not "Will you take a class?" but "Can you teach?"

What is your preparation? Are you teaching a class of adolescent boys because no one else would take them, or are you teaching them because you love boys and think they are a great field in which you can plant God's Word and expect a harvest? There is no greater mission field today than the Sunday School. Many of us cannot go across to other lands to carry the good news, but all of us can find a place in a field that is already waiting to be harvested. If we cannot win the boys and girls of America to Christ, why should we expect to win the children of other nations to the same Christ?

The Seed: The Word

The Word is the seed. This is what we, as teachers, will sow. God has given us His Word, but there is a false impression that all of God's

Word can be adapted to every age. I believe the Bible clearly teaches that the Word contains "milk" for babes, "bread" for youth, and "strong meat" for men. All of the Bible is not for everyone at the same time. I believe it would be impossible to adapt the teaching in Revelation, for instance, so that a six-year-old would understand it. Suppose you took a primary child to school and on the desk to which the child was assigned you found an algebra text and a chemistry book. You would take them to the teacher and exclaim that your child could not understand them. "Oh," the teacher would probably say, "we will adapt the material so that your child can understand it." It can't be done! It is out of the realm of that child's experience and knowledge. So there are portions of God's Word beyond the realm of the experience of the child, but there is much that is within a child's grasp so that nothing need be substituted for the Bible in teaching any child. The seed is the Word; this we know. But good seed can be lost on the wrong soil.

The Word is the seed.
This is what we, as teachers, will sow.
God has given us His Word.

The Soil: The Student

When a sower goes out to plant, the sower knows not only the seed but also the soil. No agriculturist will try to raise tropical plants in the Frigid Zone. The art of sowing is bringing the right seed into contact with the right soil. You, as a Sunday School teacher, have in your hand a Living Seed, which is the Word of God. This will bring forth a glorious harvest if it is planted in the right soil. Your success as a teacher demands a knowledge of human nature. How can we adapt our teaching if we do not know the age to which it must be adapted? This is your business as a sower. No teacher can teach without knowing his or her students, any more than a farmer can farm without studying the soil.

Remember, the teacher is the sower, the Word is the seed, and the heart of the child is the soil. Are you placing the seed carefully in ground that has been cultivated by prayer and the Spirit? Do you understand the field in which you are scattering the seed? This field in which you are sowing week after week is the hearts of boys and girls, young people, and men and women. Are you getting a harvest? Why not? You know the Seed is all right; it must be that you don't understand the soil. What do you know about the age group of your class? This knowledge will determine your success or failure in teaching them. It is not enough to know the Word and be a willing sower. You must know the soil, or your crop will be a failure.

You, as a Sunday School teacher, have in your hand a Living Seed, which is the Word of God. This will bring forth a glorious harvest if it is planted in the right soil.

Many people think that children are just little men and women. This is a very false idea. They are absolutely different from adults—physically, cognitively, emotionally, socially and spiritually. They are constantly growing and changing. Children open up like flowers. They develop like the lilies of the field. One year may make all the difference in the world in a child's interests and capabilities. Children are all alike, yet all are different. As we "consider . . . how they grow," we find out what they need (Matthew 6:28; Luke 12:27).

There has never been a time when so many people were students of human life as today. The psychologist, the psychiatrist, the businessperson, the politician, the teacher and the parent are all matriculated in the college of life. They are trying to discover how life develops, how it may be influenced, how it may be motivated. Once we can recognize the stages of development, we can adapt Sunday School lessons accordingly.

Train Up Children in Our Midst

Training the young involves the two processes of telling and teaching, but it goes farther. It provides the student with the ability of doing and accomplishing in life—of applying to everyday life the biblical principles learned. God's Word tells us that we are not to be hearers of the Word only, but doers. So our training of children must have an upward lift. "Train up."

A growing youngster is like a vine seeking a trellis. If you do not provide a pole around which the vine can climb and to which it can cling, then it will trail along the ground. This is just what is happening to too many young people today. They reach out the tendrils of their senses and desires and, finding nothing to lift them up, they crawl along the ground. Place the Lord Jesus Christ as a stake in the midst of young life, and see how His presence will lift the child. The child's personality will become an integrated one around this great Savior and lifter of men. Put a child's face between your hands and lift it heavenward. Let each child see the Savior, God's "only begotten Son, that whosoever believeth in him should not perish, but have everlasting life" (John 3:16). Let the Light of the Word shine into the heart of every child.

Place the Lord Jesus Christ as a stake in the midst of young life, and see how His presence will lift the child.

As mentioned earlier, God said that we must train up *a child*. Christ puts great emphasis upon the child. Jesus "took a child, and set him in their midst" (Mark 9:36). In contrast, we are likely to push a child into any corner of the church building where he or she will be least in the way. We must put each child where Christ put the child if we are to succeed in our teaching—in our midst.

Great stress today is placed upon the need of training the individual. The training must progress with the individual's years and according to the individual's experience. We must deal with individuals. Children are not born in crowds; neither do they die in masses. Each is born with a divine right. Follow a child and watch as the child passes from infancy to childhood, and thence from adolescence to youth and adulthood. Children are not little adults. They are a "species" all their own, but they lack the knowledge and experience of their elders. Physically they are still growing. Cognitively and emotionally they are still grasping. Spiritually they are still groping. Give them a chance! Each one needs to be individually trained. Always remember that in your class there may be a boy with a longing to unlock the secrets of nature like a Washington Carver. Or there may be a girl dreaming of adventuring in life like an Amelia Earhart. Or perhaps there may be one who longs to have communication with the vast world outside and beyond like an Alexander Graham Bell. There may be one who longs to serve like a General MacArthur or a Florence Nightingale.

Begin now to build a strong and growing school. Don't be satisfied with what you have. Set a goal!

Yes, Sunday School is big business. Your Sunday School may be small in numbers, but it is of tremendous importance as far as the youth of today are concerned. There is no end to what can be done in any Sunday School in any community of this great country of ours. Begin now to build a strong and growing school. Don't be satisfied with what you have. Set a goal! I am going to try to help you with your task.

Sources

1. Marion Laicrance and P. H. Welshimer quoted in Edwin W. Thornton, *Common Sense: A Study of Mind and Method* (Cincinnati, OH: The Standard Publishing Company, 1913), p. 110. http://www21.us.archive.org/stream/commonsensestudy00thor/commonsensestudy00thor_djvu.txt.

2. Luther Allan Weigle and others, *The New Standard Teacher Training Course: Disciples of Christ Edition* (St. Louis, MO: The Christian Board of Publication, 1917), pp. 329-330. http://books.google.com/books?id=PSxFAAAAYAAJ&pg=PA329&lpg=PA329&dq=%22untrained+jurists%22+and+%22athearn%22&source=bl&ots=3FVodLcyM8&sig=uXZQphB0TD2-ssQIUXEBLi2eVHU&hl=en&sa=X&ei=DKJ0T8CqIaXW2AWa6bHWDg&ved=0CC4Q6AEwAA#v=onepage&q&f=false.

PART 1

Children's Sunday School

As stated earlier, Sunday School exists for its students. So study of the student is the all-important thing in this book. Everything is based upon the human heart, the soil in which the Sunday School teacher sows the truth. As a child grows from infancy to adulthood, there are three distinct periods of development that are passed—childhood, youth and adult—that have characteristics so definite that they may be easily marked. All are part of the sowing field of our Sunday School.

Although this section of the book centers on Sunday School for children from birth to 12 years of age, every teacher should be familiar with the characteristics of each age group that makes up your Sunday School; then you will know what organization to build, what kind of teachers you must have and where you must have them.

Period of Development	Sunday School Group Name	Ages
Childhood	Nursery	Birth–2
	Preschool	2–3
	Prekindergarten/Kindergarten	4–5
	Elementary	6–10
	Preteen	10–12
Youth	Junior High	12–14
	High School	14–18
	College	18–25
Adult	Business and Professional	25+
	Young Couples	25+
	Adults	35+

1

Nursery

How do we start with the child? The planting begins in the nursery. So many have just a paper roll of blue booties on pink ribbons—a list of names but no real live children. You may ask, "Why should parents bring their babies to Sunday School? They are just a lot of work and take up a lot of room." Well, we want them there because papas and mamas have to bring them. And for young couples, the person in charge of the nursery is important, because that person can help advise parents what to teach their children. Take care how you start.

These little people are like pieces of modeling clay held in the hands of all those who have a part in teaching them. The clay is so soft now that it can be molded into whatever form we wish. When children are so very little, they absorb the world of people's emotions and attitudes: of safety or fear; of truth or deceit; of devotion and loyalty or neglect and betrayal. They long for protection from those who are nearest. When they cry out at night, we should comfort them. When they are hungry, we should feed them. These little ones love to be cuddled. The warm arms of parents are their comfort.

Child development experts tell us that the first two years are among the most important in a person's life. These early years powerfully influence all of a child's subsequent development. Attitudes toward self and others are formed very early and can be changed later only with great difficulty. The loving care given in the nursery builds wonderful foundations of trust, affection and security—all of which will go a long way in helping children be receptive to instruction about God.

When Jesus places each of these precious babies in our care, He says to us what the Egyptian princess said to Moses' mother when she called her to nurse the baby: "Take this child away, and nurse it for me, and I will give thee thy wages" (Exodus 2:9). Each baby is loaned for life to parents, and it is the caregivers and teachers who will aid in increasing the value of that loan. Take to heart the words Mamie Gene Cole wrote in "The Child's Appeal":

I am the Child.
All the world waits for my coming.
All the earth watches with interest to see what I shall become.
Civilization hangs in the balance,
For what I am, the world of tomorrow will be.

I am the Child.
I have come into your world, about which I know nothing.
Why I came I know not;
How I came I know not.
I am curious; I am interested.

I am the Child.
You hold in your hand my destiny.
You determine, largely, whether I shall succeed or fail.
Give me, I pray you, those things that make for happiness.
Train me, I beg you, that I may be a blessing to the world.

Goethe once said, "Only the best is good enough for the child." And Kate Douglas Wiggin, the author of *Rebecca of Sunnybrook Farm,* said, "Every child born into the world is a new thought of God and an ever fresh and radiant possibility." It would do us well to take the words of all of these writers to heart.

Never forget that when parents brought their children to Jesus, He considered blessing those children to be such an important act that He became angry when He saw His disciples turn them away! May our attitude be that these little ones and their families are of prime importance! Never let anyone on your nursery staff think that his or her job is not important! The nursery may seem to be a "small" ministry, away from the public eye, but it can be one of the most vibrant and life-changing ministries of your church! Let the little ones come—and let Jesus' love flow to each family through your ministry!

What to Expect

Healthy babies come in a wide range of sizes and exhibit myriad personalities and behaviors. And while all children grow physically following a fairly predictable pattern, what follows here should be regarded as general in nature. Never grow impatient because every child does not accomplish the same thing at the same time. Remember that God made every child and that every child was born for love.

Birth to Six Weeks

Newborn babies may sleep up to 20 hours a day. Their responses are mainly reflexive: sucking, grasping and startling. Although newborns change mood easily and are quite aware of and sensitive to their surroundings (especially the emotional "feel" of those surroundings), sleeping and eating are the order of the day. The optimal visual distance of newborns is 8 to 10 inches (20.5 to 25.5 cm), and they will track slow-moving objects with their eyes. As newborns mature, they bring hands to mouths and will also mouth objects placed in their hands. Babies this age have little control of their heads.

Six Weeks to Six Months

Around six weeks of age, *babies* begin to show curiosity by swiping at or reaching out to touch items that interest them (often bringing objects to their mouths) and to notice and separate their fingers. Their eyes are able to focus on a variety of distances; babies this age will often stare at their hands, at a smiling face or at a mobile for a sustained period of time. By the time babies are able to roll over, they will be laughing and experimenting with making other sounds as well. Smiles come easily, and brief, gentle tickling usually prompts giggles. There is usually good head control, and they love to kick and squirm. By five and a half months of age, most babies recognize the voices and faces of their parents. They also about double whatever they weighed at birth.

Six Months to Eight Months

Babies may become *sitters* at around six months of age. They can usually turn over from stomach to back and firmly push their legs when pressure is applied. Now that their range of vision is broadened, they love to reach (and perhaps even roll after) small objects, and drop, throw or bang them. Babies this age love to play little games with an adult or older child. Since these babies now clearly know who is a stranger and who is not, expect some anxiety when separating from parents or other familiar people. Teeth may begin to show at this age—along with the low-grade fever, earaches and teething pain that may accompany them.

Crawlers are now able to explore a brave new world! From the coffee cup to the full wastebasket, there is nothing that doesn't interest them. Once crawling is mastered, expect lots of pulling up, standing and attempts at climbing. This progresses into "cruising," walking a bit while holding on to something, and, finally, into walking (and falling). As crawlers move toward toddlerhood, their minds grow by leaps and bounds. Babies this age stare as intently as a scientist at most everything. What may seem to be random acts of discovery—banging, tasting and staring—serve to inform these little explorers of the nature of their world. Teething continues!

Eight Months to Fourteen Months

Toddlers are curious about everything. They continue to experiment with climbing, standing and cruising (walking while holding on to something) until they master walking, although they do so clumsily. Exploring objects, usually by mouthing them, helps them to know their world; and they will actively stack, insert and open things. They will also often stare intently at something that has caught their interest. Toddlers learn to respond to a variety of words and sentences. Although they show affection for familiar people, they are shy with strangers. By about 12 months old, they about triple whatever they weighed at birth. They continue to develop more teeth!

Fourteen Months to Two Years

Toddlers of this age walk well and often run. They now use objects with intent: stacking, opening and/or throwing them; and they demonstrate evidence of reasoning in problem solving. They are likely to show frustration when their desires are thwarted. They enjoy conversations with adults, their responses ranging from single words to complete sentences. They show strong attachment to regular caregivers.

What to Do

There should be at least one caregiver for every two babies. This makes it possible to keep a close eye on every child's safety, as well as to give each child individual attention. If possible, the same caregiver should care for the same children from week to week. This continuity is especially important when babies begin to distinguish between strangers and friends.

When a baby arrives, give the child and his or her parents a friendly greeting. Your helpful attitude and warm friendliness convey a powerful first impression of what your church family is like. Remember that for first-time parents, giving their baby to a stranger for any reason can be stressful. If it's clear to them that your nursery is a clean, friendly and safe place, both parents and child are likely to have a positive experience that they will want to repeat. Parents are deeply influenced by their children's reaction to being at church. Young parents who are not deeply committed to church attendance are often influenced to continue by the caliber of care their baby receives and by their child's positive response. Parents are looking for caregivers who are reliable, trustworthy and responsive.

Talk to and watch the child; listen carefully to any comments the parents make. After check-in is completed, take a moment to talk to and sing to the child. To interest older babies in an activity, begin to do the activity yourself. If the baby cries, talk to the child and sing to him or her first. Hold the child if necessary.

For the child, this may well be a first time away from mother or father. That's why it's so important that there be plenty of loving adult arms available in the nursery. Accept each little one in Jesus' name, just as if you could see Jesus standing right beside you.

When it's time to change or move a baby, don't pick up the child without warning; rather, talk calmly to him or her about what's going to happen. Never underestimate the power of showing loving respect for each small person through your calm voice, relaxed attitude and gentle actions. Such small, "unseen" acts of love may go unnoticed, but they build the invisible structure of the kingdom of God even among the youngest. It will likely rub off onto the babies you care for.

Remember to *watch, ask,* and *adapt* yourself to the children's changing interests and activities. Your enthusiasm for the theme-related activities suggested in your curriculum and your interest in each child are what make this a time of effective learning.

Birth to Six Weeks

Newborns need a quiet place to sleep and nurse. In the "awake" room, position colorful mobiles and hang them in such a way that babies can see them. An occasional change of scenery and the gentle talking, rocking and comforting that accompany feeding, changing and sleep preparation should keep them happy and content. Be sure to support the head of a baby this age, even if he or she appears to have good control. Remember that frequent burping is necessary when feeding a newborn.

Six Weeks to Six Months

Babies between six weeks and six months of age like to have objects placed within their view. A mirror mounted about 7 inches (18 cm) from their heads, where babies can look at the reflection, fascinates them. Colorful toys and pictures can also be provided to interest babies. Give these young ones some time in positions other than the one in which they usually sleep. As these babies become able to roll over, they will be ready for more changes of scenery and more play and conversation with adults. As they near six months of age, they will enjoy frequent one-on-one playtimes. An infant seat or other device that puts the baby where he or she can see what's going on nearby is helpful, though such a device should be used for only a limited time each day.

Six Months to Eight Months

Once a baby can sit up, try playing peek-a-boo or some other simple game with him or her; or try pushing gently on the baby's feet so that the child can push back. Provide a number of safe small toys (rattles, fabric or vinyl blocks, containers, etc.) and other objects for discovering. As you interact with a baby, describe his or her actions or responses to your actions, linking the two.

For the crawler, freedom to explore within safe limits is key. Provide lots of space for crawlers to roam without hazards. Crib mattresses and firm washable pillows can provide a variety of safe crawling, climbing and sitting surfaces. Carpet-sample squares can provide interesting textures to crawl across. Your calm and happy interaction with babies on the floor helps them learn ways to explore and communicate. When correcting or giving directions, speak in positive terms. Instead of, "Don't pull Mark's hair, Paul!" say, "Paul, pat Mark's hair. It feels soft. Here is a lamb you can pat, too." Provide balls and toys babies this age can operate, and begin to tell them brief, simple stories.

Eight Months to Fourteen Months

For curious toddlers, a safe environment for exploration is paramount, and one would do well to be ever alert to their activities. A variety of toys—fill-and-dump toys, stacking and nesting toys, balls 8 to 24 inches (20.5 to 61 cm), and so on—should be offered to these active explorers. They feel most comfortable interacting with familiar people, so a consistency of caregivers would be best. Talk with them and begin to share with them books with thick, stiff pages.

Fourteen Months to Two Years

Older toddlers need a combination of loving firmness and flexibility. These young ones have fun playing with push-and-pull toys, and plastic people and animals. Large, stable toys (rocking horses, ride-on toys, etc.) on which toddlers can sit and move may also be enjoyed. Paper and jumbo nontoxic crayons can be introduced for play, and plastic and rubber containers can be provided so that toddlers can experiment with pouring. Vocabularies grow, so conversations become easier and more natural.

How to Teach About God

Yes, we're dealing with babies in the nursery, but in addition to the necessities of being fed, changed and rocked, babies also can start learning about God's love. While no one thinks it's vital to post charts of major theological concepts on the nursery wall, it is vital to think about what babies can learn. The goal of teaching in the nursery is not to get a baby to say "God." Rather, our goal is to teach each baby what he or she *can* learn about God's love.

The goal of teaching in the nursery is
not to get a baby to say "God."
Rather, our goal is to teach each baby what
he or she *can* learn about God's love.

Such teaching is done by your every look, word and act while you are in the presence of a baby or toddler. Work in the nursery is ministry just as surely as if you were teaching a theology class to adults. Remember that you represent Christ to each little person in your care and that learning for these very young ones takes place all the time, as a natural part of living. Using a curriculum with monthly Bible themes and learning activities will help bring consistency to your efforts to help little ones learn about God and His love.

What do you communicate to that baby who seems to cry every time you hold him or her? Do you tense as you pick up the child, steeling yourself against the inevitable? That baby senses your tension! A baby is very sensitive to such subtle things. Your attitude tells the child how you feel about him or her! Conversely, when your words, looks and actions are relaxed and gentle, loving and kind, you not only teach each baby that people at the church nursery can be trusted, but you also begin to build a foundation for that little child's trust in God!

The attitude in which you meet a baby's needs greatly influences his or her developing personality. As a baby associates you with pleasant experiences and lovingly having his or her needs met, he or she also forms foundational opinions about trusting and about being loved that will affect his or her whole life. This is why it is important, whenever possible, to care for the same babies each time you are in the nursery. Continuity of care means the baby becomes familiar with one person, building the baby's trust and comfort.

Talking with babies and toddlers about God and Jesus is also a reminder to yourself of your overall purpose in serving in the nursery. Your example in ministering to these little ones will help parents begin to develop these same skills in communicating spiritual truths to their children.

One-on-One Time

Play simple games lovingly with babies (such as gently pedaling a baby's legs and saying, "Erica, God made your strong legs!"). Sing short, simple songs about God's love to even the youngest baby.

Remember that no baby cares about your vocal quality! Your low, gentle song relaxes, calms and teaches trust. As a baby often hears his or her name associated with God's love, he or she begins to associate song, self, God and love. These experiences build a foundation for faith in the perfect Father who loves all of His little ones.

As a baby often hears his or her name associated with God's love, he or she begins to associate song, self, God and love. These experiences build a foundation for faith in the perfect Father who loves all of His little ones.

Toddlers will enjoy hearing brief Bible stories and verses and short, simple songs about God and Jesus. Use toddlers' names often and show you enjoy them. Toddlers understand repeated, short, direct sentences, even if they don't make any verbal response.

Do a finger play as often as children seem interested. (To interest children in an activity, do the finger play once or twice yourself. Never ask, "Would you like to do the finger play?" Simply launch into it once or twice, and you will see interest on some faces by the third time!)

Older babies and toddlers also enjoy looking at books with you. (Books for babies and toddlers need mainly pictures, not words.) With a picture book and a toddler in your lap, you are in position to look at the pictures and talk with the child about the pictures in the book. "Look, Elisa! There's a big, red apple. I like to eat apples. God made apples for us to eat."

Guided Conversation

Guided conversation will help you make the connection between the Bible theme and the child's actions. Guided conversation is simply informal but planned conversation in which you look for opportunities to connect what children are doing to the month's Bible theme. Relating the child's activities to the Bible theme helps the child understand the relationship between what he or she is doing and what the Bible says.

When children are absorbed in an activity or are playing together, don't leave the area. Place yourself at the children's eye level, listening and observing. It is not necessary to interrupt a child's activities or force conversation. Use the natural opportunities that arise to step in with a comment or question. "I see that you built a tower with the blocks. God made your hands, so you can build." "We're putting the animals in the barn. God made animals."

With the month's Bible theme in mind, you are ready to listen, observe and comment in ways that will help each little child understand more about how God's love and God's Word relate to his or her world.

Curriculum

Although using curriculum in the nursery may seem unnecessary, there actually are several reasons why using curriculum is a very good idea. First of all, curriculum is designed to help you, the teacher/caregiver, use the time you spend with little ones in the nursery to build spiritual foundations. Curriculum provides ideas to use as you interact with each baby or toddler one on one—playing, talking, caregiving, singing and doing finger plays—teaching in ways that familiarize each child with God's name and His love.

Second, using curriculum also benefits you, the caregiver, as much as the child. Singing and talking about Jesus are powerful reminders that what you are doing is not just custodial care, but also ministry in its truest sense. The same is true for parents. Parents need to begin talking comfortably about Jesus with their children. The model the church provides of how we care for and "teach" babies and toddlers is intended to help parents catch on to the fact that they can and should do the same things at home.

Singing and talking about Jesus are powerful reminders that what you are doing is not just custodial care, but also ministry in its truest sense.

Third, curriculum provides you with ideas and words that help make your natural teaching effective. Since the best kind of teaching for babies and toddlers is primarily one on one, don't expect that babies or toddlers will sit in a circle, have a group time or even remain interested in what you are doing for very long. But as you sit on the floor and talk and play with two or three babies, make frequent use of the conversation ideas and songs suggested in your curriculum. Plan to provide at least one or two of the theme-related activities. Play portions of the music, repeating the same songs frequently. The sounds, words, actions and, most of all, the feelings that are created in this casual setting will flow into a natural pattern of teaching and learning that will eventually build a young child's understanding of God, Jesus and the loving comfort found in the people around him or her at church.

Fourth, using a curriculum with monthly themes also helps provide continuity to the activities in the nursery, especially when caregivers change frequently.

How to Use Music

Music can be a wonderful gift to share with babies and toddlers. Music can create a mood, promote familiarity and comfort, make children familiar with concepts about God, increase language and listening skills, provide the basis for large-muscle activities—the list is endless. Songs are fun for both children and caregivers!

Repeatable Songs
If you sing the same "Hello" and "Goodbye" songs every week, children will become familiar with them. Repetition builds security for a

young child. Such songs also cue children about what comes next, and they make the nursery seem a more comfortable place. A song to signal any new activity can make the transition easier.

Try singing a spontaneous song when you see a child is becoming upset. The song need not rhyme, and it may only have two or three notes. For instance, "I see Jenny dropped her cracker. It's okay; I'll get another" sung to a simple tune (such as "Skip to My Lou") can refocus the child and head off tears. It acknowledges the situation, uses the child's name and tells the child that you will help. The same song may be used over and over, substituting another child's name and another situation.

Think about ways you will use music as you care for children. Your nursery curriculum may provide a song or two that reinforce each unit's theme. Play it for the children. Learn it well enough to sing it spontaneously throughout the month at appropriate times during the session. Although it is rare for most young children to sing with you, they do love to hear you sing; and your voice, even if a bit off-key, is fine to them.

Recorded Music

If you have a large collection of music available for use, take time to plan how and when you will use it, considering the age and needs of the children as well as the activity and noise levels you want.

If you play recorded music in the background, turn it off before it becomes background noise and children are no longer interested. Even quiet music may increase the tension level, if children must raise their voices to be heard above it.

Rather than playing recorded music for the entire group, consider using music in small groups of two to three children at a time. Provide adequate space for babies or toddlers to move, and seat yourself on the floor, with a music player on a child-sized table. Let the children bounce or move in response to the music; when they lose interest, invite several other children to participate.

Using quiet songs to help a baby relax and go to sleep is as natural as breathing. Such songs will not only comfort the little ones but will also communicate God's love and calm your spirit as well. Recorded quiet songs and lullabies may be played at a low level in the sleeping room. Always be observant to see if the music calms or enlivens the mood in the room, and adjust the music accordingly.

How to Reach Out to Families

In the nursery, the only member of a family we may often focus on is the baby or toddler. But each child is part of a family to which we also should minister; families with young children need the support and encouragement of others in the Body of Christ so that a growing walk with God can be a reality for the entire family. So building solid relationships with the baby's family is an essential part of the nursery ministry.

Building solid relationships with the baby's family is an essential part of the nursery ministry.

Learn About the Family

While a child's family may consist of two parents, be aware that you may also be dealing with other family types: single parent (mother or father), blended families (a step-parent), extended family members with primary caregiving roles (grandparents, aunts), foster families, and others. Use your nursery's records to acquaint yourself with each child's family. Once you know the family, be alert for ways to build your relationship with them.

Build Relationships at the Church

When a parent brings a baby or toddler to the nursery, your friendly greeting and a personal comment to or about the child sends the message, "You and your child are important to us. We care about you!" Parents feel comfortable when they know that the caregivers in the nursery see their child as an individual. When parents bring the child, ask a question or two to show your interest in the child's welfare. ("What types of toys does he most enjoy?" "What new skill has she been working on this week?") When parents pick up the child, tell them about something the child enjoyed. If your church uses a form or note to communicate with parents about diaper changes, feedings, and so forth, read one aloud occasionally to the parents (if time permits) and add your observations.

Use informal moments around the church to talk with family members. You don't have to be outgoing, just caring!

Build Relationships During the Week

Often, time to talk with parents before or after a session is limited. So take a few minutes during the week to strengthen the connection with each family. Consider calling, emailing or writing each family during the week, communicating in whichever way would best fit the situation in each family.

For example, if a child cried during the nursery session, ask, "What suggestions do you have for helping Barry feel more secure at the nursery?" If a child had a good time, tell the parents about something you noticed. If a child bit, hit, or pulled the hair of another child, ask for tips on how best to redirect the child's behavior. (Keep in mind that when dealing with a problem behavior, approach the parent with the understanding that the parent knows the child better than anyone else and is thus likely to be the best source of insight into the child's behavior. Be very cautious about seeming to criticize either the child or the parent.)

Another way to build the relationship is to invite the family to become involved in other ministries that are likely to be of interest to families with young children. Adult study groups and classes, including parenting classes, Parent's Night Out Programs, baby-sitting cooperatives and play groups, potlucks, and volunteering in the nursery—whatever your church has to offer—all draw the family into a deeper relationship with the Body of Christ.

How to Arrange the Nursery

No one has yet surveyed babies and toddlers to find out what they like or don't like about a nursery; but by carefully watching the behavior of little ones, we can begin to "think like a baby" about our nursery's environment and the ways in which it could better meet the needs of babies and toddlers.

See the Room from a Child's Perspective

Once we begin to think like a baby or toddler, the next step should be to see the room with the eyes of a baby or toddler. Literally, sit on the floor of the nursery in several different spots and look at the room from that perspective.

How does the carpet smell? Is the floor clean? Are the floor pillows firm or squishy?

How many things are there for the children to pull themselves up on? Climb over? Crawl in and out of? Rest on? Is there space for children to crawl without being stepped on? To walk without being knocked down?

What places can children reach under (especially where the vacuum cleaner can't clean) or over? What can children climb up on?

Are there different textures to touch? A variety of sounds to hear? Places to be quiet as well as places to be active and noisy?

Are there interesting things to see on the walls at the children's eye level? Are they safe for children to touch? Are they free of pins, thumbtacks and staples that children might put in their mouths?

Are there different places (cribs, swings, bounce chairs, blanket on the floor, etc.) for children to stay for a time? Will children have to stay in just one place for a long time? May children move about freely if they want to? Is the floor safe to explore?

Does the toy shelf look inviting or forbidding? Do the toys offer lots of ways of exploring? What things can children push? Pull? Stack? Manipulate? Collect? Dump? Throw? Can children get these things into their mouths and safely out again? Will a grownup make sure the toy any child puts in his or her mouth is cleaned before another baby puts the toy in his or her mouth?

Do children get to explore "messy" things like sand, dough or water?

Keep looking around. Seeing the room from a child's perspective will help you think of the parts of a nursery environment that are important to a baby or toddler. Then you can adapt your room to suit the needs of your young ones.

Establish Activity Areas for a Large Nursery

In a large church nursery where there are many children and adults in the same room, designate certain activities for each adult to provide for children throughout the session. For example, one caregiver may position him- or herself near several books, looking and talking about them with interested children. Another adult may sit near an open area of the room with a music player nearby, playing one or two action songs and doing the suggested motions with children in that area of the room. However, as the session progresses, adults need to be ready to move to where the action is. Flexibility is key.

Source
Sheryl Haystead, *Nursery Smart Pages: A Guide for Nursery Directors and Caregivers* (Ventura, CA: Gospel Light, 1997).

2

Preschool

(AGES 2 TO 3)

The Lord Jesus taught us the great importance of the child. He always had time for these little ones. He put out His arms and said, "Let the little children come to me, and do not hinder them, for the kingdom of heaven belongs to such as these" (Matthew 19:14). The most striking thing about Jesus' encounter with these little ones is not that He interrupted an adult meeting to take time for some children. Nor is it surprising that He physically picked up the children and loved them. The remarkable part of this incident is Jesus' words. Most adults would have said something like "Let the little children come to me, and don't prevent them, for some day they will grow up and become important."

The Worth and Value of Little Children

Jesus saw something in childhood besides the future. He recognized worth and value in the state of being a child, for He told the waiting adults in the crowd that children are important for what they are right now—"For the kingdom of heaven belongs to such as these."

We adults always seem to be looking to the future. This push for preparation robs childhood of much of its essence, as parents and teachers urge little ones hurriedly through the present in search of a more significant future.

The Future—Now

"I know it's hard for a three-year-old to sit quietly and listen, but I have to start getting him ready for later when he will have to sit still."

"If she's going to be a success in life, she'll have to go to college. And to make sure she can stay ahead in school, I'm going to teach her to read before she starts first grade if it kills us both!"

"If a child is going to grow up with an appreciation for the great hymns of the church, you just can't start too young to teach them."

These and many similar statements are used repeatedly by parents and teachers who are earnestly concerned about helping young children get ready for future roles and demands. Unfortunately, these well-meaning adults sometimes actually do more harm than good, because in their long-range view of growth, they have lost sight of the value in just being a child.

Children are more than people in transition, waiting for some future date of real meaning. The qualities that come from being young are not flaws or imperfections; rather, childhood is a marked and definable stage of development.

You may think, *But an adult has so many capabilities and accomplishments far beyond those of a child. Surely the years of productive and responsible adulthood are more significant than those of infancy and early childhood.* But what adult experiences could replace the laughter of children that gladdens the hearts of all who hear? How many hours of labor would it take to equal the smile of a little girl or little boy? What a sterile world this would be were children not present to add their unique joys and sorrows!

The Value—Now

Has any parent ever seen more deeply into him- or herself than when holding a newborn child and looking into that child's eyes? All the writings and research of humankind couldn't provide the insights that come with observing the experiences of a child starting out on his or her own unique adventure. The child's fresh enthusiasm for everything seen, the child's honest questions and powerfully simple logic—all combine to peel the scales from our encrusted adult eyes.

What is the value of a child—as a child? Incalculable!

This is no plea for attempting to stop the progress of maturation. This is simply a call to recognize that just because a phase of life is brief and is replaced by another more sophisticated, we should not rush past it; for if we bypass the unique stages of childhood, we strip each succeeding developmental stage of some of its finest ingredients. The best preparation for any phase of life is the proper completion of the previous one. The second coat of paint must always wait for the first to dry. Harvest never begins when the first green shoots appear in the spring. Human life has an aching void when childhood is squeezed away.

Just because a phase of life is brief and is replaced by another more sophisticated, we should not rush past it; for if we bypass the unique stages of childhood, we strip each succeeding developmental stage of some of its finest ingredients.

Is this what Jesus had in mind when He took a small child in His arms and said, "I tell you the truth, unless you change and become like little children, you will never enter the kingdom of heaven" (Matthew 18:3)? Is there a place in our homes and churches for children to be children? Do we wholeheartedly accept them as they are, not as we wish they were? Do the rooms and materials we provide sound out "Welcome!" to a young learner? Are the adults who surround young children deeply sympathetic and understanding of what these special years are all about?

Or do we merely see little ones in terms of their potential, enduring them until they get old enough to really matter? Is the church's objective in providing children's ministries a means of attracting their parents or of getting ready for the church of tomorrow? Is our goal to train young children to act like miniature adults because their noisy spontaneity might somehow mar our sacred corridors?

W. C. Fields wrung many laughs from his famous line, "Anyone who hates dogs and kids can't be all bad." But have you ever met a person who wanted to live in a world where everyone shared Fields's dislike of children?

It's far better to follow the Lord Jesus' pattern with children. His loving response to children lets us see into His heart's feeling of the worth of a young life.

Childhood is not a disease to be cured or endured. It is a God-ordained part of human life with value and significance that continually enriches the experiences of those who may have forgotten what it is like to see the world from a fresh, unspoiled point of view.

Age-Level Characteristics

Physical

Preschool children are very much alive and lively. Their bodies are active. They are wiggling, wide-eyed question marks who need love. Three-year-old children love to jump and run and climb and tiptoe and march. They enjoy finger play. They like to fill bottles and empty them, put things in drawers and pull them out. They cannot sit still for any length of time. You will find that they cannot stand in a straight line with other children, for they must move to balance themselves.

Three-year-olds can really do things with their hands. They can build towers and houses and trains with blocks; they can help dress themselves; they can wash their own hands. And it is amazing to watch them master riding a tricycle. They enjoy stringing beads, putting together simple puzzles and playing with dough. They may begin to use scissors.

Two-year-olds are not so sure footed, although they run about constantly. Although their large muscles are developing, their small hand and finger muscles are not yet developed; but they can scribble on paper, throw a ball, turn pages of a book, build with blocks and begin to do the things mentioned above. They enjoy simple songs with movement and large-muscle activities. They need room to roam as well as quiet-time activities. Two-year-olds also are often in the process of being potty trained.

Cognitive and Emotional

Two- and three-year-olds are earnestly trying to discover what lies in the world around them. They see everything and want to handle everything they see, because they are learning what things are. Two-year-olds typically develop a vocabulary of between 200 and 300 words, which they begin to put together in very simple sentences, and baby talk begins to disappear. A two-year-old uses "no" frequently as a way to define his or her separate identity. The vocabulary of three-year-olds may be close to 1,000 words, and you will find that they will talk in longer sentences. They may be able to write part of their names and can usually identify colors. Of course, children this age understand many more words than they use.

Except as they are taught, Bible words are not in the vocabulary of preschoolers. This is the privilege of the Sunday School teacher as the child learns to talk. Teach these preschoolers to talk of the heavenly Father and to pray to Him. And since the attention span of preschoolers is relatively short, mainly use short and simple sentences when talking with children this age. They will sit and listen to simple stories, and usually enjoy retelling a story or activity, which increases their sense of mastery. They can learn rhymes, songs and finger plays. Three-year-olds can wait for short periods of time and may show more sympathy for others.

The natural curiosity of children this age is their greatest aid in learning, as they learn a great deal through their senses. Their curiosity makes them love to touch things and listen to sounds and taste and see what things are. They love to take things apart and put them together. They are eager to do things without help.

If they draw, it is with big sweeps of the crayons. Put up an easel and let them express themselves with large sweeping motions. Get a roll of newsprint and let them have all the room they need to draw.

Preschoolers are learning very rapidly. And they are wonderful imitators. If Daddy crosses his knee and reads the paper, his child is quick to pull up a little chair and try to balance him- or herself as one chubby knee is put over the other and the paper is held up, invariably upside down—but it is like Daddy. In fact, he tries to do everything you do. If Mother cooks or sits reading a book, then the child must cook or sit reading a book—just like Mommy. This imitation takes place in the Sunday School preschool as well, so teachers must be mindful of all that they do. Both parent and teacher are challenged to give the Lord Jesus Christ control of their own lives so that they may be examples of love and patience and Christian living. Parents and teachers cannot teach lovingkindness except as they show it.

Social

Preschoolers have social limitations and are only slowly learning to live and play with others. The preschool teacher who realizes the social limitations of these children is better able to cope with discipline problems, which are better handled with distraction and redirection rather than reasoning. Two-year-olds have only a casual awareness of other children. They are more likely to ignore other children and go about following their own interests. One day Billy may push Judy out of the way as if she were an inanimate object. The next Sunday he may speak to her and hug her. "It's mine! It's mine!" is a constant cry of two-year-olds, and they will go to any extreme to claim ownership of a toy. They have no idea of how to share with other children, but they are beginning to understand what taking turns means. When you talk with them, get on their eye level, and talk about what you see them doing to help them know you notice them and love them (this applies to three-years-olds as well).

Three-year-olds have made more progress. They still enjoy playing by themselves, but they can also play with others, although sharing and taking turns are still not habitual. By now they seek the approval of adults, and this helps them have a willingness to share. They understand the meaning of "Wait until it is your turn." Yet at times, like two-year-olds, they may go to extremes to gain possession of the things they feel belong to them.

Three-year-olds pay great attention to adults. They listen to adults and watch their faces, looking to see if the adults approve or disapprove. They are willing to accept some suggestions by this time.

These little children long for love and affection. Don't be afraid to show love to them. Tell them you love them. Your displays of affection won't adversely affect them. You will often find that children brought up in a foster home or in a house that is stern in its discipline and cold in its dealings are much more timid than children who have had personal attention. Children want to feel that they belong. Love gives them a sense of security.

It is not unusual to find that children act very differently at home from the way they do in Sunday School. Compare notes with the parents. Discover each child's weaknesses and strengths. A child who is naturally very shy should not have too much attention forced upon him or her. A shy child will be much happier and will adjust more quickly to the group by being left alone and talked to very little. The too-forward child is best handled by being removed from the center of interest. If the child will not cooperate, consider using another child as an example. If the uncooperative child is naturally a dawdler, it may be best to let him or her poke along at his or her own pace. This characteristic may be seen in a two-year-old, but it will not be long before he or she is a bustling three-year-old.

It is not wise to give direct commands to preschool children. If you do, you will find that you are too often disobeyed or defied. Rather, put your command in the form of a wish or a tactful suggestion. In this way you can avoid a direct conflict with the child.

Probably the greatest problem in the preschool is the child who habitually strikes, pinches and pushes other children around. Often this is an indication of a deeper need than appears on the surface. In order to deal effectively with these problem behaviors, the teacher must study the child who exhibits them, learning about the home environment and seeking to learn the reason for the behaviors. No matter what the child's problem, and no matter what the child's personality, prayer will help the teacher deal with the child, always remembering the promise, "If any of you lack wisdom, let him ask of God, that giveth to all men liberally" (James 1:5). How much wisdom we need!

Spiritual

Two-year-olds can learn that God made everything, that God cares about them, that Jesus is God's special Son, that the Bible is God's special book and that Jesus and Bible stories are true. Talk and sing about God often. *Three-year-olds can understand that Jesus was born as a baby and grew up to do kind things, that God is good and that Jesus loves us, and that God forgives when people are sorry for doing wrong.* Three-year-olds understand more about God's love and nature through loving actions than through spoken words.

A Quality Program

If the teachers in your church are like most teachers, they want to feel as if they're making a significant difference in the lives of the young children they teach and care for. As busy people choose whether or not to be involved in ministry to children, they want to know that they are doing more than baby-sitting or filling time; they want to know that their time will be well spent. Sometimes, however, either from a lack of awareness or from misguided priorities, a church misses the opportunity to effectively nurture young children. Instead of creating purposeful programs that help young children begin to build a lifelong foundation of faith, a minimum of Christian education is given.

By focusing on your church's early childhood programs, you will reap significant benefits and results in the Christian growth of preschoolers. The development of a quality early childhood Christian education ministry starts with careful consideration of the ways in which young children learn and grow in their understanding of who God is and how His Word gives direction for everyday life.

A quality early childhood Christian education ministry starts with careful consideration of the ways in which young children learn and grow in their understanding of who God is and how His Word gives direction for everyday life.

Choose a Loving Staff

The teacher must have a natural love for children and must have the ability to see as little children see, if he or she is to succeed. (If God has given to you the gift of sympathy that opens up the child's heart, do not pray for a higher gift. There is none.) The teacher of little children must exude a glowing love for Christ. The warm radiance of the sunshine of His presence in the teacher is necessary to both the soil and the seed-life that is in the teacher's care.

Because little children have a natural tendency to imitate, it is not only necessary for the teacher to be the kind of person that each child should become, but the teaching itself should be the thing the teacher wishes the child to do, as often as is practicable. In other words, if the children are to bow their heads, the teacher must bow his or her own head. If the teacher wishes the children to kneel, the teacher must kneel, too.

Recognize How Young Children Learn

It is generally assumed that learning follows four steps:

1. Gain new information.
2. Come to understand the meaning of the new information.
3. Develop attitudes and beliefs about that meaning.
4. Put the information into practice.

With young children, however, a great deal of learning occurs almost in reverse:

1. Experience something that is true.
2. Accept that experience as true.
3. Repeat the experience often enough so that the truth begins to be understood.
4. Hear words that describe that truth, giving the truth a new richness and resulting in additional understanding.

As this cycle repeats itself over and over, a child's learning and understanding grow in significant ways.

An effective early childhood ministry gives teachers the tools to help children learn through everyday experiences coupled with the words of Bible truth. Such a ministry will truly make a difference in the spiritual nurture of children.

This cycle of learning applies to education in all areas of life, including Christian education. Therefore, an effective early childhood ministry gives teachers the tools to help children learn through everyday experiences coupled with the words of Bible truth. Such a ministry will truly make a difference in the spiritual nurture of children.

Incorporate Active Play

The hallmark of Christian education for preschoolers is active play experiences that engage each child with loving Christian adults. Play is not only the way the young child learns about objects, people and relationships, but it is also the best way for a young child to learn about God and His love. The Christian faith we share with children must be more than mere words or information. It is not enough for the young child to hear God's Word or even to memorize it. The child must live it. A child is not yet able to listen to explanations about the concepts and beliefs of the Christian faith: The child must play with materials. In order to learn effectively, the child uses all of his or her senses—seeing, touching, tasting, smelling and hearing.

Therefore, we can best help children learn Bible truths by providing active play experiences that a teacher connects to Bible stories and verses through comments and questions. As a teacher uses words to describe ways children are putting God's Word into action, the child's play takes on the qualities of Bible learning. The combination of words and actions, frequently repeated, expands and clarifies the child's thinking. This kind of active, experiential learning cannot be rushed.

As a teacher uses words to describe ways children are putting God's Word into action, the child's play takes on the qualities of Bible learning.

It takes time! Early childhood programs that allow for significant active learning time provide the most benefit to young children.

Include Music

Listen to the children sing. Two- and three-year-olds seem to be innately rhythmical. They love to sing the same songs over and over again. And they like to make up their own songs.

By the time children are two and a half, they can learn several short songs. Three-year-old children learn more quickly, but they still enjoy singing the same songs each week. The teacher's aim with music is not musical perfection but the happy expression of little hearts.

Effective Teaching Methods

Most efforts to teach young children focus on the things adults want children to know. While accurate information is important and is expressed through words, words and facts are very imperfect vehicles for learning children. In order to see long-term results for your efforts, all dimensions of children's learning must be involved. The teacher's role is not merely to transmit truth; the teacher must also demonstrate truth in practical everyday activities.

The teacher's role is not merely to transmit truth; the teacher must also demonstrate truth in practical everyday activities.

Through the Senses

As stated earlier, two- and three-year-olds learn best when all of their senses are involved, and this type of learning takes place best during active play. The minds of preschoolers are not yet capable of handling ideas expressed only in words. These young children do not have the ability to give real meaning to a word unless the word is a very familiar part of experience and evokes ideas and feelings from memory.

Firsthand experiences, then, are the hard core of learning for young children. Efforts to produce learning must involve as many of the children's five senses as possible. Watching videos, sitting in large groups to sing songs and drawing on coloring pages are activities of limited value, as they involve only portions of children's senses. Quality Christian education requires much more. Building with blocks, exploring natural items and participating in art and dramatic play are activities of great value, as they often engage all of the senses.

By Repetition

Repetition is a necessary and natural part of a young child's learning. Children who feel happy and satisfied with learning experiences will want to repeat them. Songs and stories become favorites only when they are enjoyed over and over.

By Practice in Play

Practice in play will reinforce learning. Children also need opportunities to practice behaviors that reflect Christian values. Repetition through play strengthens habits, attitudes, knowledge and understanding. Children learn because they are doing. And for young children, doing is play.

Play does not sound very educational or spiritual. But play is the full-time occupation of children: It is the activity through which children learn best. Adults often distinguish between work and play. Not so with young children! Blocks, crayons, dolls, play dough and toy cars are the tools children use in play. They also are tools by which the children can learn Bible truth when guided by alert teachers.

By Imitation

Imitation is something used by children from infancy on; they continually pick up ways of doing things from the observation of others. A teacher's role, therefore, is not just to do "teacher things" but also to participate with children in the midst of their activity. If you show kindness by sharing a crayon or marker, children will learn to share. If you thank God for making the colors in a fabric collage children are gluing, they will learn to pray in the midst of daily activities.

By Connecting Words to Actions

Connecting words to actions eliminates any worry about the limited vocabularies and experiences of young children and, therefore, their limited ability to understand and combine concepts. When you and a child are building a house with blocks, you may think, *I'm glad I have a house to live in. God shows His love for me by providing a house!* The young child, however, may only think, *I like the way this house looks!* You must provide words that help the child respond to the activity and relate God to the event. Once this relationship is made, the child is able to think about God the next time he or she builds a house. Without your words, the activity would be simply another of many fun play experiences.

You must provide words that help the child respond to the activity and relate God to the event. Once this relationship is made, the child is able to think about God the next time he or she builds a house.

The Preschool Room

It is very important for preschool children to meet in suitable surroundings. Adults may excuse the limitations of the church, but preschool children do not understand such things. Preschoolers may not be conscious of unpleasant details, but they will sense an unpleasant atmosphere, and this might color their attitude toward spiritual matters as a whole. A damp, dark, unused basement corner just won't do. You may not have the ideal place, but you can choose the *very best spot* for these little two- and three-year-olds.

The ideal preschool room should be large, airy, light and attractive. Remember that the room is important, even though the place you must use seems inadequate. A lot may be done to make an otherwise drab room bright and attractive. All you need for a start is adequate space and a loving heart. Work will do the rest. Something as simple as paint can work wonders. Although there are no hard and fast rules about what colors to use, many people find light green restful, and soft yellow imparts sunshine.

Have you ever tried sitting on the floor for an hour? If so, you have had a view of the world as two- and three-year-olds see it. You probably found that chair seats were on a level with your eyes. You couldn't even see what was on the table, because everything was so high above you. If you try this experiment of sitting on the floor for an hour, you will understand the need for a specially equipped room for preschool children. The children's experience in the preschool room is the introduction of these children to the Lord's house, and we want them to think of it as a delightful place. Study *Early Childhood Smart Pages* to discover the details for carrying on a Preschool Department. So much information is given in the *Smart Pages* that repetition of all of it here isn't necessary.

Sources

Sheryl Haystead, *Nursery Smart Pages: A Guide for Nursery Directors and Caregivers* (Ventura, CA: Gospel Light, 1997).

Sheryl Haystead, *Early Childhood Smart Pages* (Ventura, CA: Gospel Light, 2002).

3

Prekindergarten/Kindergarten

(AGES 4 TO 5)

When a child reaches the age of four, he or she should graduate into the Prekindergarten/Kindergarten Department. Send a birthday card to the child and invite him or her to join the group.

Although these little ones have graduated to a new class, the way they learn is the same as it was when they were two- and three-year-olds, so it would be good to review what was written in the previous chapter. And as true as that last statement is, we must also recognize that every child develops in a unique way. At any given chronological age, children's developmental differences will vary greatly. But some basic guidelines can help you become both a better observer and a more effective teacher.

Learn the Age-Level Characteristics

Physical

At four years of age, children begin a period of rapid growth. Coordination catches up in both small and large muscles. They still need a great deal of space and time to explore and enjoy the creative process.

Five-year-olds are doing some things by themselves. They are learning to tie their own shoes, to cut with scissors successfully and to draw pictures that are recognizable to others. Girls move ahead of boys in development. Coordination has usually become excellent.

Cognitive and Emotional

Four-year-olds begin to ask why and how. Their attention spans are still short, but they can concentrate for longer periods. They may often test the limits of what is acceptable behavior.

Five-year-olds are often able to write their own names, copy words and letters and may even read some words. They can talk accurately about recent events and speak understandably. They love to learn why, still seek adult approval and love to discover for themselves through play and experimenting. Encourage them to think by asking what-could-happen-next and how-could-you-solve-this open-ended questions.

Social

Four-year-olds begin to enjoy being with other children in group activities. They want to please adults and usually love their teachers. Give each child a chance to feel successful by helping in some way. Provide ways they can sing, pray and talk together.

Five-year-olds enjoy extended periods of cooperative play, usually with one or two others. They enjoy group activities and need to feel that they are seen and heard. Need for attention may cause them to act in negative ways. Give attention before negative actions occur. Give good eye contact at eye level and be sure to show that you see, hear and love them.

Spiritual

Four-year-olds begin to understand more about Jesus. They can grasp that Jesus is God's Son, that He died to take the punishment for the wrong things we have done and that He did not stay dead but rose again and is still alive. They can also be taught that the Bible tells us ways to obey God and that we can talk to God in prayer.

Five-year-olds are the most likely to respond by talking about the Bible story or Bible verse, and some children will understand that being kind as Jesus was is something they can do. Some children, especially those from Christian homes, may be interested in becoming members of God's family. Help them feel confident that God hears their prayers and that God wants to help them. As with all young children, they think literally and concretely and cannot understand abstract ideas like "Jesus in my heart" or "born again."

The most important way we teach young children about God's love is to show them! As we get on their level, listen to them, encourage them and make them feel secure, they begin to link God's love with the joy, excitement and security they feel from you.

Understand Different Learning Styles

To be the most effective teachers or parents we can be, we need to be aware of each child's style of learning. God made each of us unique and loves our uniqueness. Once we understand styles of learning, we are better able to provide an environment that helps children know the reality of God's love for each of them as individuals!

Research is constantly finding new ways people learn and express their knowledge. As you read the broad descriptions of these ways given below (a few known by more than one name), first recognize your own learning styles; these affect the choices for activities you plan. Then read again to pinpoint the strengths of the young learners you know. Most children will display a combination of these approaches to learning.

When you provide activities that challenge and stimulate children in the ways they learn best, they are more focused and ready to learn. It may not be easy or interesting for you to do some activities because of your own learning styles; but as you understand the needs of each child, you'll find it worthwhile to try the activities you never thought you'd do.

Visual (Spatial)

Visual learners learn best when there is something to look at. They enjoy creating pictures and building with blocks. They usually are eager to learn to read and write because they want to see the information. They like to imagine the scenes of the stories they hear, enjoy worksheets and prefer complete quiet to background music or sound. They are bothered by visual clutter, so they prefer an orderly environment. (It's estimated that most schoolteachers are mainly visual learners!)

Verbal (Linguistic)

Verbal learners learn best by talking and conversing. They process ideas as they talk about them; they like to listen to stories read aloud or audio versions of books. They remember things that are set to music. They like to have music or sound in the background and are not very bothered by visual clutter. They ask many questions, not because they weren't paying attention, but because they want more understanding.

They may be considered too talkative or distracting, but verbal youngsters challenge us to provide those opportunities to talk and listen so that they can learn.

Physical (Kinesthetic)

Physical learners learn best when their bodies are in motion. They often have good coordination and may use their hands as they talk or may act out what they say. They process information with their whole bodies. Tactile learners learn well through touch. They like to take things apart. They fiddle with things constantly and learn far more by doing than by seeing or hearing. Physical and tactile learners respond to touches and hugs, a cozy environment and soft lighting. They need lots of hands-on activities that involve more than one sense. Large-muscle activities (such as an action to help them remember a word and so forth) help keep these children involved.

Relational (Interpersonal)

Relational learners are keen observers, noting body language and tone of voice. They process information by realizing how people feel and they respond accordingly. They like cooperative, interactive activities; they are "people persons" who are energized by interaction.

Reflective (Introspective)

Reflective learners don't shun group activities, but they tend to think more about who they are and where they fit; they are sometimes drained by too much group interaction and express themselves more often through one-person activities.

Logical (Mathematical)

To some degree, every child is a problem-solver and explorer, but some take to it and enjoy it more than others. These learners see the patterns in the world and can think through problems. They are glad to have point-by-point explanations of how things work and enjoy games and puzzles that challenge them. They often count things without being asked to count. They may enjoy sorting toys into categories (things that are red, things that fly, and so on).

Musical

Most young children enjoy music, but some are more sensitive to rhythm and pitch and to the musical quality of spoken language (such as poetry). They tend to be good listeners but probably won't sit still when music is playing. They express themselves through making up songs of their own on the spot and through dance and movement whenever they hear music.

Naturalistic

Naturalistic learners learn best when they are involved with the natural world—being outdoors and interacting with natural surroundings. God's creation is a constant wonder to be explored, investigated and categorized. They want to experience and interact with their environment. These learners enjoy having windows in the classroom, so they can gaze out of them and see what's happening outside. And they are glad to participate in activities that use nature items.

Use Effective Teaching Methods

Many young children can repeat advertising jingles verbatim. They may count in foreign languages or quote entire children's books! When these feats of memory are applauded, adults often comment, "You know so much!" Young children do have a great facility for memorization. But as much fun as it may be and for all the approval it might gain a child, memorization does not reflect understanding. In fact, a child's ability to memorize may erroneously lead adults to assume that a child really understands what he or she is repeating! Especially when it comes to spiritual truth, it is imperative that we connect with young children's minds and hearts in ways that build true understanding.

When it comes to spiritual truth, it is imperative that we connect with young children's minds and hearts in ways that build true understanding.

Concrete Experiences

Children younger than seven or eight are concrete thinkers—that is, they don't think symbolically and do not reason in the same way that adults do. They are still in the process of learning very basic things about the material world around them and of developing the words to describe it. They understand best what they experience, touch and see. Concrete experiences lay a foundation for more advanced symbolic thought later on. However, teaching spiritual truth presents an interesting difficulty: How do we communicate truths about someone we cannot see?

Jesus' Method

The Christian faith and the Bible are full of word pictures, metaphors and symbols. When Jesus lived on earth, He often taught in parables or stories that connected to people's everyday lives (planting seeds, watching birds, building a house, and so forth). Jesus knew that learning about God's kingdom would be better understood if He related spiritual ideas to experiences that were familiar and related to people's previous knowledge.

Good teachers always connect new learning to students' prior knowledge. However, it's important to remember that the prior knowledge of four- and five-year-old children is quite limited! They still need to learn what a seed is and how it grows. They still need to learn about flowers and building a house. Since they cannot yet understand abstract concepts and metaphors, we should follow Jesus' example of teaching effectively by relating new ideas to children's real lives.

We should follow Jesus' example of teaching effectively by relating new ideas to children's real lives.

Practical Pointers

Use stories and lessons that teach one main idea at time. Plan to focus the entire session around that one concept so that the same idea is presented repeatedly in a variety of differnt ways. This repetition will provide a broader base of experience from which the children can gain understanding.

Begin where these young children are. These little ones can understand loving and helping because they have experienced both. They can understand Jesus' physical birth as a baby because they have seen babies. But they cannot understand the idea of spiritual rebirth. If they hear about Jesus "living in your heart," they wonder how a grown man could fit inside them! Because they have experienced being part of a family, it is better to talk about being a member of God's family. They can understand that David took care of sheep and wrote songs about God but not that we are "the sheep of God's hand."

Choose stories, lessons and songs that relate to children's real lives. Try not to use similes or metaphors to describe what you want to teach children. Say, for example, "The Bible is a special book. It tells us about God and what He wants us to do." Avoid, for example, "The Bible is like food we need to eat daily."

Remember that time is meaningless to four- and five-year-olds. For children this young, it doesn't matter if Jesus was born 2,000 years ago or two years ago. They haven't lived long enough to have a concept of the past!

Choose songs that mean exactly what they say. For example, "Jesus Loves Me This I Know" would be a better choice than "Jesus Wants Me for a Sunbeam." While many traditional songs may be appropriate for older children (say, "Deep and Wide" or "This Little Light of Mine"), such symbolic meaning is lost on children who are only four and five years old. Don't be afraid to change some words to favorite songs to make the meaning more literal. For example, in "The B-I-B-L-E" substitute "I like to hear the Word of God" for "I stand alone on the Word of God" (which preschoolers often interpret as someone standing on a Bible).

Above all, pray for guidance as you teach children. Jesus said that "with God all things are possible" (Mark 10:27) and "apart from me you can do nothing" (John 15:5, *NIV*). As you pray, observe and do your best to teach as Jesus taught, and you'll see children grow in remembering *and* understanding God's Word!

Challenge Kindergarteners

In any group of children entering kindergarten, developmental maturity might range from that of a three-year-old to that of a seven-year-old. This is neither good nor bad—it simply *is*. Every child develops at his or her own unique pace. Because of such differences, teachers need to be ready to either simplify or expand activities in such a way that every child gains understanding, competence and feelings of success.

At some point during the kindergarten year, many children's minds seem to suddenly kick into high gear. Fascinated with learning, they ask wonderful questions that show they are thinking deeply: "Where is heaven? Why does the water look blue? What makes your brain think?" These children are eager for greater mental challenges, so be prepared to expand activities and increase the challenge, keeping every child excited and involved!

Thinking Skills

Any activity, at any moment, can be given an increasing level of challenge with kindergarteners.

Invite children to observe and then categorize. "What is the same about these pumpkins and these watermelons? What is different?" "What other fruits are the same color as these apples?" "How many sheep do you see in the picture?" "How many horses with brown spots do you count? How many goats have black tails?"

Invite children to find common characteristics either in something or someone observed. "Who else is wearing red?" "Where is another person in the picture who is wearing a sweater?" "What are Jack and I wearing that is the same?"

Stop at various points when reading a story and invite children to predict what they think will happen next. To expand the prediction work, invite children to make up endings to the story or draw a picture of what they think could happen next, or invite children to suggest outcomes if a character did something different. "What would have been different if Jesus had told the blind man to be quiet?" "What if Samuel had not asked Eli what he wanted?"

Begin an open-ended story. Invite each child to take a turn contributing one or two sentences. You may also show a picture and ask children to tell what they think happened before the picture or what they think might happen next. Such simple activities challenge and sharpen thinking skills.

Change an item of your clothing slightly and challenge children to detect what was changed.

Play charade games of any kind. Charades help children to learn the nuances of body language and think of ways to communicate without words.

Word Skills

Take advantage of children's natural curiosity regarding words and reading in the natural situations that arise during class time.

When children are asked to name people whom they can help, print the names on a large sheet of paper.

As part of a prayer time, ask children to name items for which they are thankful. Print each word on a large sheet of paper. "Read" the list aloud after each child has contributed.

If children in your class are beginning readers, print the words of a Bible verse on separate cards. As each word of the verse is said aloud, give a child the appropriate card. Then ask children to place the cards in order.

Label classroom items so that interested children may read the names.

While it is impressive when a young child can recite a Bible passage, memorization is no guarantee of understanding. Adult approval for memorizing will likely make a child feel successful but may also send the message that Bible words are just phrases to be spoken, not God's Word that gives direction to our lives. If children are to memorize Scripture, the verse should be one whose meaning you can make clear. Help the children understand what they are repeating. If you are not able to make the ideas in the passage clear to the children, perhaps that passage should be left for later!

Since a kindergarten-aged class usually contains children not yet reading, children in the process of learning to read and beginning readers, incorporate activities that include children at any skill level. Give children books to "read" to each other (whether or not the actual words are read); let them listen to recordings of a story while looking at books that contain the same words. These kinds of enrichment activities will help to span the gap in reading skills among children.

Number Skills
Counting anything is fun for kindergarteners!
Teach the names of the first five numbers in a foreign language.
Measure items with a measuring tape or measuring stick.
Bring a scale and weigh a variety of items.
Invite children to sort manipulative items (small building blocks, large beads, plastic animals) into a variety of categories, or create patterns in the way items are placed on the table or floor.

Include these challenges in such a way that children feel it is simply good fun. They are learning far more by these simple experiences than we can classify. Don't, however, test them later or expect right answers.

The heart of these expansion ideas is not so much achieving specific educational goals as much as it is stimulating children to explore and discover, keeping their involvement high. Most of all, make learning challenges fun! Don't pressure children to perform. Simply play with them, give out information and remind them of God's love for each one. Express your gratitude to God for the abilities He gave them.

Use Guided Conversation

Why do we need to guide conversation with young children? Don't we simply talk to them? Certainly there are many times when simple conversation is spontaneous. However, guided conversation helps children remember and recognize ways to apply the Bible truth that is the foundation for the day's activities in Sunday School.

What is guided conversation? Does it mean the teacher spends every minute spouting Bible verses or repeating the day's lesson focus? Talking only when a problem arises? No! Guided conversation is simply informal but planned conversation in which the teacher looks for opportunities to connect what children are doing to the Bible learning content of the session. Relating children's activities to Bible truths helps the children understand the relationship between what they are doing and what the Bible says.

Step 1: Know the Session's Lesson Focus and Bible Verse
Knowing the session's lesson focus and Bible verse prepares you to share these ideas whenever natural opportunities and teachable moments occur.

Guided conversation is simply informal but planned conversation in which the teacher looks for opportunities to connect what children are doing to the Bible.

Step 2: Listen

The biggest part of being a skilled teacher is being a good listener. When children are absorbed in an activity or are playing together, don't take a break or leave the area. Place yourself at the children's eye level, available to hear what they are saying. Listening and observing provide you with helpful insight into children's thoughts and feelings. Watch and listen for clues to their interests, how they see themselves and what things might bother them. Resist the temptation to tune out any child or race ahead mentally.

Step 3: Ask Questions

Invite children into conversation that involves more than answering yes or no. Ask open-ended questions that invite children to describe and discuss. For instance, when you see a child stacking blocks, you could say, "What do you think will happen if you put this big block on top? This little block?" Or you could say, "Tell me about your construction." Questions and comments that cannot be answered with a yes or no help children learn verbal skills, help them express their feelings and give you greater insight into their thoughts and feelings.

Step 4: Relate the Child's Thoughts and Feelings to God's Word

Relating children's thoughts and feelings to God's Word helps them to associate Bible truths with everyday living. You might begin by commenting on what you see. "Daniel, you helped Jake! You are obeying our Bible words. God tells us to help each other. Thank you!" You may also rephrase a child's words. "Bella, it sounds as if you had a happy time with Jaden. The Bible tells us that God gives us friends. We can thank God for Jaden. Thank You, God, for Bella's friend Jaden!"

Relating children's thoughts and feelings to God's Word helps them to associate Bible truths with everyday living.

When you identify acts of kindness or helpfulness, children then learn what it means to help each other, share or take turns. Relate a child's actions immediately, before children forget the circumstances. And use the child's name. Often, a child who does not hear his or her name assumes you are talking to someone else!

As you see children experience satisfaction, curiosity or even frustration, you are witnessing teachable moments. Children are especially receptive to new ideas at such times. Step in with a comment or question that will help the child resolve the problem; affirm a child's accomplishment with an "I see . . ." comment; answer a child's question and thank God for the child's curiosity on the spot.

With the session's Bible truths in mind, you are ready to listen, observe and comment in ways that will help each child understand more about how God's love and God's Word relate to the child's world.

 With the session's Bible truths in mind, you are ready to listen, observe and comment in ways that will help each child understand more about how God's love and God's Word relate to the child's world.

Include God's Word

It doesn't seem logical that a book completed nearly 2,000 years ago would have much to say to young children. But the Bible is far more than an ancient classic. The Word of God is living and active. It applies to every life in every age! For those who teach young children, however, it's up to us to help make the words and ideas of an ancient book something that relates to a young child's world.

The Bible is far more than an ancient classic. The Word of God is living and active. It applies to every life in every age!

The Bible is listed in curriculum as a necessary material in every activity for a very good reason: Although you can easily quote Bible verses, children need to associate the words with the Bible. This way they will know that the Bible is the source of these words. Frequently emphasize that the stories in the Bible are true.

The most direct use of and application of the Bible will come during conversation as natural opportunities arise. With your Bible open to the day's memory verse, say the verse aloud. Children will naturally associate using the Bible as a source of information and guidance in everyday situations. Because young children are "here and now" people, they need to have you see and interpret their actions in light of what the Bible says. Young children have a limited grasp of ideas, so this kind of natural, direct Bible teaching can help them know what Bible ideas can look like, sound like and act like.

Consider keeping a large-print Bible in your classroom. Display it prominently and use sticky notes or colorful bookmarks to help children find Bible verses. You'll find children enjoy pretending to read (or reading) the words you have marked.

While some older children may memorize Bible verses easily (especially when the words are sung to familiar music), don't pressure all young children to memorize the Bible verses. Make your main goal to help children understand the content of what God is saying to us and how we can obey Him.

Provide Play Activities

As Christians, we have far more to teach children than facts and words. It's not enough for children to hear us read from the Bible or even for children to memorize it. Words alone are the least effective way humans learn. When we hear words only, we must build a mental image based on previous information. Because the knowledge and experience of young children are so limited, they are not likely to gain a real understanding through hearing words alone.

For an idea to make any sense to young children, they must *do* something with it. And the word that describes most of what young children do is "play." However, young children are not yet able to play with *ideas*. So children must build understanding through playing with something they can touch. That's the reason for hands-on activities. Play-based activities are the most effective way for young children to learn. Young children can learn Bible truths effectively through active play experiences. As children draw, play games, build with blocks or hold dolls, natural opportunities arise for the teacher to link the children's actions to what God's Word says. When we describe the ways children are putting God's Word into action, we turn play activities into Bible learning. Play then takes on a greater purpose.

For instance, during a simple beanbag toss game, we can comment, "Kenna, you gave Josh a turn to toss the beanbag. Thank you! That is a way to be kind. The Bible tells us to be kind." As we effectively link a Bible truth to Kenna's actions, she now has a concrete example of a way to be kind.

> When we describe the ways children are putting God's Word into action, we turn play activities into Bible learning.

Providing repeated opportunities to think and talk about Bible truths creates more and more of those mental building blocks. As you participate with children in an activity, it's important to watch for opportunities to acknowledge and encourage children you see acting in ways that you can relate to the Bible truth.

Play-Based Activities Have Many Advantages

Play-based activities are opportunities for children to explore, create and discover with the materials you provide. There is no predetermined pattern that the children must follow. During these activities, you can talk informally with children, asking questions and guiding the conversation toward the Bible learning goals, rather than just issuing instructions. And children can talk with each other as well as with the teacher. These activities focus on the process (including the use of materials), group interaction and the connection to the Bible truth, not the product. Children have the ability to choose from two or more activities and choose how they want to complete the activity, as opposed to having to do the one project that is offered and being expected to produce the same result. Small groups work with one activity at a time and move freely from one activity to the other; everyone need not work on the same project at the same time.

Busy Hands Mean Open Minds

When children are fully involved in an activity they enjoy, we have the privilege of seeing them simply being themselves. When we observe them, we understand more about how they think. Also, children whose hands are busy are often eager to talk. Ask open-ended what-do-you-think questions. Avoid questions that have one-word answers. This chance to listen helps us determine what a child does or does not understand. Then we are able to respond in ways that truly meet that child's needs.

Watch for moments when a child experiences curiosity, expectation or frustration. In that moment of heightened interest, a child is most receptive to a new idea or the security of a familiar truth. Remember the words "acknowledge" and "encourage" as your conversational cornerstones. For example, when Zachary's block tower is finished, he looks around with satisfaction. He's eager to know you see him and share his joy. "I see you finished your tower, Zachary. It looks very strong. God has given you good hands and a good mind. You're a good builder!"

Choice Creates Interest

Children are usually more content to stay with an activity they have chosen, rather than one they have been assigned. When you provide several play-based learning activities (each led by a teacher) that appeal to different learning styles and interests, discipline problems often diminish and children enjoy finishing what they began. Children who are absorbed in an activity they have chosen are in prime positions for learning.

Some children find it difficult to begin an activity when they first arrive to a class. They need help in learning to choose. Allow each child to move at his or her own pace. "Liam, when you're ready, you may build with blocks in the corner with Mr. Sanchez or glue these pictures with me. Watch for a while if you like."

When we provide a choice of several activities, we should not expect young children to stay focused on one activity for more than a few minutes. The younger the child, the shorter the attention span; again, this is part of helping a child learn. When the child moves back and forth between activities, remain quietly observant for ways you can connect his or her play to the Bible story or verse being taught.

Children need to use every sense—tasting, touching, smelling, hearing and seeing—to learn effectively. This is why it's important to provide activity choices that may not appeal to you personally. When we give children activity choices that involve as many senses and learning styles as possible, we send them the message that we want them to choose, learn and enjoy. It's another way to show the loving acceptance Jesus modeled.

Guide the Children Toward Jesus

Each of us moves through the spiritual development of life in as much of an individual rate and way as we do in any other area. God knows each person intimately; therefore, He works differently in every life. Whatever one's rate of growth or plan of development, God is tirelessly at work to bring us into closer relationship with Himself. Acknowledging this helps us rest in His good plan and look for His hand in the experiences that cause us and the children we care for to develop spiritually.

When we present Jesus consistently by both our actions and our words, we lay a foundation for children to receive Christ as Savior. When is a child ready to receive Christ? Remembering God's ceaseless work, we need to be sensitive facilitators of that process. God's Holy Spirit calls a child into relationship in His time, not ours. We should never put up walls, but we also should never push or manipulate children. We need to give children time and opportunity to ask questions, think through ideas and respond at their own pace. While some children at this age level (especially from Christian homes) may indeed pray to become members of God's family, accepting Jesus as their Savior, expect wide variation in children's readiness for this important step.

When we present Jesus consistently by both our actions and our words, we lay a foundation for children to receive Christ as Savior.

To help a child give words to thoughts and feelings about Jesus, ask many open-ended what-do-you-think and tell-me-more questions. "Tell me what you like best about Jesus" will help you gain insight into what a child does or doesn't understand. This will also help you to give a child the information he or she needs, instead of an answer that doesn't apply. Prekindergarten children especially want to know more about many aspects of God. Every question we answer creates an opportunity to help the child understand more about a personal relationship with Jesus.

Talk individually with children. Something as important as a child's personal relationship with Jesus Christ can be handled more effectively alone than in a group.

Talk simply. Phrases such as "born again" or "Jesus in my heart" are symbolic and far beyond a young child's understanding. Focus on how God makes people a part of His family:

- God loves us, but we have done wrong things (sinned).
- God says sins must be punished.

- God sent Jesus to take the punishment for the wrong things we have done.
- We can tell God that we have done wrong and tell Him we are sorry for our sins. We can ask Jesus to be our Savior.
- Then God forgives us and we become a part of God's family.

 Talk individually with children. Something as important as a child's personal relationship with Jesus Christ can be handled more effectively alone than in a group.

Consistently share this information whenever a child seems interested but only for as long as the interest lasts. Lay a good foundation for a lifetime of solid spiritual growth!

Source
Gospel Light, *Preschool Smart Pages* (Ventura, CA: Gospel Light, 2010).

4

Elementary

(AGES 6 TO 10)

Activity is the keyword of this group of children. This is the time when both mind and body must be kept busy every minute. Success in teaching these active and curious children depends upon this.

Learn the Age-Level Characteristics of Children in Grades 1 and 2 (6 to 8 Years Old)

Physical

Children in first and second grade are growing rapidly. Younger first-graders may be physically more like preschoolers, while children moving toward third grade have hit a new level of physical maturity that shouts "I'm not a little kid anymore!" Although these children may be expected to sit in school at this age, they still need frequent opportunities for movement during every class session. Small-muscle coordination is still developing and improving. Girls are ahead of boys at this stage of development.

Teaching Tips: Use activities that involve simple folding, cutting and writing skills. Always offer drawing in place of writing for those who struggle with writing. Give them frequent opportunities to change position and to move around the room or outdoors. Vary the kinds of activities to help keep attention high and discipline problems to a minimum.

Cognitive

Children of this age have an intense eagerness to learn. They ask many questions. They like to repeat stories and activities. Their concept of time is limited. Thinking is here and now rather than past or future.

Listening and speaking skills are developing rapidly; girls are ahead of boys. Each of these children tends to think everyone shares his or her view. Children see parts rather than how the parts make up the whole. They think very literally.

Teaching Tips: Consider the skill and ability levels of the children in planning activities. For example, some children can handle reading and writing activities while others may do better with music or art. Use pictures to help them understand Bible times and people. Avoid symbolic language, which often confuses them. Use a variety of activities to keep brains alert and functioning at optimal levels.

Emotional

Children in these grades are experiencing new and frequently intense feelings as they grow more independent. Sometimes the children find it hard to control their behavior. There is still a deep need for approval from adults and a growing need for approval from peers.

Teaching Tips: Seek opportunities to help each child in your class *know* and *feel* that you love him or her. Show genuine interest in each child and his or her activities and accomplishments. Learn children's names and use them frequently in positive ways. Smile frequently.

Social

Children this age are greatly concerned with pleasing their teachers. Each child is struggling to become socially acceptable to the peer group as well. The Golden Rule is still a difficult concept at this age. Being first and winning are very important. Taking turns is hard, but this skill improves by the end of the second grade. A child's social process moves gradually from *I* to *you* to *we.*

Teaching Tips: Provide opportunities for children to practice taking turns. Help each child accept the opinions and wishes of others and consider the welfare of the group as well as his or her own. Call attention to times when the group cooperates successfully and thank children for ways you see them sharing and taking turns.

Spiritual

First- and second-graders can sense the greatness, wonder and love of God when given visual and specific examples. The nonphysical nature of God is baffling, but God's presence in every area of life is generally accepted when parents and teachers communicate this in both their attitudes and their actions. Children can think of Jesus as a friend but need specific examples of how Jesus expresses His love and care. This understanding leads many children to belief and acceptance of Jesus as personal Savior. Children can comprehend talking to God anywhere and anytime in their own words, and they need regular opportunities to pray. They can also comprehend that the Old Testament tells what happened before Jesus was born and that the New Testament tells of His birth, work on earth, return to heaven and what happened in God's family on earth.

Teaching Tips: The gospel becomes real to children as they feel genuine love from adults. Teachers who demonstrate their faith in a consistent, loving way are models through which children can understand the loving nature of God.

Learn the Age-Level Characteristics of Children in Grades 3 and 4 (8 to 10 Years Old)

Physical

Children in third and fourth grade have increasingly good large-muscle and small-muscle coordination. The girls are still ahead of the boys. Children can work diligently for longer periods but can become impatient with delays or their own imperfect abilities.

Teaching Tips: Give clear, specific instructions. Allow children as much independence as possible in preparing materials. Assign children the responsibility for cleanup.

Cognitive

Children are beginning to realize there may be valid opinions besides their own. They are becoming able to evaluate alternatives, and they are less likely than before to fasten onto one viewpoint as the only one possible. Children are also beginning to think in terms of the whole. Children think more conceptually and have a high level of creativity. However, by this stage, many children this age become self-conscious about their creative efforts as their understanding grows to exceed their abilities in some areas.

Teaching Tips: Encourage children to look up information and discover their own answers to problems. Provide art, music and drama activities to help children learn Bible information and concepts. Encourage children to use their Bibles by finding and reading portions of Scripture. Bible learning games are good for this age, and children are often eager to memorize Bible verses. Help children understand the meanings of the verses they memorize.

Emotional

This is the age of teasing, nicknames, criticism and increased use of verbal skills to vent anger. At eight years of age, children have developed a sense of fair play and a value system of right and wrong. At nine years, children are searching for identity beyond membership in the family unit.

Teaching Tips: Here is a marvelous opportunity for the teacher to present a Christian model at the time children are eagerly searching for models. Provide experiences that encourage children's creativity. Let all children know by your words and by your actions that "love is spoken here" and that you will not let others hurt them nor let them hurt others. Make your class a safe place where children feel accepted, where they are comfortable asking hard questions, and where they may express their true feelings without fear of teasing.

Social

Children's desire for status within the peer group becomes more intense. This often leads to acting silly or showing off to gain attention. Most children remain shy with strangers and exhibit strong preferences for being with a few close friends. Many children still lack the essential social skills needed to make and retain friendships.

Teaching Tips: This age is a good time to use activities in which pairs or small groups of children can work together. Create natural opportunities for each child to get to know others and to take on greater responsibility.

Spiritual

Children are open to sensing the need for God's continuous help and guidance. The child can recognize the need for a personal Savior. There may be a desire to become a member of God's family. Children who indicate an awareness of sin and concern about accepting Jesus as Savior need clear and careful guidance without pressure.

Teaching Tips: Give children opportunities to communicate with God through prayer. Help them understand the forgiving nature of God. Talk personally with a child whom you sense the Holy Spirit is leading to trust the Lord Jesus. Ask simple questions to determine the child's level of understanding.

Select Appropriate Activities

Children learn best by what they do, not by what they hear or see. Thus, choose activities that reinforce the focus of a lesson.

Selecting Learning Activities

Suitability—As you look at activity ideas in your curriculum, determine whether the activity is appropriate for the age, number of children, interest and skill level of your class. While young children may enjoy using puppets, they may not be able to actually make puppets. Older children may feel that some activities are too childish. Because of their learning styles, the students may enjoy doing certain activities more than others. Inner-city churches may have different challenges than suburban or rural congregations. An effective curriculum will provide you with varied activities from which to choose so that you can customize your lesson to the needs and abilities of your class.

Don't let having a small classroom or limited budget prevent learning from taking place. Rather than focusing on limitations, think of ways to creatively use the available resources. Instead of buying expensive maps of Israel, ask a church member who has visited there to share slides and photos of the trip. If there is no money for art supplies, ask church members to donate paper and markers. If a classroom is too small for games, make arrangements for the students to use the fellowship hall or an outdoor patio.

Teachability—Determine whether the activity supports the objectives of the lesson or is only a fun time filler. While children love to have fun—and your classroom should provide times of fun—it is also necessary to provide a good balance of activities that help students discover how to apply the Bible concept to their daily lives. If the activity is too complicated, if it hides or distorts the teaching objective, find another activity that requires less explanation. Look for activities designed to help students learn to use the Bible and Bible reference tools.

Life-related—Your lesson may have one Bible truth for the students to grasp, yet student learning should connect that truth to everyday life. For example, the lesson may focus on obeying God by being honest, but an effective game activity will help each student to name situations and ways in which to show honesty.

Your lesson may have one Bible truth for the students to grasp, yet student learning should connect that truth to everyday life.

Leading Learning Activities

Tell the purpose. Tell students why they're doing an activity. They may see the activity as a fun thing to do, but use your conversation to point students toward a higher purpose. "We're going to make a scene of the Israelites escaping from Egypt to help us remember that we can trust God to take care of us."

Give clear directions. Children grow frustrated if they don't understand what to do. Explain clearly what is expected and how students can accomplish their tasks. Write directions on a chalkboard or large sheet of paper for reference. Have supplies nearby and organized.

Let children work at their own pace. Once the project is explained and students begin working, avoid micromanaging. Avoid the temptation to do it for them. Let students make choices and mistakes. Allow students the freedom to ask for help, instead of anticipating their needs. Have additional activities on hand or books to read for students who finish quickly, instead of making the slower students rush.

Use guided conversation. Use comments and questions during the learning activity to help students connect the activity to the lesson's Bible truth. "I see you've drawn a picture of a way to show patience at home. What is a way to be patient at school?" "Thanks, Nathan, for helping clean up the spilled glitter. That's what the Bible tells us to do."

Summarize what was learned. Near the end of the session, ask students to summarize what they learned about today's Bible truth. "What was one important thing learned by the boy who shared his lunch?" If students cannot answer the question, then more learning is needed. Ask additional questions, or tell an example from your life to extend students' interest and learning.

Share learning with others. Information is best used when it's passed on to others. Teaching is the best way to learn. Encourage students to share what they learned in class with their parents and friends. Let students lead an activity for a class of younger children. Students can share their learning by giving short talks to the congregation during worship or a church event. Children who are shy about public speaking can write statements for other students to read. Artwork can be displayed during an open house.

Tell Stories to Teach Spiritual Truths

Make spiritual truths come alive in stories. Children can receive them in no other way. Jesus used parables. Never despise the story method of teaching truth. There is no substitute for a carefully prepared story given by a spiritually prepared teacher. "If there is attention, there will be retention." You may find difficulties in holding the attention of your students when you go over their heads in your instruction. But the greatest difficulty will be found when you forget their active minds and bodies. Remember, discipline problems will be prevented when these active children are kept constantly busy with that which interests them.

The stories you choose for elementary children should center on people, life and living things. Stories from the lives of men and women that illustrate simple lessons in character building or present simple principles in living are excellent.

Abstract ideas have no value when you are teaching children. Lessons of obedience are more needed by children than lessons of doctrine. Children can feel before they can understand. They can love before they know why they feel that emotion. Always keep in mind that they care nothing for the abstract.

Teaching children of this effervescent, slam-bang age is not easy. Laughter and noise from these enthusiastic children will fill the premises. You cannot teach an elementary child with a long face. They coin new words and seem to be entering a "silly" stage. When they say something funny and everybody laughs, generally they repeat the same thing again. Instead of reprimanding such a behavior, assure the child that the first time such a thing is said, it is funny; but the second time, it is silly. A joyous laugh at some amusing happening will do much more good than harm, even in Sunday School. Vary the mood of the class. Don't be afraid to have moments of relaxation and freedom, but do quickly bring these responsive minds within bounds again.

Tips for Becoming a Storyteller

Everyone is a storyteller. Storytelling is how people communicate important, heartfelt information. Whether it is a promotion at work, moving into a new house, getting engaged or a child's hitting the winning Little League home run, we all love a good story—and when we are "full of" a good story, we're eager to tell it!

Storytelling is how the Bible was written. For centuries, stories of the patriarchs and matriarchs were handed down from parent to child. After the resurrection and ascension of Jesus Christ, His followers preached about Him through telling His stories until the New Testament Scriptures were completed. When a teacher tells a Bible story, he or she is continuing in the grand tradition of the ancient storytellers who passed on God's Word. It's a responsibility and a privilege.

Tips for Effective Storytelling

Know the material. Study the story. Understand the main theme, know the central characters, research the setting if needed and be able to answer questions about the story (especially why and how questions). (Remember how important it is to be "full of" your story!) As you read the story, focus on finding the answers to these questions: Who is the main character(s)? Where does the story take place? Does the setting need to be explained to the students? What elements of the story (characters, objects, feelings, actions, etc.) are similar to the experiences of your children? How does the story illustrate the lesson aims? What one Bible truth do you want the children to remember and use during the week? What is the conflict in the story? Every good story has a conflict and a problem to be solved (Joseph is in jail, the soldiers are chasing the Israelites leaving Egypt, Paul is arrested, the lame man can't get into the pool, etc.). How is the problem solved? How is God involved with solving the problem? How are the characters' lives changed?

Use words familiar to the children. Rephrase Bible passages that children may not understand. Avoid talking down to children. Use modern language, not "thee" and "thou." Consult a children's Bible for easy-to-understand vocabulary if you have no curriculum resources.

Use a lot of details in the story. Do not present a number of truths in the lesson. Rather present one truth in many ways. Picture in detail the characters and make them live before the children. Describe their garments, their hair and their eyes. Children can have a vivid picture of David and Daniel. They will be able to see in their mind's eye just how they look. A vivid picture formed in the imaginations of children stirs their emotions and impels their action.

Avoid memorizing and reading. It is not essential to recite the story exactly as written in the Bible or your curriculum manual. While you should always have your Bible open to the story reference, storytelling is more interesting and spontaneous when the teacher doesn't read from a page. Telling rather than reading makes the presentation more natural and exciting. Reading the story from a book keeps your face buried in the pages and unable to look at the children. This is why preparation is essential: The better one knows the story, the less one needs notes. Know the plot points well enough to get back on track if the story digresses.

Practice, practice, practice! Many people feel uneasy about storytelling simply because they have little experience speaking to a group. Skills and confidence are built by repetition. Practice the story at home in front of a mirror. Tell it to your own family. Record the story on tape and as you play it back, listen for areas that need improvement. One can always erase a bad tape!

Be bold. Bring the story to life through dramatic gestures, movement, and facial expressions. "Larger than life" and "over the top" are good rules when telling a story. Feel free to emphasize words, be expressive, even look silly. Vary your voice—loud in some spots and soft in others. Some people use different voices for various characters, although this is not essential.

Be confident. Have faith in the story. Bible stories are powerful because they contain God's Word for today's people. Be enthusiastic. Think about how excited people get when telling about their children or accomplishments. Carry that same energy into biblical storytelling. If you are full of and interested in the story, the children will be, too! Maintain eye contact with the children.

Be relevant. Show why the story is important for today. The Bible is not a collection of 2,000-year-old fairy tales that are read for entertainment. Draw parallels between the story and children's lives. In the Joseph story from Genesis, discuss sibling rivalry and family relations in the children's homes. For Noah and the flood, ask how students might feel if they were teased for doing the right thing.

Tips for Involving Children

Children learn by doing! Incorporate the children into storytelling. This is particularly beneficial for children who already know the story and may feel bored by its retelling.

Act it out. Have students pantomime or dramatize the story as it is being told. Students may use puppets, hold up pictures or put felt figures on a flannel board. If a student already knows the story, let him or her tell the story for the class or assist you with the telling. Invite a student to retell the story in his or her own words. Play "What happened next?" with a child who is familiar with the story: "And Moses came down the mountain. What happened next, Jake? What did he see?"

Make sound effects. Have children make appropriate sounds when they hear a cue word. They can make animal sounds when they hear an animal's name. They can gurgle for "river," stomp their feet for "walk" or "march," or say "grumble grumble" when characters are tired or hungry. Look through the story for repetitive words or ideas and think of sounds the children can make. This keeps children alert and listening so as not to miss a cue.

Use the Bible. Have students look up the story in the Bible. This familiarizes students with the books of the Bible and shows that the stories are not made up. Even young children can find chapters and verses with some help and even locate the name of a Bible story character.

Carry out research. Older children can look up unfamiliar words in a Bible dictionary, locate cities in a Bible atlas, and read more about story characters in a Bible encyclopedia. Let the children find more information on the Internet or dramatize the story by making a home video.

Encourage Memorization

God's Word is too important not to commit it to memory! Memorization lays a strong foundation and provides a rich spiritual resource from which a child can draw throughout a lifetime. In times of doubt, stress or grief, an adult or teen will remember verses learned as a child. Telling about their faith to others is easier with the memorization of key Scriptures. When it's hard to put theological concepts into words, children can rely on Bible verses to express basic beliefs.

Tips for Memorizing with Understanding

Learn with meaning. The goal is for children to understand what they memorize and not simply recite words. Memorization has little value unless the child can apply the Bible verse to life situations and use it for spiritual growth. Demonstrate and model for your children the principle of learning a verse and what it means before memorizing it. In class, explore the application of a Bible verse through discussion and learning activities. Explain any difficult or unusual words. Look at the verse in its context and help your children understand how it fits in with the rest of the paragraph or chapter.

Memorization has little value unless the child can apply the Bible verse to life situations and use it for spiritual growth.

Learn with purpose. Avoid learning verses for the sake of learning or to win prizes. Select verses that children will find interesting and helpful to learn. Know why a child should know this particular verse. Does it explain the way to salvation? Does it provide a promise of God? Does it make an important statement about Jesus? When choosing a curriculum, look for one that presents Bible memory verses that focus on life application of Bible truth, rather than on Bible facts.

Find it. Part of verse memorization is to become familiar with the Bible. Be sure each child has a Bible to use rather than having to share one. Have extra Bibles in the room for children who do not bring one. Teach children how to use the table of contents to find a book and how to interpret the chapter and verse numbers in a verse reference. Help children locate the book and page where the verse is written. Accuracy is more important than speed. Always memorize the chapter and verse reference along with the words.

Provide a modern Bible translation. In order to help children not only memorize but also understand God's Word, consider having a modern Bible translation available that children can easily read. If a child brings a Bible from home that is different from the Bibles you provide in class, take advantage of this opportunity to enrich the child's understanding of the Bible. Help the child compare the words used in the different translations.

Tips for Ways to Increase Memorization

Repeat and review. People memorize simply by hearing or saying something many times, such as saying multiplication facts every day at school. Repeat the verse together several times throughout the class session. Use various activities (games, music and discussion) so that the children can hear, see, write and use the verse. Over time, children will find they have learned the verse without realizing it! And don't forget to return to learned verses periodically. Apply the principle of "use it or lose it." Children will forget verses unless they are reviewed often.

Use music. Set the words of the verse to a familiar tune so that children can sing the verse. Many contemporary praise songs are taken word for word from the book of Psalms. Many children find that music helps them remember words. Long lists, such as the books of the

Bible or the Ten Commandments, can also be learned easily when set to music.

Use artwork. Incorporate short verses into art projects. Children can write the words on bookmarks, boxes, scrolls and clay tablets or string together beads with letters. The class can write verses on posters or banners that are hung on the classroom wall or in church hallways for several weeks.

Use games. Incorporate the verse into noncompetitive games that are enjoyable and educational. Children like learning when they don't know they are being taught! Use the games suggested in your curriculum. You may also be able to purchase board or card games that teach Bible verses. However, some of these games can be too expensive for a limited church budget. Before investing in a game, be sure that it can be reused many times, that it is suitable for several age groups, and that the children will not grow tired of it. Of course, many simple games can be adapted for use with Bible verses:

- *Matching Game*—Write each word of the verse onto a separate card and lay the cards facedown on the table. Children take turns flipping over one card at a time, trying to turn the cards over in the correct verse sequence. Correct cards are left face up. If the card does not match the sequence, the card is placed face down again.

- *Scavenger Hunt*—Write each word of the verse on a separate card and hide the cards in the room. Children find cards and then put them in verse order.

- *Balloon Game*—Write words of verses on separate narrow strips of paper and hide the strips inside balloons. Blow up the balloons. The children pop the balloons, read the words aloud and put the words in verse order.

Use rewards. The goal of learning verses is not to get rewards, but children do like appreciation for their efforts. Plan cooperative memory contests in which children work together to reach a common goal of a specified number of verses memorized. When the goal is met, all children receive a prize (e.g., popcorn party, ice-cream treat, game day).

Teach Children How to Pray

One of the most awesome responsibilities of the teacher at church is to give children the tools of prayer. Even young children can approach their heavenly Father with the confidence that He hears their prayers. It's never too soon for children to establish a habit of daily prayer.

What to Teach

God listens. Children may feel that they are too young or insignificant for God's attention or that God is only interested in grownups. Assure children that God cares and wants to hear from them at any time (see Matthew 7:7-8).

Some children may feel that when they pray, they must feel or express deep emotions. Let your children know that God hears, even if they don't feel like anything happened!

God provides. God is the source of everything on earth. Children can give prayers of thanksgiving for food, shelter, clothing, friends, family and safety (see Psalm 103:1-5).

God is not a magician or Santa Claus. Prayer is often seen as something magical that grants instant requests. Children may feel sad or angry when prayers do not "come true" right away. Sometimes prayers are answered after a long time. For example, a chemistry set is a great birthday present, but a very young child would not be able to use it. The child would need to get older and learn more before using it. Sometimes God waits for children (or adults) to mature before answering a prayer.

People commonly pray when they want something. Children often pray to get certain gifts for Christmas or that their team will win the championship. Sometimes God answers prayer not by giving us what we want but by giving us the strength and wisdom to work for it. A child who works hard to earn an allowance can save money for a bike. A team can win a championship with practice and with good sportsmanship.

Reassure children that God wants them to pray about all their needs and concerns and that they can depend on God to always love and care for them (see Philippians 4:6).

God likes to hear prayers for others. Besides praying for their own needs, encourage children to think about and then pray for the needs of others. Children can pray for their parents (especially absent or divorced parents), siblings, friends, schoolmates, teachers and pets (see Matthew 5:44; Ephesians 6:18; James 5:16).

Why didn't God answer my prayer? In an imperfect world, bad things happen. A child can be caught in an ugly custody battle during a divorce. A child may be the victim of abuse or a criminal act. Natural disasters and accidents can destroy a family home. A family member or favorite pet dies. Children may wonder why a caring God would allow things to happen that they consider tragic.

Reassure children that God understands how they feel and that God can make something good come out of a bad situation (see Romans 8:28). For example, when a disaster happens, people in a church or community often help each other. God is still present and working through these people to see that needs are met.

How to Pray

Keep it simple. Children may feel that they need poetic language and "thees" and "thous" to pray. Children can talk to God in ordinary language.

Keep it honest. Children may feel that God will punish them if they are angry, upset or doubtful. It's okay to talk to God about unhappy feelings. God wants to hear how we feel.

Keep it short. Prayers don't need to be long or cover every subject. Young children can begin with short sentence prayers as they learn to pray.

Be a role model. Children will become comfortable with prayer when they see adults praying in ways that are appropriate and appealing. Make prayer a regular part of your class. Talk about personal answers to prayer during class.

Use a simple format. ACTS is a common acronym you can use to teach children how to pray:

Adoration: Praise and thank God for His love and power.
Confession: Admit actions and attitudes that do not show love for God and others, and say "I'm sorry" for sins.
Thanksgiving: Thank God for the good things He gives us.
Supplication: Ask God for things you need.

Keep a prayer journal. Older children can write down their petitions, thanksgivings and answers to prayer. They can record biblical prayers that they use in class. Lead children to make prayer journals by decorating a notebook or attaching sheets of paper together with a ribbon and cardboard cover. Prayer journals may be kept as personal, not to be read by other students.

Create a Welcoming Environment

The room for elementary children is very important. First-graders enter into a new realm of experience physically, cognitively, emotionally, socially and spiritually. They ought not be put with the smaller children in Sunday School. The first, second, third and fourth grades should have classes of their own as soon as it is possible. As they begin to read the Bible for themselves, a new world is open to them.

Don't give up because you don't have a room. You can convert a corner in the sanctuary into an elementary room, if necessary, or divide a larger room. A screen with some appropriate cover can be put up and removed with ease. Hanging something age appropriate will accomplish much. The point is that we need to create a welcoming place—a place in which we honor the children whom we want to disciple into being wholehearted followers of Jesus Christ. And as we honor them, we honor Him who said, "Let the little children come to me!" (Matthew 19:14).

We love to see children come to our classroom doors full of enthusiasm and ready for whatever is coming next. But some children reluctantly sidle up, act clingy or are clearly anxious. Although their negative reactions may be unrelated to their being at church, we're wise to be aware of the ways we can head off some of that negativity by making each child feel welcomed.

A Welcoming Place

Take time to look thoughtfully at the areas of your church where children's ministries take place. Then consider the places in your town where children love to gather. What are those places? What features of those places send the message to children, "This place is for you. It was created especially to make you want to come here!" (In addition, consider what features are designed to actually appeal to adults so that they want to bring their children!) Based on features that have genuine child appeal, look at your children's ministry area again. Ask, "If we could make this place more child friendly, how would it change? What features could it incorporate? What might this physical space look like?" Changes need not be cutesy or especially appealing to adults. The space may not need to be a particular color or have special lights or fog machines. But it is important that the features of the room tell a child, "This place is for you because we think you are important. We welcome you into this place!"

No matter how visually appealing and exciting a place may look, children are still human beings. They look for other human beings to whom they can relate, whether in a nursery, an elementary room or a preteen hangout room.

Welcoming People

The first moments of a child's experience at church will have great impact—for better or for worse. When a child comes to the door of a room whose interior looks like a famous pizza restaurant or an amusement park and he or she seems overwhelmed and hesitant, we may wonder, *What is wrong? Didn't we make it look welcoming?* But if a child is ignored at the doorway of an attractive room, this tells the child that no matter how much fun this place looks to be, he or she is not likely to be treated as an individual. "You can be part of this gang if you are bold enough to step inside!" is what the environment alone can tell a child. No matter how visually appealing and exciting a place may look, children are still human beings. They look for other human beings to whom they can relate, whether in a nursery, an elementary room or a preteen hangout room.

Ministry to children begins by welcoming them. Making children feel welcomed and comfortable is life-changing stuff! A friendly person at the door sees a child. He or she gets at the child's eye level, smiles, gives a pat or hug around the shoulder and talks to the child, repeating the child's name. This amazing person then explains the activities in which the child may engage. Something powerful happens—a child is included! Community is created, there and then!

Greeters should work in teams so that one may always be at the door while another guides a child to an appropriate area. Even in very small classes, greeters at the door free the teachers to interact with children already in the room. Instead of being constantly distracted, teachers and children can integrate new arrivals easily and effectively. And don't forget to give greeters the honor they deserve—they are tremendously important.

A Welcoming Program

The program is what happens to a child once he or she is inside the door. It may be large group or small group, entertaining or interactive, quiet or loud. But what makes a program say "Welcome!" to a child? What program makes a child feel, "They value me here. They care about me. They think I can do things!"

Make sure the program is age appropriate. For example, second-graders yawn and roll in their seats, counting ceiling tiles, during a program that is absolutely riveting the attention of the fifth-graders. Are the second-graders feeling as if the adults chose this program especially for them? Not at all! Rather, they are exhibiting normal signs of restlessness that result from a program that is not designed in an age-appropriate way.

Make sure the program is different from what children do at school. When a program seems like school, children quickly revert to school behavior (that skill we all learn—feigning attention while ignoring the proceedings around us!). Most children believe that if they wait quietly and patiently and don't volunteer (what some schoolteachers call "being good"), they can wait out this experience, too. So a program needs to catch children's interest and engage their minds and bodies to tell them, "This is not school!"

However, this does not mean that a program needs to scream, "Fun! Fun! Fun!" every minute. Children are already distracted and over-entertained. We do them a disservice if we do not provide the meat of what matters forever and show them how to chew on it! Children need some quiet time and a safe place for age-appropriate, interactive discussion that helps them not only learn Bible facts but also understand how Bible truths work out in their own daily lives.

Fun is not the only purpose of children's ministry—because God did not create us with a need for perpetual fun but with a need for relationship with Him. No amount of fun will satisfy that need. Fun is often the by-product of activities that engage and excite children about what matters.

Rather than asking if a program is fun, determine whether a program is lively, engaging, interesting and conducive to children's discovering truth for themselves. Refuse to be intimidated by those who whine, "This is boring!" Determine what their actual concerns are. Then address those concerns by involving those children in the learning process.

Children need some quiet time and a safe place for age-appropriate, interactive discussion that helps them not only learn Bible facts but also understand how Bible truths work out in their own daily lives.

Determine if the program is going to make a difference in children's lives. First, understand the aims and goals of the program itself. List aims you believe should be achieved in your situation. Without knowing specific aims for ways a program may effect change, there will not be clarity about what result to expect. Because this is spiritual ministry to children, don't settle for childcare or entertainment. Talk with and listen to teachers to see if they feel that the aims of the lesson are being met.

Meet the Children's Needs

Keep your groups small. Ideal classes do not have more than six or seven boys and girls. This small group makes it possible to keep each one in direct range of your eye when you tell the story. Elementary-age children must be kept physically close in order to be mentally close. When the class is small, you can know your boys and girls personally. This is of great value.

When the class is small, you can know your boys and girls personally. This is of great value.

There are other concerns besides keeping groups small, because children don't arrive at the classroom with a blank slate. They have physical, emotional and social needs that can interfere with learning. They bring baggage of what has happened to them outside of class that can distract them from learning. Think about ways you can begin to recognize and deal with such needs so that the children's minds are free to learn. Do realize, though, that although you can do much to help meet students' needs, you cannot solve every problem, make every student's life perfect, force people to change or make every situation right. You can forgive yourself for your human limitations, do your best to minister to your students and turn all things over to God. When you show that you are secure in your faith in God, your students are encouraged to also be confident of God's care in their own situations.

Types of Needs

Spiritual needs—Every child needs a relationship with Christ and to know that his or her sins are forgiven. Sometimes this important goal is lost when you struggle to provide for all of the student's other needs. At times you may need to step back and evaluate the ways in which this spiritual goal is being reached. Look for opportunities to share with children appropriate examples of how being a Christian has helped you. Invite children to tell what they know about becoming members of God's family. Listen to their responses to observe when a child indicates readiness to become a member of God's family. Pray for each child and ask God to give you wisdom in discerning his or her spiritual needs.

Physical needs—A child may have a difficult time focusing on learning if he or she is hungry or uncomfortable. Make sure that the classroom temperature is not too hot or cold, the air is not stuffy or smelly, outside noises are not too distracting and chairs are not too hard or wobbly. Clean up and brighten the room to make a pleasant learning environment. If children arrive without breakfast, provide granola bars, fruit, bagels or juice. A church located in a low-income neighborhood may want to sponsor a free meal program or a food pantry. The church may also need to provide clothing for children without warm coats or shoes.

Safety needs—Children need to feel secure and safe from harm. Establish an atmosphere of trust and love so that children feel comfortable in class. Follow your church's written procedures to protect children when they are picked up after class, being aware of restraining orders and not releasing children to noncustodial parents. Make sure there is an area in your classroom where children's belongings can be left without being stolen or destroyed. Let children know that you will not allow bullying in your classroom.

Every child needs a relationship with Christ and to know that his or her sins are forgiven.

Social needs—Children want to be with those who love, affirm and accept them. They want friends and need to feel part of the group. They don't want to be ridiculed, criticized or ignored. Be sure that all children are included in class activities. Provide team-building and trust-building exercises. Let children pray and sing together to form community. Demonstrate acceptance of a child who may appear to be different in some way. Your caring actions will teach more about God's love than your words.

Children want to feel important and respected. They want their contributions to class (singing, reading, art, discussion, etc.) to be valued and welcomed. They like their artwork displayed, their photos on the bulletin board and their names listed in the church newsletter. They like to hear the teacher say, "You did a good job!" A child who does not feel valued will be more likely to withdraw from the class and be unwilling to participate.

Areas of Special Concern

Sometimes children will tell you about a special concern or worry; most often, however, they will not. Without prying, make an effort to learn about students' everyday lives and be sensitive to children's emotions. Some children clearly express their feelings; others are quiet and moody. Some children who have ongoing emotional needs or who are experiencing difficult times in their lives may need you to be nearby for support.

Family problems—Children are affected by the problems faced by their family members: an older sibling facing trouble with the law, parents getting a divorce, a parent dealing with unemployment, or parents dealing with financial difficulties. Even a normally happy event—moving to a new house, going to a new school, the birth of a new sibling, the remarriage of a parent, among others—can cause stress and anxiety. You can provide support, comfort and love. In extreme situations, you may need to intervene. (*Note:* If you see signs of possible physical abuse in a child, notify your supervisor and follow your church's established procedures.)

School situations—A student may have difficulty at school with low grades, a dislike for the schoolteacher, no friends, encounters with a bully, and so forth. Parents may demand that their child achieve high grades. Children may be overburdened and tired from too many after-school activities. Children want to feel popular among their classmates. There may be peer pressure to start dating or to have a "boyfriend/girlfriend" even among elementary-aged children. Students may feel pressure to buy expensive clothes or toys. Some children may even be approached by street gangs recruiting new members. All of these concerns can prevent a child from concentrating in the classroom.

Emotional needs—A child may be dealing with an illness or disability that prevents him or her from functioning at peak efficiency. A child may have ADD/ADHD, depression, a mental illness or a learning disability. A child may be shy and find it difficult to socialize with other people. Some children may have deeply rooted feelings of inadequacy or rejection. Some students come to class with "chips on their shoulders" and uncontrolled rage.

Intellectual needs—There are children who truly want to learn as much as they can. They are fascinated by the Bible, eager to serve God and willing to work hard. However, they feel discouraged and hindered by the students who don't share their interests. The effective teacher may need to find additional learning experiences for such children to keep their interest high.

Reach Out to the Homes

Keep in close touch with the home of each child and know from what kind of environment each child comes. The personal call, the letter, the telephone conversation, the email—all communication will do much in holding interest. Don't forget to send birthday cards and Christmas greetings.

Once a teacher has prepared lessons, played games, told stories, taught Bible verses, shared snacks and sung songs every week, it may feel like quite a stretch to try to connect with each child's family as well! But learning about the family of each child doesn't really add more work. Rather, it helps give understanding of the home roots from which each child has grown. This enriches teaching and improves a teacher's ability to minister to that child and his or her family. Teachers and families are blessed in the process.

Make it clear that your church values family outreach and support as an important task. Consider recruiting a Family Outreach Coordinator. The coordinator serves as the point person to both organize and administer a variety of programs and outreaches for families within and outside the church.

Any extra work you do is a real investment, and you will discover that it pays high dividends.

Let Parents Help

In most instances, we have found delightful cooperation from the parents, even though more than 50 percent of our children come from unchurched homes. Take-home papers help parents know what their children are doing. We find that most parents like to help if they know what to do. Direct contact with each child's home is most desirable. Your success will depend a great deal upon the sympathy and cooperation you receive from the parents. You will find that most parents wish to help their children, as is evidenced by their sending them to Sunday School, even though they themselves may not attend church. Give the parents an opportunity to help and you will be surprised at their response in almost every case.

Arrange a time for teachers and parents to meet. The church pastor, the children's pastor, a parent and a teacher can each give a short presentation about some phase of children's lives.

These parent-teacher meetings are not anything new. We have done it for years—as have many others. But the results are always gratifying. If your Sunday School is to grow, you must gain the interest and confidence of the parents. They must be impressed with the kind of work you are doing with their children. Would you be proud to have your parents see what you are doing in your department? This is an excellent way to do a self-checkup.

Post Rosters and Get Acquainted

Help teachers know the families of their students by providing teachers with up-to-date rosters. List each child's name, address, phone number, birthday, family or parent email address, and both first and last names of parents and siblings. Compile rosters from Registration Forms or Family Information Sheets. Update the information throughout the year.

At each classroom door, display a roster of names (including pictures, if possible) to make it easy for parents and children to find classrooms and feel welcomed.

If teachers' rosters also list the names of children from church families that are not actively involved, teachers can then periodically contact these children and families to personally invite them to attend a class or special program. Suggest that teachers use lists to make contacts informally (in the church parking lot, at an adult event, in the grocery store, at the mall, at the park, and so forth).

Communicating by card, email or phone call with each child during the week could be overwhelming, but an attainable goal to encourage your teachers to strive for is to communicate with at least one child and his or her family each week. Make the goal seem possible by giving each teacher a contact kit: a class roster, enough note cards to send one to each child, a pen, decorative stickers, postage stamps, and so forth. Seal all items in a resealable bag. Label with the teacher's name.

To help parents get to know a child's teacher, give parents copies of a Teacher Get-Acquainted Form at the beginning of the term. Parents may use this as a guide for getting to know their child's teacher(s) and get the information they need most.

Thank Visitors

Pay special attention to the ways in which visitors are contacted in the week or two after their first visit. In addition to mailing personalized "thanks for visiting" cards or letters, consider giving each visiting child a small bag containing several inexpensive gift items (stickers, crayons, etc.) as well as printed information about your church.

Give visiting families a Welcome Pack when they visit. Include information about church programs, stickers or inexpensive books, registration cards, letter from a parent describing the benefits of participating in church programs, refrigerator magnet with church information, and so on.

Plan Parent Support

Plan a series of parent events that include Parent-Education Classes to provide parents with strategies and guidelines related to common parenting issues. Invite a speaker (a knowledgeable person in your church or community) to address an issue of interest to parents—discipline, family activities to do at home, holiday celebration ideas, safety in the home, and so forth. Include a time for parents to talk together and trade ideas and thoughts about the challenges of child rearing. Offering six to eight sessions over a period of several months will encourage participation by parents whose time is limited.

One to three times a year, plan a Family-Growth Meeting that focuses on ways to teach children spiritual truths to help the family grow in Christ. Present information found in relevant articles as the basis for this meeting. Allow time for brainstorming as well as questions so that parents can both learn new information and share their best ideas on the topic.

Send out copies of articles of special interest to parents from reproducible parenting resources.

Plan ways the church can support a family when a new baby is born or when a child or parent is ill (meals, transportation, child care, etc.).

Develop an Intergenerational Prayer Partners Group: Link older members of the church family with parents of growing children. Encourage growth of these relationships by providing complete contact information, birthdays, ages and interests of children. Prayer partners can share requests and encouragement by phone, email or personal meetings.

Establish a library area near children's classrooms. Stock it with books about child rearing, activities to enjoy with children, age-level characteristics, and so forth. Encourage parents to sign out these books, returning them in a week or two. Invite parents whose children have grown older to donate books or other resources they found helpful as parents of young children.

Connect grandparents to young families by forming a Grandparents' Club. Invite senior adults who do not have grandchildren or whose grandchildren do not live nearby to join in informal meetings with young families—particularly those whose parents are no longer living or who do not live nearby.

Once a month, offer babysitting free to parents of young children during the dinner hour. Parents can eat at home or at a restaurant, enjoying a special time of "adults only" conversation. Include these guidelines: (a) parents reserve space a week ahead of time; (b) when checking in their children, parents leave a phone number where they can be reached; and (c) parents sign a permission slip.

Hold Family-Friendly Outreach Events

New families may feel that everyone else at church seems to know each other. This can cause them to feel like outsiders. To help new families get acquainted and feel that they are part of the group, design several outreach events yearly. To inspire you, here are a few ideas for social times and simple parties that include fun activities:

- *Game Night* (families bring table games to play together)
- *Kite Day* (families bring and fly kites together at a nearby park)
- *Music and Potluck Evening* (families bring food, instruments and music to share)
- *Pet Show* (families show real and/or stuffed animals)
- *Cookie Share* (every family brings a batch of their favorite cookies or children bake cookies together with adults)
- *Indoor Picnic* (every family brings a lunch and a blanket to share)
- *Movie Night* (every family brings a favorite flavor of popcorn to share; stop the movie for a popcorn-related game)

These simple ideas can be made as elaborate as your imagination allows! Keep in mind the goal of developing the time in ways that will make new families and children feel welcomed and included.

Source
Gospel Light, *Children's Ministry Smart Pages* (Ventura, CA: Gospel Light, 2004).

5

Preteen

Preteens are filled with uncertainty. Everything is changing and all at one time! No wonder our students sometimes seem as if they are on a roller coaster of emotions. And it's no wonder that leaders, teachers and parents of early adolescents have a difficult time understanding who these students are! As Michael A. James wrote:

> Upon entering the world of the early adolescents, the observer immediately faces what seems like an unfathomable array of differences and discontinuities. The early adolescent is at one moment coordinated and awkward, shy and aggressive, astute and absentminded, attentive and distracted, loving and "squirrely."

Early adolescence is perhaps the most misunderstood period of human development in our society today. We now understand that early adolescence is that period of transitional development that exists between childhood and adolescence. It involves the transition from concrete thinking to abstract thinking, from a child's body to a young adult's body, from emotional dependence to independence, and from primary focus on parents and family to interaction with peers.

For too long, we have treated preteens as immature high school students or hard-to-handle elementary children. This developmental period does not belong to either childhood or adolescence. Preteens are not between two stages of life. They are traveling through a specific, identifiable, wonderful period of transitional growth and maturation. The potential of preteens is incredible!

Age-Level Characteristics

Physical

The rate of growth and changes in preteens vary widely. This variation is seen between individual preteens and between the genders. In general, girls will grow more quickly and oftentimes will be taller than boys during the early adolescent years. Although the timing may differ, the experience is similar. Growth in each individual rapidly accelerates before pubescence and decelerates after pubescence. At some point after the body reaches sexual maturity, the growth hormone seems to stop its work.

Growth comes in spurts. Sudden spurts of growth cause the preteen to be awkward and clumsy. Bones grow faster than muscles, leaving children's new bigger and better bodies uncoordinated. Hands and feet mature before arms and legs. Children's feet are causing particular troubles. They are simply too big for the rest of their bodies, and the extra three inches (7.5 cm) inevitably trip up the children! Legs and arms grow faster than the trunk and are often the source of growing pains.

Sudden growth causes fatigue. Just as in younger children, sudden growth creates fatigue in early adolescents. Their bodies are working overtime to grow and change, and they are left with low energy and a greater need for sleep.

Early adolescents are very physical. Preteens like to be active, and they move about constantly. Outside activities are popular at this age, because this environment allows for large-muscle movement and loud, boisterous activities. It is difficult for early adolescents to sit still for long periods of time. Their growing bodies need to be active and moving. Although they are easily tired, they also have surges of energy that need to be burned up. Growth spurts make them need more food, yet eating more gives them more calories to burn. Exciting activities or competition can overtire early adolescents, since their stamina and endurance are not adequate to match their love for activity. They are poor self-regulators when it comes to balancing fun activities and rest or sleep.

The preteen is bombarded with hormonal changes. The early adolescent's life is complex. The onset of puberty causes a flood of hormones into the body. New hormones affect the child physically by causing dramatic growth and physical changes. They also affect far more than the child's body. The raging hormones dramatically affect the early adolescent's emotions.

Cognitive

Here again, preteens are in transition. Preteens are able to sit through a worship service and enjoy it, but they are certainly not at an adult comprehension level.

Preteens are very curious and, therefore, also quite distractible. Attention span continues to increase with all activities, but the most impressive advances are in problem-solving activities. Preteens are capable of making judgments and are quickly developing the ability to use hypothetical reasoning, a product of formal or abstract thinking. Their brains function best when they are stimulated enough to cause them to focus on the issue at hand.

Preteens are beginning to move from concrete to abstract thinking. They are able to reason much more than ever before, but they still may have trouble with symbolism. At church, preteens who have attended for years will start to question their beliefs as they continually seek to understand and personalize their faith on deeper cognitive bases.

Practical experience of preteens is lacking. While the brain and neurological system are almost fully developed at this point in life, preteens simply lack the experience necessary to acquire and evaluate the data needed to process every situation. They are, therefore, unable to solve adult problems in appropriate, mature ways. This is one reason that preteens must still have adult guidance and should not be given more responsibility than they are ready to handle.

Early adolescents have little concept of time. When a teacher tells a preteen that a report is due in a month, this has little meaning to the child. The knowing teacher will help set short-term subordinate deadlines to help accomplish the big project. At church, it's no wonder that deadlines for deposits and registrations are not heeded unless the communication somehow gets to the parents. The preteen teacher needs to be prepared for students to be late.

Preteens' interests are in the present and in the real and the practical. In large part because preteens lack the concept of time, they are most interested in what they can see, touch, hear, taste, smell and do—here and now. Our learning activities and lesson applications need to focus on what the preteens can experience and put into practice immediately in order for them to be relevant.

They are prone to daydream. If what you are doing is not exciting and meaningful, preteens won't stay with you. Their entire world has opened up with so many new experiences. Their relationships have changed dramatically. They are beginning to realize they have a future and that they will one day grow up. This, joined with their growing ability to think abstractly, creates fertile soil for daydreams. The more involved we get preteens (mentally and physically), the less likely they are to daydream.

Preteens enjoy activities that include writing, drama or painting. They enjoy expressing themselves in creative ways. Each may choose his or her own medium for expression, but finding ways to communicate individuality is a common theme among preteens. It is profitable for early adolescents to be exposed to a wide variety of creative arts so that they can experience a number of different means for self-expression. With some training, preteens who have specific talents can blossom at this age.

Preteens want to be challenged, but they have limits. Although they want to be challenged intellectually, they are ambivalent about having to do the work if it seems hard or unfair. It is common to hear them say that their teachers ask too much of them at school.

Emotional

Early adolescents are subject to tremendous mood swings. These sudden changes are often confusing for the parent or teacher, as well as for the child. The preteen's mood jumps suddenly and dramatically between love and hate, happiness and fear, interest and boredom. These mood swings influence every area of the preteen's life, from their relationships to their desire to attend church. We need to remember that they have little control over their emotions. We must be patient with preteens who seem to overreact emotionally to any given situation. They may laugh one minute and cry the next. It is not their fault that their changing environment and changing chemistry collide and create wide swings in how they feel about themselves, their peers and their leaders. Our job is to help these preteens learn to respond or act appropriately in spite of their emotional states.

Early adolescents can *control their actions and words*. It's possible, but it's not easy! Preteens need consistent training from loving, calm, patient adults to learn to react appropriately in spite of how they are feeling. Those who lead early adolescents must be able to deal with their own emotions in such a way that they can model appropriate behavior and true Christian maturity. The teacher or parent who has trouble handling frustration or anger constructively will not get very far helping early adolescents with their own emotional turmoil. This is a very real part of discipling preteens, as is getting their teachers and their parents together to compare notes with one another and recognize their common challenges.

Preteens are angry. Anger is one of the most common emotions that emerge in the life of preteens. They are often quick-tempered. This anger comes from a variety of sources, including fatigue or feelings of inadequacy, rejection or uncertainty. Any number of negative issues may be understandable sources of anger in the lives of preteens, and they must be taught skills for releasing or appropriately expressing their frustrations and have modeled for them patterns for processing feelings of anger positively. For some preteens, ongoing counseling and training to provide them with practical ways to avoid inappropriate reactions may be necessary.

Preteens are fearful. The fear of preteens comes in the form of worries. They have increasing demands upon them in every area of their lives, and they have anxiety about being able to perform to an acceptable level, as they desire to please both their peers and their parents or teachers. Non-acceptance and rejection are preteens' biggest worries in life. They are constantly evaluating whether they are fitting in and receiving approval. Things like report-card grades and peer criticism are vital to every preteen's self-evaluation process.

Preteens deny having fears. If you ask an early adolescent about fears, he or she will most likely deny them. Especially when those fears seem to be identified with younger years, like being afraid of the dark. The fears, however, are real. Because they don't want to admit their fears, maybe not even to themselves, preteens may be somewhat of a mystery to adults. Preteens will protest against having a babysitter stay with them, but then they'll lock themselves in a closet when they hear a scary sound outside and no one is there to protect them! They don't want a baby's nightlight, but they will hide a flash-light under their pillows in case they hear a sound in the night. As adults, we must not discount these very real fears, because preteens may well feel discounted.

Preteens are often threatened by competition. This is another area of seeming contradiction for preteens. One day, they will seem to love competition; the next, they hate it. It's possible that this has a lot to do with whether or not they win! Almost everyone loves competing if they are so good at something that they are assured a victory, but not many of us like losing. Competition points out even the most minor of chinks in our armor, and preteens are already too self-critical.

Early adolescents have a love of humor. Preteens enjoy jokes and lead-ers who can see the lighter side of life. Humor should be included in every part of the ministry for preteens. Make your classrooms and programs fun places to be. Humor must never be used as a weapon, though. It must be used in a mature manner. No child should ever be the subject of the joke. Even those who seem to be able to handle it and who laugh along with us are not normally laughing inside. Sar-castic humor directed at someone can make your whole youth group an unsafe place for preteens. Any child may feel as if he or she could be the next victim of a joke. But good, positive humor and lighthear-tedness should be the flavor and tone of our ministry to preteens.

Preteens are private. Although at times it appears that they will never stop talking, during the later years of early adolescence, pre-teens will develop private areas of their lives that they do not want to share with anyone else, especially not with authority figures. These private areas include their fears and questions about themselves and their peers. Great care must be taken during group discussions to show respect for the privacy of preteens. Teachers should allow some freedom in choosing discussion topics and never pressure preteens to divulge personal information.

Preteens need encouragement, support and unconditional love. We need to give them strong, frequent affirmation. Because preteens are con-stantly changing and experiencing conflicts and emotional upheavals, they need to be reassured over and over that at least one significant adult unconditionally loves and accepts them, even though their be-havior may not be to the adult's liking.

Preteens need to be needed (and to get positive emotional feedback). This is why preteens, both boys and girls, are frequent volunteers for the church nursery. They truly enjoy caring for small children, because they get to feel needed and loved by the little ones. Having young teens and preteens work with other people's children for a few hours a week gives the teens and preteens some positive emotional feedback. It also gives them an appropriate and serious look at the long-term commitment of becoming a parent. Preteens benefit greatly from being placed in positions to extend care and to know that they are making a difference in the lives of others.

Social

For preteens, peers are incredibly important. Early adolescents are greatly influenced by their peers. As preteens begin to break away from their families and express individuality and independence, they immediately reach out to surrogate families to fill the void: the church youth group, an athletic team, a small group of friends or a gang. Their fear of non-acceptance leads them to want to look like, act like and talk like others their own age. The group is all-important. Failure to achieve a certain status of belonging in the group can result in an introspective self-pity for the preteen.

Early adolescents are self-critical and critical of others. Preteens feel awkward. They often wonder if they are good at anything. They wonder how their intelligence and athletic ability compare with others. Failure or poor performance in any area, whether it be sports, academics or other observable indicators of intelligence or physical prowess, is sure to cause a crisis. A facial blemish, big feet or wearing the wrong brand of clothes can cause a crisis. In addition, the fact that they are surrounded by critical peers who are typically quick to point out these differences causes preteens to become increasingly critical of themselves (to fit in with what others say about them) and others (to get the critical glare off themselves).

Preteens need good friends of the same gender. Early in the adolescent years, preteens often do not like members of the opposite gender. This is the age of buddies and best friends. It is not only normal for preteens to feel close to a same-gender peer, but it is also a must for building a foundation for positive relationships with members of the opposite gender later in life. Any fears about such a relationship being a precursor to a homosexual orientation are completely misplaced. This is a natural, healthy stage of the preteen's development toward social maturity.

Later in early adolescence, friendships develop with members of the opposite gender. This is one more area of transition for preteens, so it is important for the teacher to make at least some small-group activities coeducational so that leaders can help preteens learn how to relate appropriately to the opposite gender.

Early adolescents are seeking independence and autonomy from parents. Although preteens want to feel separate and independent from their parents, they still need and truly desire adult guidance and emotional support. This is why staffing preteen ministry programs with people just like Mom and Dad works so well. The church is at its best when one parent is supporting another by being that significant adult for a child who is searching for independence from his or her own mom and dad.

Preteens are increasingly concerned about their physical appearance. Preteens are typically overly aware of their own bodies and the changes that may or may not have begun to occur. In fact, one could say they are obsessed with their physical appearance. Because of this obsession about their own looks, early adolescents are very vulnerable to the expectations and perceived expectations of their peers and society as a whole as observed through the media. The magazine, movie and TV industries serve up a constant parade of desirable, admirable images with which these awkward young adolescents compare themselves unfavorably. This is another area in which preteens feel they must do anything in order to fit in. Externals, like clothing and physical beauty, become a measuring stick that they believe will make the difference as to whether or not they are accepted.

Early adolescents become more reflective. In striving to preserve their self-identity and emerging sense of individuality, preteens need privacy and time to just be alone with their thoughts and their interests. They will sometimes choose to read alone in order to have the privacy and quiet to think. Although this may seem very different from other characteristics of this age group, it is still an important part of their makeup, and we must attempt to provide them with these quiet, reflective times as well.

The preteen does not enjoy anything that seems like work. This is especially true at home and especially during the earliest years. This seems contradictory at first, since they love to be needed. If the task is presented correctly, washing cars, doing dishes and babysitting will all seem like exciting challenges. It's when they become routine tasks and take on the drudgery of a job that preteens tend to lose enthusiasm. Schoolwork can be particularly challenging for some preteens.

Spiritual

Spiritually, a preteen is very open to having a personal relationship with God. As the student shifts from a parent-given faith to a personalized faith, it may appear that he or she has become interested in spiritual things for the first time. This transition sometimes causes the casual observer to assume that children this age cannot make significant spiritual decisions. In reality, children can make incredible decisions for God, but they must rethink them and re-own them as they transition through early adolescence.

Preteens' consciences become more fine-tuned—especially about the behavior of others. They are extremely aware of the fairness and honesty of the adults around them. They will constantly evaluate the values of their parents and teachers. However, they may be more relaxed about their own behavior. For example, their own cheating in school or shoplifting is rationalized and makes sense to them while they are quick to condemn others who do the same things.

Fairness is extremely important to preteens. When adults are inconsistent, they are quick to point out, "That's not fair!" They have a sense of justice that must be satisfied, especially by the teachers and parents in their lives.

Egocentrism

Egocentrism is the lack of ability to differentiate between one's own responses and the responses of others and between one's own thoughts and reality.

God wires a two-year-old child to define the world in terms of him- or herself, and we understand this to be a normal developmental process for the young child. We need also to understand the egocentrism of a preteen to be a natural characteristic of the emerging adolescent. The preteen also sees the world in terms of "me." In fact, some have said that early adolescents are two-year-olds with hormones!

The preteen's brand of egocentrism may be identified most clearly in two mental constructions: imaginary audience and personal fable.

Imaginary Audience

The early adolescent cannot differentiate between a preoccupation with him- or herself and what others are thinking about him or her. The preteen assumes that others are as obsessed with his or her behavior and appearance as he or she is, so the preteen is always anticipating the reactions of other people. The child is constantly constructing an imaginary audience and then reacting to it. For example, a preteen with a new pair of athletic shoes may walk by a crowd of peers and imagine that they all are looking at him or her.

All this makes the preteen very self-conscious. The preteen assumes that everyone is focusing on him or her. This explains the early adolescent's desire for privacy and his or her obsessive drive to wear the currently popular brand of clothes. This explains the increasing amount of time the preteen spends in the bathroom each day getting hair and face just right. This self-consciousness is also why so many preteens have difficulty staying plugged into church programs where they do not feel that they belong to the group. The self-conscious preteen walks into a Sunday School classroom and assumes that everyone in the room is wondering why he or she is there and why in the world he or she wore that outfit!

Self-admiring also becomes common at this age. The preteen boy can convince himself that the image in the mirror will cause a girl he admires to drool, when in reality the girl will be so concerned about her own appearance, and her own imaginary audience, that she won't even notice the two hours of grooming that he went through to make himself presentable.

Because preteens are so self-absorbed, they do not give the same emotional support and positive feedback that they are looking to receive from others. Unfortunately, both parties tend to be takers looking for this support to come from the other person but not offering it in return. This is why it is imperative to staff preteen ministry with adults who are mature and trained to focus on others instead of themselves. These people will effectively encourage the preteens and be emotionally supportive to them.

For some preteens, the importance of self is so high that the value of others cannot even be understood. Stories about preteens who plan and carry out ways to hurt others because they believe people are ridiculing them exemplify the incredible power that the imaginary audience can have over the early adolescent.

Personal Fable

A personal fable is a fictional (untrue) story that an early adolescent tells him- or herself. Personal fables may include these ideas:

- The preteen's feelings are special and unique.
- No one else understands how the preteen feels.
- The preteen is invincible. Accidents or bodily harm only happen to others, not to him or her.

This intellectual construct dovetails with the imaginary audience construct. Since the child believes him- or herself to be so much the center of attention to so many people (the imaginary audience members), the preteen's feelings and life become very special and important. The preteen believes his or her experiences are unique. Only he or she has ever experienced such pain. Only he or she can truly understand the situation. And because he or she is unique, the dangers that might hurt someone else would never affect him or her.

Personal fables can lead to extremely risky behaviors. A motion picture called *The Program* (released in 1993) depicted the protagonist and a few of his teammates lying down in the middle of a busy highway to show how brave they were and as a show of unity. In the movie, the movie characters who engaged in this incredibly risky activity were never hit by passing automobiles. This behavior in the movie struck a chord with preteens who, already believing that bad things happen only to other people, thought that they could do the same thing and not get hurt. Several early adolescents from around the country were in fact killed or injured copying this behavior. The motion-picture maker finally cut this portion of the movie.

Societal Pressures

The casual observer might conclude that preteens are maturing faster than they used to. Their bodies seem to be blossoming at an earlier age. They are involved in far more sophisticated activities, social interactions and issues than previous generations. The world is confronting them with much more serious problems and questions than we had to address at their age. They know more than their preteen predecessors did.

But are they truly maturing, or are they being forced to grow up before their time? While their bodies are advancing at earlier ages, are their emotions and cognitive arenas keeping pace?

Watch movies or TV and you'll quickly see that various media are capitalizing on these physical changes. Younger children are more interested than ever in their appearances and the look of their peer group. Preteens are "big game" for advertisers and moviemakers, and they are being drawn in as never before as consumers.

Socially, emotionally and mentally, preteens are being exposed to more mature material but may be no more ready to deal with it than we were at their age. Children are being forced to grow up more quickly than they ought to be. Through the media and other sources, society is exposing our children to more mature concepts and visuals than ever before. Any evening of TV watching exposes young children to more than most of our parents ever saw in the movies.

The fact that preteens are being forced to deal with all of this does not mean that it is good for them or that they are ready for it. Society has forced children to be more sophisticated. In some ways they are maturing; in others, they are encountering things they are not equipped emotionally to face. The world of the early adolescent is very complex and they are very socially aware, but what many do not realize is that the skill development of preteens does not match this level of sophistication. Their social contacts have pressured them to act like adolescents before they become adolescents.

Preteen-Specific Programs

Even as researchers grapple with how to transform education to meet the unique needs of the preteen group, churches have to adapt ministry for them as well. Knowing what preteens are like and what they need and want, we need to design our programs to fit those characteristics. We can no longer do preteen ministry the way that we've always done children's ministry, nor can we attempt to throw preteens into traditional youth ministry. It's time for the church to design programming and ministry opportunities specifically for preteens—and their friends!

The Needs of Early Adolescents—According to Them

What do preteens want? We can learn a lot about their perceived needs by listening to the questions they typically ask at church. Here's a top-10 list of the questions your students are most likely to ask:

10. Are we going to have a snack?
9. Who's coming?
8. What are we going to do now?
7. Are you sure?
6. What are we going to eat?
5. Really?
4. Is it time to go yet?
3. What did you say?
2. Do we have to?
1. When are we going to eat?

We may wish that preteens would ask, "What Bible verse can we memorize today?" or "Is there a needy person in our group that we can show love to right now?" But these aren't the issues foremost on most preteen minds. Their questions show their felt needs.

Food! As mentioned once or twice above, food is both a felt need and a real need! Preteens are a lot easier to work with when their stomachs are full.

Friends! Preteens want to know who's coming, because relationships are central to their existence. They want to be around peers by whom they feel accepted. Friends are a must. Our style of ministry needs to maximize development of relationships.

Fun! They want to know what they're going to do, because they want to have fun playing and being active with their friends. They also want to be sure that they won't be embarrassed by an activity that makes them feel awkward. Preteens demand fun, so a certain amount of our ministry must be devoted to entertainment.

Focus! Early adolescents want to be the center of attention—but only in certain ways. They desire to be noticed by their peers and the significant adults in their lives. So some of the things they say and do at church may simply be to get the attention they desire.

Although it is important for us to be sensitive to the likes and dislikes of our students, we must avoid building our preteen ministry solely on what the students say they want or on what we assume they want. Just as we would not consider parenting children by meeting the children's every whim, we should not design our ministries with only the desires of the students in mind. We must provide bold leadership in our ministry and carefully craft our preteen ministries according to the desires of the students along with what we know preteens need and what we know will help them grow spiritually—needs that even the early adolescents may not be able to express or understand.

The Needs of Early Adolescents—According to the Experts

Young adolescents have seven key developmental needs according to research done by Peter Scales of Search Institute:

1. Positive social interaction with adults and peers
2. Structure and clear limits
3. Physical activity
4. Creative expression
5. Competence and achievement
6. Meaningful participation in families, schools and communities
7. Opportunities for self-definition

Each of these developmental needs may be understood better in light of the age-level characteristics of preteens described earlier.

Learning-Style Activities

Plan to minister to preteens by using a variety of activities, depending on the learning styles of your group (for broad descriptions of the different learning styles, see "Understand Different Learning Styles" in chapter 3).

Visual (Spatial)—Challenge visual learners to express themselves by creating visual representations of what they've learned: drawing, building or completing art projects. Don't be surprised to find these learners doodling ideas.

Verbal (Linguistic)—Verbal learners will enjoy reading assignments and writing activities. They can use words creatively and are sensitive to the spoken word. They enjoy talking, discussing and storytelling, so use discussion and creative storytelling ideas. Challenge these preteens to memorize.

Physical (Kinesthetic)—Physical learners like to participate in a variety of short learning activities that include moving, touching, playing, acting and running. Minimize furniture in your room so that you may quickly, easily and frequently shift the activity from one part of the room to another. Have preteens role-play Bible stories and applications of lessons.

Relational (Interpersonal)—Because relational learners enjoy activities that involve small groups, teams, social settings, and projects that include working with others, you should make cooperative learning (working in pairs or small groups) a regular part of your learning environment. During each session, allow get-acquainted times for these preteens to talk and build friendships.

Reflective (Introspective)—Introspective learners appreciate activities that include meditation, reflection and prayer. They find self-study projects and one-on-one times with teachers and other students enjoyable. Allow for some quiet reflection during each session, and don't assume that quiet students are shy.

Logical (Mathematical)—Logical learners like to be involved in experiments, analyzing topics, problem solving, and answering tough questions. Help these students challenge and defend the faith. Stretch their thinking by asking open-ended questions.

Musical—Occasionally use music to set the mood for the Bible story, and make singing and listening to Bible words set to music part of some of your lessons. Have your students help supply popular Christian music recordings from which you can choose appropriate mood music for before and after class. Play and sing along with recordings of Bible passages set to music.

Naturalistic—Naturalist learners learn best when there are outdoor activities in God's creation, in natural surroundings. Include activities that utilize plants, animals, and other nature items. Occasionally take your class outdoors and/or plan class outings, camps and/or retreats. Have windows in your rooms.

Preteen-Specific Curriculum

Good Bible teaching is, of course, the number one priority in evaluating curriculum for our preteens, but there are some age-specific considerations that should be met by the curriculum chosen for this particular age group.

To Meet the Physical Needs of Preteens

Each lesson must provide ideas for movement and activity. The curriculum you use with preteens should have an active-learning style of education. Think of it this way: For many early adolescents, if their bodies are not moving, their brains are not switched on. Read through several lessons, and evaluate how often the students are encouraged to get up and move, discover, interact and discuss. When this is done well, the movement will be a natural outgrowth of the activities rather than just an occasional stretch break.

The lessons should shift focus at least every 10 to 12 minutes. The attention span of 10- to 12-year-olds is 10 to 12 minutes. Our lessons need to account for this by shifting focus frequently. This does not mean that there has to be a new activity every 10 minutes, but the focus needs to change. Activities that last for short chunks of time will also help preteens' need for movement and change of physical activity, making the class much more desirable and successful for both teacher and students.

To Meet the Emotional Needs of Preteens

The lessons should be fun, both for the students and the teacher. Preteens learn best when they are having fun. Teachers teach best when they're having fun. The ultimate goal is for the students to go home thinking they played the whole time, while the adults realize they taught the whole time! And research has shown that when emotions are involved, memories are stronger and will last longer. It's often true that the louder the laughter coming from a children's classroom, the better the chances that good ministry and good education are happening.

The teaching style should allow preteens to feel secure in the classroom. The curriculum should help you set up a comfortable environment in which everyone is welcome to share and be a part of the community. The questions provided should include a significant number of open-ended questions so that students are encouraged to think out loud and enabled to expand their concepts and explore their thoughts without fear of being put down if they give a wrong answer.

To Meet the Social Needs of Preteens

Each lesson should provide frequent opportunities for preteens to discuss the focus of the lesson. Preteens learn best when their education is interactive, when they are able to talk while learning.

Activities should include group efforts so that preteens can talk together. Peers and friends are important, so there should be opportunities for preteens to share and exchange information and goals. A mission or outreach activity, at least occasionally, would be a plus for these children eager to help others.

Activities should include group efforts so that preteens can talk together. Peers and friends are important, so there should be opportunities for preteens to share and exchange information and goals.

To Meet the Intellectual Needs of Preteens

The scope and sequence of the curriculum should be made up primarily of topics relevant to the world of preteens. Some of the topics that interest or concern these early adolescents and that you will want to address at various times throughout your years with them include the following:

- Friendships and relationships
- Setting priorities
- Peer pressure
- Death and eternal life
- Fear
- Popularity and success
- Substance abuse (drugs, alcohol, inhalants)
- Justice, world hunger and poverty
- Violence and gangs
- Respect for parents and other authorities
- Self-esteem and God's view of us
- School, grades and handling pressure
- The future
- Dating, love, marriage and sex (in that order!)

This is the time to talk about topics that involve the opposite gender, because preteens are close enough to being involved with the opposite gender to be interested but far enough away to be open to discussing them. We need to establish correct standards before they are involved in the activities. They're already seeing more than they are ready to see on TV, so they need to know what God says about this issue.

Each lesson should attempt to teach only one major Bible truth or concept. Better retention comes from looking at one key Bible truth over and over in different ways throughout an entire session. If we can get our preteens to enjoy church enough to attend fairly regularly (say, 30 to 40 times each year) and if we can get them to understand and apply just one Bible concept each time they come, they will still end up having more than 30 spiritual principles added to their lives annually.

Every aspect of the lesson should help reinforce, explain or make application of the one Bible concept. We don't have enough time with our students to add lots of extra stuff. We need to make sure that the music, the art projects, the prayers, the activities and the games all help repeat, reinforce, explain and explore the Bible concept. Repeated exposure to one point throughout the session will cause our students to learn and retain what is taught.

Good lessons will include thought-provoking questions that cause preteens to use higher-order reasoning skills. We want to challenge our students intellectually. Good questions will do that, but we must plan our questions (or have them planned for us in our curriculum). Beginning teachers will especially need help in this area. (Don't minimize the value of purchasing good curriculum with the right questions.) The questions also need to be open ended so that students are made to think and analyze the information before answering. Yes-or-no answers, or simple repeating of information that has been presented, will prove whether the student was listening and has some short-term memory of what was said, but those questions don't advance the student's thought process and understanding of the material.

Make sure that each lesson accounts for the various learning styles of your students. You may not be able to utilize every learning style in each lesson, but each style of learning should be included regularly and all should be accounted for within each two- to three-week period.

To Meet the Spiritual Needs of Preteens

The lessons must be doctrinally and theologically acceptable to your church or denomination. Ask the publisher for a copy of its curriculum scope and sequence. Most have a printed brochure or chart that tells you what stories or Bible concepts are taught at what age levels. If you need help in evaluating the scope and sequence, ask a church or denominational leader to sit down with you as you look at specific lessons that might be of concern to your church.

Each lesson should have the preteens opening God's Word for themselves. Preteens need to see that the Bible is practical and usable for them in their own lives. Choose a curriculum that gets them to look up verses, read short passages and even search for truths in the Scriptures on their own.

Preteens need to see that the Bible is practical and usable for them in their own lives.

Lessons must be practical and must emphasize life application. Early adolescents want to know that what they're doing has value for them. They no longer are interested in the stories that younger Sunday School classes emphasized. Now they want to talk about real issues, meaning how these stories can help them and how they can apply them to what is happening in their lives. Early adolescents aren't very interested in theory; they want to know how to apply this to their lives and what will happen when they do.

Lessons must be relevant to the student's search for a more abstract understanding of faith and God. As preteens move into the realm of abstract thinking, they want and need to rethink faith in God. The purpose of this search is to make God real in their new way of thinking.

Sources

Michael A. James, "Early Adolescent Ego Development," *The High School Journal* (March 1980), p. 244.

Peter Scales, *Portrait of Young Adolescents in the 1990s: Implications for Promoting Healthy Growth and Development* (Minneapolis, MN: Search Institute, 1991).

Ross Campbell, M.D., *How to Really Love Your Teenager* (Wheaton, IL: Victor Books, 1981), pp. 29-30.

Benjamin S. Bloom, ed., *A Taxonomy of Educational Objectives* (New York: Longmans, Green, 1956).

Gordon and Becki West, *Preteen Ministry Smart Pages* (Ventura, CA: Gospel Light, 2005).

PART 2

Youth Sunday School

Period of Development	Sunday School Group Name	Ages
Youth	Junior High	12-l4
	High School	14-18
	College	18-25

6

Junior High

(AGES 12 TO 14)

"Adjustment" is the keyword of this age. There are adjustments of new physical powers, new emotions, new ideals and conceptions of life, and new spiritual experiences. Junior high is the continuation of the roller-coaster ride begun in preteen. These changes from the old life to the new, from interests narrow and selfish to interests that are far reaching are often accompanied by a terrific upheaval mentally, physically and spiritually. This then is a period of readjustment, and the duty of the teacher is to understand this most misunderstood youth of all ages.

Adolescence is the age so fraught with danger and so filled with opportunities that it may rightfully be considered one of life's most important periods. Mistakes at this age are more disastrous than at any other because they affect all of life. On the other hand, right choices have eternal values, for the choices of adolescence are apt to be the choices of eternity.

> The Moving Finger writes; and, having writ,
> Moves on: nor all thy Piety nor Wit
> Shall lure it back to cancel half a Line,
> Nor all your Tears wash out a Word of it.
> — Omar Khayyám, *The Rubáiyát of Omar Khayyám*

This age group is the most baffling of all to the educator. The very word "adolescence" fills us with terror. I often wonder how our forebears raised us without even knowing the word "adolescence." These youngsters are neither children nor adults. Boys' voices are doing stunts on the vocal trapeze. Girls' hair seems stringy. Their stomachs are bottomless pits. They are either very shy or very bold. They just don't seem to fit anywhere, and they can be exasperating to the nth degree.

Junior highers offer particularly trying problems—but also great opportunities.

A Distinct Species

Most people do not understand the fact that junior highers do not fit with any other age group. They will not mix with younger children or older children anymore than oil will mix with water. They are a distinct species. You cannot put junior highers with preteens without disastrous results, and to put them with the high school students is to lose them, for this older teenager will look upon them with contempt.

Too many Sunday Schools do this very thing. They do not separate children into distinct groups. They push junior highers in with preteens, where they stay for a while, possibly making trouble for the younger group, and then drop out one by one; and the teacher sighs a sigh of relief because the troublemakers are gone at last. If you put junior highers in with high school students, one of two things happen: Either the older students will assume leadership and overshadow the junior highers (who will leave for lack of challenge); or the junior highers will take the lead and show up the older students (who will leave because they will not follow their underclassmen). Every Sunday School should make a careful study of their enrollment and create a separate class for each age group.

Watch this group carefully. Too great an emphasis cannot be placed upon the teacher's responsibility in dealing with junior highers, as with preteens. Physical and mental changes are taking place too rapidly for either group to make perfect adjustments to all that is happening within them. Sometimes you will think that fifteen-year-old Mary has really grown up at last. She displays the wisdom of her mother. But the next minute she is as petulant as her younger sister. She is now the most baffling problem that science has ever attacked.

Be kind to them. They are very sensitive because they constantly feel misunderstood, and it is at this age that many children consider leaving home. And statistics on truancy and irresponsibility tell us that the average minister, physician, educator, lawyer and businessperson of now-irreproachable standing will confess to having been guilty of lawless pranks and devilry in their early teens. Sometimes the activities even bordered on the criminal. You must put yourself in the shoes of these young people and you must remember your own youth, or you will never be able to hold on to them long enough to lead them onto the right path.

During these years the student is most susceptible to outside influences, which impel and incite them to action. These influences determine the course of their lives; changes in tendencies and character are rarely made after people reach full maturity. Therefore, in all probability as their lives emerge from adolescence, so will they be for eternity. What kind of men and women is your Sunday School producing?

Age-Level Characteristics

Upheavals are many, and battles rage within these tempestuous personalities. Their capacity for emotional thrills knows no bounds. They reach out for new continents to explore. Their whole lives are filled with stress and storm. They think they know more now than they will ever know again. This is the time when the child is least understood. They long for someone who can understand them. We just need to love them and feed them. Be friendly. Lead them into a relationship with the Lord Jesus Christ. Let their tangled threads of emotion be unified by Christ. Challenge them to live lives that are pure and noble. Christ's presence, this new hero for them, will be a tremendous driving power within them.

Lead them into a relationship with the Lord Jesus Christ. Let their tangled threads of emotion be unified by Christ. Challenge them to live lives that are pure and noble. Christ's presence, this new hero for them, will be a tremendous driving power within them.

So often teachers of this age are discouraged because they feel they are accomplishing so little. Don't lose heart! You are accomplishing wonders if you are just holding these youngsters to Christ and the Church, as this is the time of greatest loss in Sunday School. It is more during early adolescence than any other age that people are lost to the church forever!

Physical

Rapid changes are taking place physically. Junior highers are awkward and unpoised, because of the great changes going on; this, in turn, results in poor coordination. They are all arms and legs. They slam doors and trip over everything. One boy goes down the stairs and you think you are hearing a thundering herd. Junior highers must give vent to the great tides of energy that race through their whole being. You can't decide whether these youngsters should be dressed as adults or children. Nothing seems to look exactly right on them. You are constantly reminded that they are in transition. They have a superabundance of power but are in constant danger of overtaxing their strength.

Cognitive and Emotional

Junior highers are in a state of transition and change mentally. They are critical. Faith is yielding to reason. They are becoming more and more independent. Their lack of mental balance leads to instability of conduct. You will find that junior highers are extremely sensitive and very easily disturbed.

Junior highers are painfully self-conscious and, because of this, they are extremely bashful or so bold as to be brazen. A sense of approaching adulthood makes junior highers extremely sensitive to reproof or criticism, especially in public. Never make fun of them in front of their peers.

The emotions of junior highers are like TNT, easily kindled into a fire by a little friction. Slang words pepper their speech. Periods of great enthusiasm are common, but periods of depression counteract those of exhilaration. There is constant questioning and introspection, and the teacher has to be a confidant as well as an instructor. Don't ever be ashamed or shocked by what a junior higher may say or do, thus closing the door between you and the student.

Permit junior highers to decide matters for themselves. Throw these young people more and more on their own resources. They must learn much by trial and error. Remember, they pay little heed to what their elders think. One of the most serious errors on the part of parents and teachers alike lies in dictating instead of guiding, making their choices for them instead of allowing them to choose. Do not think for this group; rather, stimulate them to do their own thinking and to solve their own personal problems. If you do not teach young people to become strong and independent during these years of adjustment and transition, their lives will likely always be weak and vacillating.

Emotions are strong during these years and there is a danger in our teaching lest we permit any newly awakened feeling to be dissipated. If feelings are not converted into actions, they tend to weaken rather than strengthen the impulses to take the right stands. Lead junior highers in making life decisions. Christ knew at 12 that He "must be about [His] Father's business" (Luke 2:49). Little Samuel heard God's plan for his life. We are likely to pass by this most sensitive period of life and consider the youth's decisions too lightly.

If feelings are not converted into actions, they tend to weaken rather than strengthen the impulses to take the right stands. Lead junior highers in making life decisions.

Knowledge is growing faster than experience. They have "forgotten" more than their fathers ever knew. We must remember that an idle adolescent's brain is certainly the devil's workshop. Junior highers have vivid imaginations and spend much time in building air castles. They are reaching out for new mental continents to explore. This is the self-important age, and a 14-year-old boy is no more to be criticized for being big-headed than for being big-footed.

Junior highers do not believe that their parents understand that the things that the parents did in their day are outmoded in this present age. "Why, nobody does that anymore" is their refrain. They may quizzically ask adults, "What did they do in the olden days when you went to school?" This sort of question doesn't cause quite the shock it once would have. With technology improving all of the time, it's difficult for a lot of people to keep up with all of the changes occurring in this area.

Be conscious of the fact that junior highers have an intense longing for appreciation. They long to excel and have their talents and accomplishments appreciated. For this reason, we often find that a junior higher who is gifted will try to draw attention to him- or herself in some way. In contrast, others who feel themselves deficient in that same area will draw themselves into a shell and become very self-conscious and quiet.

Social

This is the age of growing self-consciousness and of sexual awareness. Junior highers are very curious about the opposite sex. Boys of this age usually love to tease and torment girls, so you may consider separating the boys and girls into different classrooms.

Younger members of this age group are not much affected by what others think of them, but it is not long before a desire to look good in front of the opposite sex manifests itself. As soon as a boy begins to go with a girl, you will see a new look in his appearance. Life takes on meaning due to the new love interest. This makes the girls giggly and silly. The sight of a boy throws them into a dither. This is the time to cultivate right boy-girl relationships lest there be an explosion of undesired actions and unforeseen consequences so characteristic of too many children of this age in society in general. Provide group activities for junior highers so that they can practice right actions with the opposite gender.

Junior highers are very clannish and they seek peer approval. The wise teacher will capitalize on this and see this as an excellent opportunity to teach the art of getting along with others, for junior highers are guided by the opinion of their peers. Both preteens and junior highers form spontaneous social groups, though one must be cognizant that cliques can be hurtful toward others and harmful for their members.

Junior highers want companions of their own age. At this age, they do not want to play alone; neither do they seek the company of older people. Junior highers always seem to move in crowds of their peers. Their play turns into games with teams and competition. They seem to have laws and ethics all their own. Each junior higher adheres to the code of honor of his or her social group. I once saw a club in our Sunday School, just a group of boys, stick together through thick and thin. They would never act independently. Never would they betray a confidence. They would rather let the heavens fall than tell on one of their friends. These fellows have stuck together through a period of 12 years. This "gang" has never been broken. Loyalty was their platform.

We must orient peer groups so that their loyalties are to the church. Every junior high social group has a meeting place. It used to be the library or the five-and-dime. Now it may be the mall or a local eatery. Wherever they meet, junior highers may be planning adventuresome things, which may develop into something criminal or at least dangerous.

At no time does the influence of the home count for so little. This is because newfound friends count for so much. Junior highers are stepping out from under the roofs of their childhood homes—and the influence of their parents—into a new independence.

In order to take advantage of the strong loyalty junior highers feel toward others in their social group, we have offered different clubs, sports and even a camp program to attract the whole group to the church. Remembering that we cannot win one junior higher at a time to our church program, we have emphasized a program that includes his or her whole social group.

We must realize that junior highers are facing complex personal problems. I once received from a principal of a neighboring junior high school the following list of problems and questions that faced the junior highers:

- *Boys*: broken home, economic insecurity, belonging to gang, fear of ridicule, to be athletic, getting a car, tension, to smoke or drink, getting along with people, sex information, rules of etiquette, inferiority complex, stealing.

- *Girls*: bringing up mother, clothes, sensitive, allowance, afraid of being called names, attracting the opposite sex, tension, to smoke and drink, getting along with people, sex information, rules of etiquette, inferiority complex, to be attractive and popular, stealing.

When the ninth-grade girls were asked to write down their biggest problems, almost all of them wrote that they wondered whether it was right or wrong for a ninth-grade girl to have sexual relations. We must help them to answer this question and work out the biblical answer for themselves. The fact remains that in the lives of junior highers, the opinion of adults counts for very little. They generally go by what their peer group says. That is public opinion to them.

The concerns that are vital to junior highers must be dealt with before they can go on and develop Christian lives. From the problems and questions that the principal learned when he questioned the junior highers in his school, we find what occupies the minds of junior highers. We discussed some of these topics in our junior high club meetings. The students could not figure out how we knew so much about their concerns, but you may be assured that the meetings were popular. We did not have to create interest. It was there. Perhaps the reason that so many seventh-, eighth- and ninth-graders loose interest in Sunday School and drop out is because we are not doing anything to help them deal with what concerns them the most. Is there any reason that we in America are having such moral and juvenile delinquency problems? The questions on the minds and hearts of our young people have been ignored. This calls for the most delicate of treatment, but this is an operation that must be performed or the patients will die!

This age of loyalty is also an age of hero worship that is unreserved and wholehearted. How often I have seen a fine young man literally engulfed by a crowd of junior high boys. They climb in his car three deep or surround him on the basketball court. They love him and everything that belongs to him. All he needs to say is, "Come on, guys," and they all go. I have found that they prize what a man can do more than anything else. A man becomes a hero because of his accomplishments.

Girls are quite the same. They have their heroes too. They follow to the death the latest fashion designer or singing sensation—anyone who opens up new avenues of life to them. Club programs that touch life interests appeal to them. Life friendships are formed now. If their friends are made in the church, the junior highers will continue to come. If not, they will go where their friends are.

Life friendships are formed now. If their friends are made in the church, the junior highers will continue to come. If not, they will go where their friends are.

Everyone must have something to do. We have learned to organize everything we can in order to make everybody a definite part of the organization. Have students help choose a name for their class, and consider having every person in the class hold an office. If there are four in the class, have a president, vice president, secretary and treasurer. If there are five, add a sergeant at arms or a second vice president.

Neither parents nor teachers can solve any problem with children this age by just putting their foot down. The rules that worked in childhood will not work now. You must have a positive plan for these youngsters. Your church must develop a proactive plan to deal with early adolescents.

You must have a positive plan for these youngsters. Your church must develop a proactive plan to deal with early adolescents.

Organization helps in class discipline. With everything organized and scheduled, junior highers will know what to expect and when, so discipline problems will be minimized. To help deal with any problems that do arise, consider turning over at least some of the responsibility of maintaining class order to one of the pupils. It is an established fact that if you give your worst troublemaker at least some of the responsibility for maintaining class order, that student will take the responsibility seriously and try to help. Make him or her the chairman of a Class Personnel committee.

Organization helps maintain interest. At my church, one of the teachers who was a pilot called his class the Sky Pilots. Their room was equipped like an airplane. Flash cards with words that are used during airplane communications were used as signals to the class: "Break-break" meant prayer; "Standby" signaled the class to get ready for a discussion. This teacher mastered discipline this way. This teacher always had something that he could pull out of his pocket to capture interest. He gained the friendship of his boys by finding out their interests and hobbies. For those interested in radio, he procured tickets to one of the local broadcasting studios and went with them. If they liked to hike, a Saturday afternoon found them roaming the hills together.

Another promising group was the Loyal Knights. A room in the tower was their meeting place. A round table was built for them. The walls were decorated with swords and shields. A complete organization around the Knights of the Round Table captured the interests of this class for years. And every boy had a part in the program.

Junior highers have an increasing social appetite. When you curb a junior higher's desire to go out with the crowd to indulge in any questionable entertainment, you will hear him or her say, "But everybody else is going." This desire for a good time is paramount, and these young people see no reason why this right should be denied them. Provide a wholesome outlet and good times for junior highers in the church or you will discover that they will find it elsewhere. Remember, we were created with social as well as spiritual appetites. Frequent social outlets are essential.

Junior highers will become like those with whom they "play." Entertaining this group is not easy. If you open your home to junior highers, you will likely have a lot to clean up afterwards. If you take them on hikes, you will have to devote one of your own Saturday afternoons to the event. Junior highers have a very superficial standard for judging people, and this opens the way to very harmful influences at this critical time of life. Teachers are extremely important at this time. We want to use a patient, guiding and inspiring touch upon the lives of these young people. Encourage wholesome outdoor sports for those who are athletically inclined. Foster this spirit as a safety valve for their surplus energy. It gives them great joy just to be with their peer group. Junior highers put a premium on their athletic prowess. But remember that you must find nonathletic activities for those who are not interested in sports.

Begin to cultivate the spirit of service. Give every pupil definite tasks to perform both in the class itself and in the church. Teach them by giving them specific short-term projects. Be sure that they are finished quickly. If projects are long drawn-out affairs, junior highers will lose interest. They love to undertake something and at the end are thrilled with the sense of accomplishment. Projects may range from outreach activities to very simple services like passing out supplies or taking attendance. You can launch almost any project if the subject or object of it is enthusiastically presented as worthwhile. Follow up any interest that has been aroused.

Spiritual

Junior highers are at a point in their lives when their spiritual decisions are deliberate, not based on feelings. Even though a junior higher may be a genuine Christian, there is still a growing consciousness of God and a personal relationship to Him as Lord and Master. Up to this time, a child's relationship to God has been based mainly on feeling. Now the will begins to make deliberate choices.

The span of years from 12 to 13 is a time of great spiritual awakening. This is also the time when most conversions occur, and every child seems to be deeply religious. Typically, following this peak is a period of temporary decline, which is alarming to most parents and teachers. At this time, junior highers ruthlessly break away from the traditions of the past. Maybe the boy or girl who has loved Sunday School, has read the Bible every day and has learned all of the memory work in the Junior High Department suddenly decides that there is nothing in prayer, the Bible isn't believable and going to Sunday School is just for little children!

Don't react harshly or negatively to this sort of attitude, even if you feel frustrated and disgusted. Be patient. Give the junior higher real reasons for faith. You must be able to convince this adolescent by strong facts that Christianity is just what it claims to be.

Less stress must be placed on material and method and more on teacher-student relationship. We will find that a story presenting life situations similar to their own will have great teaching value.

Less stress must be placed on material and method and more on teacher-student relationship.

Many a parent during this period of adjustment for adolescents came to my office and was sure that he or she was a failure. Parents are very likely to blame the teacher for this change in attitude, saying that in the Junior High Department their child earned small awards and wouldn't miss a Sunday for anything, but now if the child goes to Sunday School, he or she must be forced to go. This child also assures his or her parents that when old enough, he or she certainly won't go to Sunday School anymore. But the teachers are not always responsible. The child has become an adolescent and is going through a revolutionary change—physically, cognitively, emotionally, socially and spiritually. As we have said before, if you just hold this boy or girl for Christ and the Church during this turbulent period, you have done enough. We must not lose the child now. Make your problems your partners. Attach them to yourself. If they love you, they will soon love your God. Someone once said, "First I learned to love my teacher, then my teacher's God."

Make your problems your partners. Attach them to yourself. If they love you, they will soon love your God. Someone once said, "First I learned to love my teacher, then my teacher's God."

Prove to junior highers that Christianity is practical. Few experience genuine Christian living in their homes. Some never see it. Boys and girls of this age have great admiration for sincerity and bitter contempt for hypocrisy. Teachers must establish real camaraderie with their students. Don't pity junior highers; rather, feel with them—learn to empathize. Put yourself on the level of their experiences. If you don't, you will fail! Two substitute teachers filled in two consecutive Sundays for a class of 14-year-old boys. One was called a "sour puss"; the other was "smart." The "sour puss" knew more of the Bible in a minute than the "smart" fellow knew in a day, but he did not know boys.

If the student is not a Christian and does not heed Christ's call now, that call will grow less and less distinct until the noises of the world deafen the ears to the wooing of the Spirit.

Guide junior highers to heed Christ's call to follow Him. Every teacher must remember that if the student is not a Christian and does not heed Christ's call now, that call will grow less and less distinct until the noises of the world deafen the ears to the wooing of the Spirit.

Unfortunately, once adolescents have left the Church, no evangelistic campaign, no matter how many times waged, will succeed in getting back the vast majority after they have gone. These are the men and women who a few years later are playing golf or gardening or going to the beach on Sunday. The habit of going to church has been broken. They find no time in their lives for God. We cannot blame the public schools entirely for sending our youth to hell. *We are responsible.* We have made Sunday School so unattractive that the young say that they'll be so glad when they don't have to go to church anymore, because they hate it. They are the ones who grow up to say, "I was made to go to church so much when I was young that I don't want to go anymore." The godless schools are not responsible for this. It is the fault of the Sunday School.

Use the biography and history of the Word. Tell junior highers facts and let them see the plain statements of truth. Convince them that Christianity meets the needs of the day. The process of relating fact to fact, life to life, and each soul anew to God is the paramount task of teaching adolescents. Help them to adjust their lives to a new world alive in Christ.

The process of relating fact to fact, life to life, and each soul anew to God is the paramount task of teaching adolescents.

Foster high ideals. An ideal cannot be passed to another person as one would a book. It is a personal matter. But every teacher can foster high ideals. It is in the transition period from childhood to maturity that each person decides what is to be the most worthwhile thing in this world. God in His gracious providence has made this time of life one that is most easily influenced. The teacher can play a big part to influence these junior highers in the direction they should go.

Test your teaching by the number of your students who give themselves to Christ and confess Him as Master and Lord, the friend for whom their hearts at this age yearn. Teacher, your responsibility is great. Gain the love and admiration of your class. Many tragedies in this age can be averted by understanding teachers. Remember, this is the age of transition and

If you are in a vital relationship with God and live with your students during this ambitious, discouraging, tempestuous period of their lives, you can wield the dynamic force of a spiritual, personal influence.

adjustment. Most important, you cannot lead your students to any higher place than you occupy yourself. If you are in a vital relationship with God and live with your students during this ambitious, discouraging, tempestuous period of their lives, you can wield the dynamic force of a spiritual, personal influence.

The Junior High Department

How do we organize a department to meet the needs of junior highers? Organization requires a program. Our aims require a vision. When the Holy Spirit empowers a leader who has a vision and a program, tremendous results are obtained. Make your Junior High Department a matter of careful study. Try to discover what appeals to 12- to 14-year-olds, what kind of teachers to attract, what goals you should strive to reach.

Our aims require a vision. When the Holy Spirit empowers a leader who has a vision and a program, tremendous results are obtained.

First, evaluate your present setup. Do you have an adult staff sufficient to carry out an effective program? How could you reorganize to make for greater efficiency? Are your leaders trained for their work? One junior high superintendent, a college woman of high standing, attended a training class every week every year she taught. She constantly grew. She discovered new methods. Hence the department forged ahead.

If you are not in a place where you can attend a training class, read books and find information for study on the Internet. There is no excuse for anyone to remain uninformed today. A farmer isolated from great urban centers does not go on working with the same tools indefinitely. Catalogs are sent for, and articles that present the latest methods of running a farm are read. The latest equipment is added whenever possible. But that same farmer is likely to think that he or she can run the Sunday School in the same way year in and year out without changing a single thing.

Do you have enough teachers to carry out a graded study program? Are you doing anything to train new ones? Do you have regular workers' conferences or meetings? Such get-togethers are always stimulating for the worker and provide an opportunity for the exchange of ideas.

Physical Environment

What is your physical environment like? First, take a look at the rooms in which your junior highers meet. Are the assembly and classrooms adequate? If not, what else is available? Have you made the existing rooms as attractive as possible? If not, what can reasonably be done? Maybe rearranging the furnishings would improve it. As your Sunday School grows, move from one room to another to make use of every available space. Do some shifting. Perhaps the adult class should move out of the largest room so that junior highers can meet there. Remember, we must do everything to hold these adolescents.

Worship Center

Do you have a worship center? Are you using visual aids? What about music? Plan and work to create an atmosphere of worship. Sometimes a beautiful picture is an excellent and simple way to provide a theme for the worship service. Sometimes a movable screen that can be put up quickly in a room will immediately transform the room and give a center of interest.

Curriculum

Does your curriculum include the necessary components: study, worship, service, recreation and evangelism? Is the curriculum geared to meet the needs and interests of this age group? It makes a great deal of difference *what* you teach your students.

Choose Materials Wisely

Make a careful study of the materials in your curriculum. Just anything will not do. In choosing curriculum for junior highers, we must remember their great desire for facts. Capitalize on their hero worship, and guide them in every lesson to see Christ as the hero. We must remember junior highers' susceptibility to outside influences and study the great missionary books of the Bible, like the book of Acts. We must bring junior highers face to face with personal decisions constantly and challenge them to find their places in this world of opportunity.

We must bring junior highers face to face with personal decisions constantly and challenge them to find their places in this world of opportunity.

Include Student Books

Many have questioned the value of using student books with students this age. We must remember, though, that it is especially important to encourage junior highers in their daily study of the Bible as well as to inspire their thinking for themselves concerning spiritual things. Since this is the very purpose of Junior High student books, every effort on the part of the teacher and leader to stimulate their use will be worthwhile.

It is especially important to encourage junior highers in their daily study of the Bible as well as to inspire their thinking for themselves concerning spiritual things.

Vary Your Methods

Various methods may be used to encourage junior highers to firmly establish a habit of daily Bible study. Give awards to individuals or to classes for work that has been completed. Show much appreciation for work well done. Post in church hallways samples of completed art projects that reflect biblical lessons. Publish a newsletter that lets the church know what junior highers have been studying and doing, especially in regard to outreach and mission projects.

You may want to help your students get started in their books by having them do one lesson together in class. Study the questions together and have them write the answers as they discover them. Collect the books at the end of each quarter and take them home and grade them. Find and write something good about each one, thus instilling in each student a sense of a job well done. This is important.

Give an examination at the close of the quarter. This will not keep junior highers away. More often than not, they like to see what they can do, especially if the questions are true-and-false ones or ones that they have written themselves. Organize your test like a baseball game, giving points for questions correctly answered.

Proper motivation must be given constantly. Junior highers are no different in Sunday School than they are in day school. If the teacher did not regularly check their progress, they would soon leave their books untouched.

Clubs

The good that clubs contribute to the physical, cognitive, emotional, social and spiritual training of students is incalculable and is best organized in our Youth Sunday School. The hands and eyes of adolescents are trained through hobbies and recreational interests for leisure times. Christian character through wholesome contacts and projects is developed. Clubs also give students a new sense of their responsibility to win their friends for Christ and the Church. Then the friend in turn will be led into a fellowship of service. Club activities must, of course, be adapted to individual interests and needs. You can't force a program upon a group.

A service program is particularly helpful for junior high students, and much can be done through clubs. Projects may be planned and carried out to meet the special needs of your missionaries who will be happy to make suggestions for your club group. In this way, the junior highers are given a picture of the world and its needs and are shown what part they can play in a great worldwide program. They or you can invite people of different ethnic backgrounds to speak to the club. As junior highers learn about different peoples, they will find out the needs of those different people groups.

Maybe a room or two in the church needs a coat of paint. Maybe a local shelter could use small bags of personal-care items. Maybe your local food bank needs a supply of canned food. There are many ways that junior highers can be of service—just ask them!

Clubs, by way of sports activities, are a way to bring these young people into fellowship with other churches in the area, thus broadening their interests, friendships and knowledge.

Social Activities

When you think of a whole year of teaching and then add planning recreational activities to the mix, you may think that running the Junior High Department for a year is burdensome. Things will seem easy, however, when you plan ahead for the year's activities and then divide the responsibilities for the activities. There must be great variety in the "fun" life of the junior-higher.

Begin your plans in the fall to coincide with the start of the regular school year. As you begin to look at the calendar, you will immediately see that there are many special days throughout the year that can be the basis for festive occasions. In the fall, a junior high get-together banquet would be a grand way to get off to a good start. Let the junior highers invite their friends to this fine affair. Then Halloween would be a perfect time to keep young people off the streets by giving them a wonderful evening packed full of food and games in the fellowship hall or gym in the church. The first Thanksgiving is a grand theme for a Thanksgiving celebration.

At Christmastime, have your students create a Christmas program to present to the congregation or to people living in a nursing home; have the junior highers sing carols at the homes of church members who cannot attend church. Then New Year's Eve is another time when youngsters can gather to enjoy together games and refreshments in a room they've decorated themselves. At 11 o'clock let them move to the sanctuary for a watchnight service. What a wonderful way to review the past year, make a confession and then start off the New Year with praying.

George Washington parties, lighthearted April Fools' Day celebrations, patriotic Memorial Day festivities—there are more than enough holidays throughout the year to pick from and celebrate with some sort of get-together. And you and the students can choose from a variety of things to do: play games, make and eat a meal, put on puppet shows, watch old movies and share popcorn with different toppings, hold a carnival, have a picnic, camp indoors and tell stories around a flashlight campfire—the possibilities are nearly endless.

The fellowship that will result will be well worth the effort.

7

High School

(AGES 14 TO 18)

Teenagers are individuals trying to be real people in the only way they know. They are striving to reach the goal of being grown up. They spend much of their time trying to find their way around in a world controlled by adults. However, the world they really live in is one of their own making.

How superficial this age seems to older people. We think, *They haven't a serious thought in their heads.* This is the time of hit songs and hot technology. They spend hours on their cell phones or on the Internet. The spend hours at the mall, even though there is a school paper due tomorrow. They combine loud music with geometry lessons and seem to have enough attention for both. Often we long for displays of a more serious attitude about life. We must admit that students at this age both amuse and confuse, surprise and confound us.

Not only do we need to understand this youth, but also—in fact, even more so—we need to help them to understand themselves so that they may realize and use their varied talents and abilities in the service of Christ and His Church. We must help them discover a lifework, not work for life. This process of growing up is very confusing and often painful. Don't believe it when you hear someone say, "Youth is the time of being carefree and happy." This is not always so; the problems and heartaches of teens are often greater than we can imagine.

We must help them discover a lifework, not work for life.

Henrietta C. Mears • www.gospellight.com

Age-Level Characteristics

Physical

Teens are going through physical changes. "What a lovely young lady Mary is getting to be!" we find ourselves saying when we first see Mary as a young high school girl. Her legs and arms are no longer gangling and out of control, and her hair is not stringy. Now she is definitely a young lady. She is very clothes and makeup conscious. Her hair is fixed in the latest fashion. The contrast between this somewhat sophisticated young lady with the silly, giggly Mary of junior high almost startles us. Bill no longer tumbles over his big feet, nor does his voice do the trapeze act. We who are leaders of high school young people must realize that this physical change occurs naturally during the later teen years.

High school young people are no longer children. Don't treat them as such. They are physically mature. This maturity brings with it a desire to be independent and free from adult restraint. This maturity is also evidenced by a strong interest in the opposite sex and thoughts of establishing their own homes and raising their own offspring. This is a profound situation in which these young people find themselves.

Much of what young people do that is so disturbing—and almost alarming—to parents and teachers is really due to the normal process of growing up. But we should guide teens away from maturing so fast that they lose their faith and forget biblical teaching. Teens must be led to avoid sexual experimentation and to follow biblical principles when establishing relationships with the opposite sex.

Teens are interested in sex. One of the finest ways to overcome—or maybe at least defuse—the overwhelming interest these teens have in sex is for the teens to engage in athletic activities. Many Sunday School teachers discover that this is one of the ways they can interest and hold teens. Take them on a swim or a hike; have them enter into an athletic contest of one sort or another. When you go to camp with a group of high-schoolers, you will be amazed by their boundless energy and reckless way of letting off steam. They invariably act before they think, and everything is not done as it ought to be.

Cognitive and Emotional

At this age there is a keen desire for knowledge. Beyond the seeming superficiality, there is a constant searching for something new, a discarding of the old. The reasoning power of teens has reached a new height. Their horizons are widening rapidly. There is a general intensity and extreme in everything—thoughts, feelings and enthusiasm. Let us direct this all toward Christian objectives. Let us clearly define what the goals and aims of this group should be.

This is the age of problems, not of doubts. The two most perplexing and pressing problems of high school young people are, first, their proper relationship to others and, second, their relationship to their lifework. They need guidance, and this is a place of opportunity for teachers and parents. Until children reach this age, teaching has largely been an impartation of knowledge. Now, though, discussions and logical appeals to their reason are necessary. Show your students that nothing is settled until it is settled right and that God's Word has never failed, and you will have given them a basis for solving their problems.

Show your students that nothing is settled until it is settled right and that God's Word has never failed, and you will have given them a basis for solving their problems.

Much learning by youngsters this age is best done by the method of group learning. Each teen influences his or her group, and each teen's group influences him or her. Our task in Sunday School class is to form a group whose members may learn to know how to live a Christian life. When Jesus organized a school on this earth, He chose 12 to be with Him. To be sure, He dealt with each one as an individual, but He constantly taught the group. Young people must be planted in the right environment or they will not grow.

Teens want to see proof. Always remember that your students are accustomed to the atmosphere of the classroom where most teachers speak with authority. The minds of teens are in the habit of working with mathematical accuracy, and they demand proof. What you *think* does not count for half so much as what you *know*.

High school teens are daydreamers. They draw impossible plans for the future. Unsympathetic people refer to these as air castles. This is a situation where we ought to use caution. Were the dreams of Edison or the Wright Brothers or Alexander Bell useless? It is often hard for us to believe that teens can master their dreams, but always express a belief that your students *can* succeed. Give them big things to do and challenge them to do their best. Little things have no magic in them!

When Jesus organized a school on this earth, He chose 12 to be with Him. To be sure, He dealt with each one as an individual, but He constantly taught the group. Young people must be planted in the right environment or they will not grow.

Most teens seem irresponsible. Seldom will they offer to do something around the house. They must be urged to do their homework. They put everything off. Their grades are seldom what they could be. They appear lazy and lax, but you will notice that if there is anything they want to do, they will work at it untiringly. They take initiative in the things they like.

High-schoolers are egotists. Use this as a basis of moral appeal. The Lord recognized this characteristic in Peter when He called this vascillating fellow a "rock" (Matthew 16:18). Far better for a teenager to have too much self-confidence than none at all.

Teens have critical attitudes. They despise the status quo. Their daydreams give them visions of how things ought to be. They are critical of people; they think their parents know little about their interests and feelings. The sad thing is that in some cases, they may be right. It might have been Mark Twain who said, "When I was a boy of fourteen, my father was so ignorant I could hardly stand to have the old man around. But when I got to be twenty-one, I was astonished at how much he had learned in seven years." They are especially critical of those who are older than them. They are often as disgusted with what we do as we are with them.

Teens at this age feel very superior to younger children. They think of themselves as very grown-up, but their elders think they have a long way to go.

Teenagers are exceedingly moody. One day they are ready to conquer the world, and the next day finds them, like Elijah when he was in a cave, thinking of their aloneness, and as the prophet put it, "I, even I only, am left" (1 Kings 19:10). There is a constant cry in every heart that is often expressed out loud: "Mom and Dad do not understand. Times are so different now from when they grew up." Parents and teachers, have you ever stopped to ask yourself whether you do understand? We must not only know the problems of youth, but we must also know how to meet them.

Social

High-schoolers are very social beings. At this age, children are beginning to be more selective in picking out their friends. They choose friends with whom they wish to spend time alone. They do not want family members to interfere. They are very secretive with their friends and may be heard speaking slang or seen texting messages or sending emails that parents find difficult if not impossible to understand. The greatest worry for children this age is not intellectual doubt but how to become popular with their own crowd. And, of course, young females want to be attractive to young males; and young males want to excel in athletics and be heroes of the day in order to be attractive to young females.

Teens begin a gradual separation from the family and ties to the home. Generally, teens seem to have a horror of being thought to be tied to their mother's apron strings. They no longer are interested in doing things with the family; a family picnic or trip does not appeal to them. Parents should not take any of these things personally. It is not that the teens no longer love their families, but they are becoming part of a new social world with its own whirl of activities. Teens should not be challenged about their love for their families. In fact, we should remember that these individuals should never be compelled to move in a limited circle.

Teens are passing through one of the most difficult periods of adult development. Teens are not having the easiest and happiest times of their lives; rather, they face complex problems. They must decide whether to continue with their education, how they can best earn a living, what their vocation will be, what school they will attend and how to pay for it—among so many other things. And while still in high school, they need to decide what extracurricular activities to take part in, what electives to take, whether to get a part-time job, whether to buy a car—among so many other things. This is a time when students need a great deal of the right leadership.

We as teachers must counter the alarming situation that is facing America where in some states the high school graduation rate is not even 50 percent. We must make these teenagers face the facts about what education and training will afford them. At the very least, they need to recognize that completing high school is the minimum requirement for most jobs; and with our society becoming more and more complex and dependent on technology, teenagers simply cannot afford to drop out and expect to do well later in life. We must do everything we can to prevent teenagers from giving in to wanderlust.

If these young people do not make Christian friends at this time, they are very likely to make friends that will draw them away from Christ and the Church.

Teenagers want to have a good time. They want fun. And they want it with their own social group, wherever that group is. This is the time when the church must play a large part in the lives of teens. Do not say that the Church is not responsible for the social life of its young people. If these young people do not make Christian friends at this time, they are very likely to make friends that will draw them away from Christ and the Church.

Teens are loyal. Teens have been loyal to their social groups in junior high. Now cultivate their loyalty to their Sunday School class. Teach them to be loyal to the small group at church. This is the foundation upon which we may build greater loyalties of life. Organize Sunday School classes with a real program and a challenge of service. The formation of choirs, clubs, drama groups, sports teams, camps and outreach projects is necessary along with the proper presentation of the Word of God. One loyalty will lead to another: Sunday School class loyalty to school loyalty to church loyalty; city pride and love for country and humanity will follow. But the greatest loyalty of all that we want to develop is the loyalty to the Captain of their salvation. Inspire this in them!

 Organize Sunday School classes with a real program and a challenge of service.

Moral and Spiritual

Physical changes and new emotions bring questions about morality to the forefront for teens. Every girl with a normal and natural desire to become popular has questions: "How can I be popular and yet hold my standards high?" "Is it worthwhile to be good?" "Where does being good get me?" Every boy wants to know how to find a girlfriend; how to get enough money to take her out; whether he should go steady; whether he can kiss the girlfriend; whether he can hold her; what is a reasonable hour to get home. These are real problems facing high-schoolers. These high school years can well be called the mating period, and with this mating period comes dating problems. The church that ignores this issue will lose its youth to the world, the flesh and the devil.

The problem of courtship is a serious one. Young people want the privilege of courtship (though they would probably never use that word) when no courtship really exists. Being sexually active is not unusual, and much of what passes for entertainment these days revolves around this. Its prevalence is startling. To tell teens that they should not engage in sexual activities and that good young people never indulge in such things is begging the question. In fact, it is not true. The days of dating and courtship have changed. Our teenagers live with sexual things before them all of the time: movies, music, advertising, television, the Internet. The moral bar has dropped considerably and a great laxity of standards has become the norm, even in the "best" social circles. So teens believe that because sex has become so "common," engaging in it is not anything to think much about—it's practically become a custom. Teens take for granted things that we would question very highly. This in turn makes teens question how much their parents and other adults really know and understand about what they are experiencing. Teens repeat to adults the well-worn phrase, "Oh, you just don't know about the world today. It is all so different from when you were my age." And it is.

Teens must be taught how to court and date as much as they must be instructed how to become a doctor or a nurse. In fact, it is more important. This is the basis for establishing a Christian home, one that can withstand the many storms that will assail it both from within and from without. Unless Christ is placed in the center of every home that these young Christian people inhabit, there can be no assurance that the home will last. The Church must take the lead in this. Here is the time that we must teach the meaning of the great words, "Know ye not that your body is the temple of the Holy Ghost which is in you, which ye have of God, and ye are not your own?" (1 Corinthians 6:19). Youth must know what the sacredness of the body means and how the destruction of its sanctity will affect one's whole life. Teens must learn that although God planted these great sex urges in everybody, they are not to be dissipated and dragged in the dirt but rather to be channeled into that which is the highest and finest in all of life.

Unless Christ is placed in the center of every home that these young Christian people inhabit, there can be no assurance that the home will last.

Although most conversions take place by the age of 14, teens close to this age can still be led to Christ. Their souls are soaring and seem to "mount up with wings as eagles" (Isaiah 40:31). The freedom they feel in breaking away from the past and their home ties and even church can become part of their whole religious experience. Yes, teens are going through a time of great change, but they are still open to the working of the Holy Spirit. If high-schoolers are fortified by the finest Christian habits while they are young, they can be kept from being shaken from their moorings later in life.

Teens need to see that Christ is the anchor in the tempests they're going through. There is in high-schoolers a general intensity that leads them to extremes in thought and to rash decisions. They often seem to quiver between exaltations and depressions. They change quickly from love to hate and from ecstasy to despair and from laughter to tears. They pass from one extreme to the other with such a swiftness that they cannot understand what is happening any better than anyone else. These tempest-tossed children certainly need an anchor for their lives, although they will never admit it.

Teens need to see that Christ is the anchor in the tempests they're going through.

Teens ask important questions. Help them answer the questions, "Why am I here?" "What am I living for?" and "How can I explain my presence?" Help young people to see themselves in a moral mirror. Guide them to develop Christlike personalities. Help them to see how they stand in comparison with the measure of the stature of the fullness of Christ. Never allow them to measure themselves with themselves. They will always find someone over whom they can tower. Help young people to overcome cynicism by approaching their problems positively. In your teaching, remember that you can lead these young people to facts but not to truth, work but not service, ideas but not ideals, Jesus but not salvation.

Teens need to discover great things for themselves. We want them not only to learn to obey the law but also to learn obedience. Let us confirm their faith. Let our teaching always be marked by correct information and our counsel by a calm level headedness. Let our informal conversation with them be marked by a sincerity and camaraderie that will inspire their confidence.

 In your teaching, remember that you can lead these young people to facts but not to truth, work but not service, ideas but not ideals, Jesus but not salvation.

The feelings of strength that teens feel must be challenged to grow. Let them know that the Christian life is a battle or a race. Train them how to use the sword of the Spirit in answering the flimsy argument of the modern skeptic, and let them see that God's truths cannot be overthrown. When challenged by the Lord Jesus Christ, these young people will either step out behind the banner of their King in a new loyalty and ever-growing trust, or they will lag behind with doubts, finally slipping into the crowd on the outside.

Although these young people are beginning to do a good deal of reasoning for themselves, they need to be provided with a background of biblical knowledge. We, therefore, ought not to enter into futile arguments or permit our students to do so. Rather, establish their faith by presenting the

 Let them know that the Word of God has never failed. . . . Let them think of the Word as a textbook that will lead them into all the truth they need to make their most important decisions.

great bulwarks of truth. Leave out petty questions. Let them know that the Word of God has never failed. They need to understand that they will find in this Book the answers to all the questions of life, whether they be personal, social or national. Let them think of the Word as a textbook that will lead them into all the truth they need to make their most important decisions.

Ministering to Teens' Needs

What do young people need from the church High School Department? What they need is not always what they think they need. Because of their basic nature, they naturally strive for adventure, achievement, enjoyment and fellowship; but the world in which they live tries to divert them from the Christian influences that would give them proper direction.

There are five great needs that teens have that the High School Department ministry should supply, and it is how you plan to fulfill these needs that will determine how you organize your department.

The Need for Security

We must remember that there is an irregularly shaped vacuum in every heart, and only Christ can fill it. Christ offers security. In his *Confessions,* Saint Augustine wrote, "Our hearts are restless until they find rest in [Christ]." Our teaching and ministry and organization must help give high-schoolers this security that they demand. One of the reasons that many want to drop out of high school is because they want the security of a job, or they want the security of a relationship through marriage. We cannot ignore this tremendous need of young people for security. We must make teens see that their security lies in Jesus.

The Need for Recognition

Teenagers like to receive credit, so give them all you can. Remember, the disciples argued over the question of who should be the greatest (see Matthew 18:1-6; Mark 9:33-37; Luke 9:46-48). Ask the retiring student to be an usher and print his or her name in the church bulletin. A new member might be asked to read a portion of Scripture that you assign the week before so that the student can read it well on the following Sunday. If you have a newsletter of any kind, do not let only the same few names have all the limelight. Be careful to satisfy this urge that lies in the heart of every teen. And encourage your young people to bring to the forefront whoever they believe is in need of recognition.

The Need for Adventure and New Experience

Keep the world and its needs before the teens. Give these young people big things to do. Challenge them to do their best. World needs have driven people to pursue missions in far-off continents, but today there are needs to fulfill on our city streets and in our local towns. Young people have stepped away from television screens and computers to don work clothes and clean up urban areas and help build homes and schools in rural towns *and* foreign countries in order to introduce other young people to Christ.

The Need for Social Life

To answer the great need for fellowship, we find that Christ chose 12 just to be with Him, not to serve Him (see Mark 3:14). Enter enthusiastically into the life of your students. Create an atmosphere in the High School Department that will help these young people forget their troubles and difficulties and shortcomings and make them realize their strength in the Lord Jesus Christ: "The LORD is the strength of my life" (Psalm 27:1).

Enter enthusiastically into the life of your students.

In building a department, remember that young people will go where their friends are. If your department does not appeal to the young people of the high school in your community, it will not appeal to any teen that you are trying to capture. This means that you must provide an opportunity for teens to date—under the proper supervision and in the right environment. Any occasion that brings young people together in a wholesome and fine way is of utmost importance in the church of the Lord Jesus Christ. What better place is there for young people, not only to make passing friendships, but also to make life-long friendships. If the church offers nothing, then you may be sure that the public places of entertainment will be crowded, and your people will be part of the crowd.

One reason young people often do not act well is simply because they do not know what to do. A few lessons in Christian courtesy would be an excellent addition to your curriculum, and what better place to practice those courtesies than at a church-sponsored function.

The Need to Help and Cooperate

Constantly look for opportunities for your teens to make use of their need to help and cooperate with others. Teens can take part in many different sorts of Christian service and usefulness. Sharing develops a sense of self-importance and a personal interest in a mutual undertaking. You will quickly discover that teens are constantly seeking to do something worthwhile. Release the dynamic power of these young people. There is no *im*pression like *ex*pression. When young people feel as if they are not needed, they soon lose interest. "Use me or lose me" is said not only of junior highers but also of high-schoolers and adults.

High School Department Organization

When you organize your department, take into consideration the teens' needs just discussed. The need for recognition, for example, may be met by having the students elect a student committee. Here the students would have a chance to develop real leadership skills. Do not neglect giving them encouragement and instruction. And do not have your officers be mere figureheads. If you were to visit any large high school, you would be astonished to see a young high-schooler presiding with poise and authority at a great assembly of his or her peers. A six-month term may be long enough for each office. In this way, more of the students will have the opportunity to gain skills and reap a bit of recognition.

Expressional Hour

It is not enough for a High School Department to have a good Sunday morning worship-teaching hour. There must be a time for expression on Sunday night or during the week. If you can add Bible clubs and choirs and deputation (or outreach) teams and boys' and girls' clubs and life-service groups, all the better.

Age Groups

When you start your department, you may find it necessary to have all of the high-schoolers meet together in one class; but you will soon learn that it is difficult to teach a tenth-grader and a twelfth-grader in the same class. As soon as your group grows, divide it into separate age groups for the study hour. Keep watching again for the time to divide your classes into more groups. Do not, however, divide the group down to such small numbers that there will be no challenge or interest left. Numbers are important to young people. *Never* put them in with all the older folks in an adult class!

The High School Teacher

An important factor in the success of any High School Department is the teacher. Not just anyone can teach a high school class. A teacher of these young people must have a Christian character that rings true. These young people are very critical, and they can recognize and have an admiration for genuineness—and contempt for hypocrisy. Many teens do not see Christianity practiced in their homes, so they look for it in their teacher.

The teacher must exhibit an understanding sympathy that encourages camaraderie. Sympathy does not mean pity but "feeling with," an empathy. The teacher must never think that what these high-schoolers do is silly or shocking. The teacher should never call their romances puppy love but regard them all as serious.

The teacher should have thorough knowledge of the Bible lesson. Preparation will, of course, give the teacher assurance, impressiveness and power. Conversely, lack of preparation will make the teacher timid, vague and weak.

The teacher must have positive convictions. In this age of doubting uncertainty, young people need a teacher who believes the Bible to be God's

Word in the fullest sense and who relies upon his or her own Christian life and Christian experience to prove it. How many can say with Paul, "Be ye followers of me, as I also am of Christ" (1 Corinthians 11:1)?

Young people need a teacher who believes the Bible to be God's Word in the fullest sense and who relies upon his or her own Christian life and Christian experience to prove it.

The teacher must be interested in the social activities of the students. The teacher must enter into the lives of his or her students. If students are interested in baseball, get some tickets and take them to a game. If students are interested in the outdoors, take them for a hike. In short, find out the interests of your group and be able to talk to them about those interests. Remember, a bore is a person who talks about himself or herself when you want to talk about yourself. Don't be a bore in the eyes of your teens. Know what your students want to know or ought to know, whatever their age. Aim to train each soul's aspirations according to the highest possible standards.

Don't be a bore in the eyes of your teens.

The teacher must have some understanding of young people this age. A parent who has or has recently raised a teen or a high school teacher might be an ideal candidate to be the teacher, as long as the other teacher qualifications are met. A person can learn a lot from reading books and searching the Internet, but actual experience with young people is definitely an advantage.

The teacher must have the time for these young people and all of their activities. It is not easy to find adults who are capable of leading these high-schoolers and who are willing to spend the time necessary to take part in every activity. Too often those who volunteer are not capable of this great task. Never suggest that anyone accept this place of leadership by letting him or her think it is not hard work. Rather, let the person know that teaching these teens will challenge all they are and have to offer—but the reward is great.

8

College

(AGES 18 TO 25)

People of college age are almost a lost generation to the average church, yet most world leaders of tomorrow—corporate and national—will come from college campuses of today. Though there are exceptions to that generality, remember that it is the exception that makes the rule. Someone has well said that the world is literally carried forward on the backs of young people. This means the Church should be vitally interested in them. Invest your time and resources to challenge these young people for Christ—to hold them in the church and to prepare them for their places of responsibility in the world.

Age-Level Characteristics

Self-confidence is the keyword of this age. Collegians are apt to think in very sweeping terms. They are sure that if they are given a chance, they can do something big in the long run. These young people have a great sense of power. It would be a crime to let anything happen to make them lose their self-confidence. Every teacher of this age group must challenge the students to the utmost, and they will respond if properly challenged. If you want to hold them, you must give them difficult tasks to do, difficult lessons to learn, difficult projects to attempt.

These young adults need definite goals. More young people of this age leave the Church because of the lack of something to do that they feel to be worthy of their time and abilities than for any other reason. This group needs to have set for it very definite aims, which could include doing research for an intellectual exercise or mission work of one sort or another.

The greatest need of young adults is an older adult who understands them and will be their confidant. They need someone who will be honest with them and will help them evaluate themselves.

> The greatest need of young adults is an older adult who understands them and will be their confidant. They need someone who will be honest with them and will help them evaluate themselves.

Teacher, be this person. Always be available. Be easy to reach. Hold your confidence as the most sacred trust. These young adults are passing through what might be called a final period of adjustment to full adulthood, and they need the counsel and guidance of a true friend.

Transition to Adulthood

After young people graduate from high school, they are never quite the same again. They now decide the next direction for their lives: go to college, start a job or enter the military. Although they might remain in the home, they will play very different roles in the family. They are no longer children. This is always very hard for parents to accept, because their children remain children to them as long as they live under their roofs. This means that real adjustments must be made between parents and their offspring.

Two Main Interests

There are two things that are uppermost in the interests of college-age young people: what job they will do for the rest of their lives and whom they will marry. These young adults are no longer looking to their family for direction but to the world.

A college education or service in the military is a very profitable thing for most young people while they determine what they will do for the rest of their lives, though another worthwhile choice might be to attend a local junior college or even work for a year. These young adults need an opportunity to become more mature. They need to learn that they must become responsible adults in order to maintain gainful employment and to help maintain a successful marriage. And although they have absorbed much during the past years of their lives as they went through periods of physical and social adjustments, now they must be concerned with the development of a new capacity for work and self-support. Whether they go on to college, a junior college, military service or even a job, they need the guidance of trained adults without feeling the restraints that they experienced in their teens. The sad thing is that virtually all of the choices of what to do next are not Christian oriented. This means that the Church must supply what the world lacks, and too few churches have assumed this responsibility.

Church Responsibility

The Church should teach these young adults the great fact that God has created them for a purpose and has endowed them with personalities and abilities that He expects them to use for His purposes. When someone asked Daniel Webster what he considered the greatest thought that ever passed through his mind, he answered, "My personal accountability to God." It is the church that teaches the young this greatest of all truths. They want an answer to the same question they had in high school: "What am I living for?" They must discover the greatest purpose of their lives—how they can best serve God and their fellow humans.

The Church must also take responsibility for providing the biblical principles of a proper Christian home in order to channel the instinct to marry and start a family that is strongest at this age. Every young adult seeks a mate in order to fulfill a desire to have a home and start a family of his or her own. The proper channeling of this divine impulse will prove to be one of the greatest safeguards to our civilization, for the Christian home is the bulwark of democracy. The busyness of divorce courts is evidence enough of the lack of training our young people have received in this most important area of their lives.

Ministering to the Needs of Young Adults

Some church leaders have said that college-age students are not interested in the Bible and that they are only interested in the opposite sex. They condemn the College Department, saying its only purpose is matchmaking. Even if that were to be true, what better place could matches be made? Far better for the Church to be concerned with Christian matchmaking than in trying to repair broken homes and reconcile broken hearts. These young people are concerned in finding the right partner and in establishing a Christian home. They are interested in biblical teachings that concern the home and family and marriage.

Resolving Their Questions

I believe that the most important decision to be made in anyone's life concerns choosing the Lord Jesus Christ as Savior. The next most important decision concerns the choice of a life partner. The person one marries will either make one feel whole or break one into bits. Many young people have come to me to ask how to know when they are really in love. The Church must prepare young men and women to answer this question and many more that concern this important relationship. Do all you can to promote friendship among members of the College Department. I have discovered that friendships formed under wholesome circumstances meet a great need.

Do all you can to promote friendship among members of the College Department. I have discovered that friendships formed under wholesome circumstances meet a great need.

Another thing a young person wants to know is, "Where can I invest my life?" These young people want to make a contribution to the world, but they don't know what to do or where to turn for help to answer the question. The most important thing in life is not to learn how to make a living but how to make a life. Too often hasty decisions lead to tragic results. Teach young people to wait on God and to find out His will for their lives.

Leading the Group

These young people must have leadership of the finest ability and quality, those in whom they can put the greatest confidence. The pastor should help the teacher in this area. These young people must be taught that if they put Christ first and "seek . . . first the kingdom of God, and his righteousness; . . . all these things shall be added unto you" (Matthew 6:33).

These young people must be taught that if they put Christ first and "seek . . . first the kingdom of God, and his righteousness; . . . all these things shall be added unto you" (Matthew 6:33).

Camps, conferences and weekend retreats should be offered so that these young people can have special periods where they can consider under proper leadership the opportunities before them and the problems they will face in the world. These group activities held away from the noise of society can be times of great discussion and study.

Every college group should also have an outreach team. This always helps the group to grow spiritually and gives them practical training that will hold them in good stead later in life.

Teaching the Bible

We will no doubt all agree that the Bible should be the textbook for our teaching, but what is the purpose in teaching the Bible? Is it merely so that young people will know the facts recorded in this Holy Book? Too many teachers are satisfied if students get factual information whether they make use of it or not. Of course, we want students to know the Bible, but Bible teaching that ends there fails.

The first reason to teach the Bible to these young adults is so that they might have a proper knowledge of God and a growing faith in Him that was revealed in the Lord Jesus Christ. The Bible, too, will give meaning to life. Here we find God's will for each individual. To know that God has a great plan for His children and that we are a part of His plan is a thrilling discovery. Jesus Christ is the answer for every life. The Word of God reveals Him in all of His majesty and power. He is the One, too, who knows and understands everything we feel and go through, for He was human like us. We must present the reasonableness of the Word of God. We should examine the internal and external evidence that proves its truth and value. Give young people a reason for the faith that is in them.

Jesus Christ is the answer for every life. The Word of God reveals Him in all of His majesty and power.

Another reason to teach the Bible is so that young people experience the truth of the Word as it operates in everyday life. Young people not only need to see Bible truths being lived out by others, but they also need to live that truth for themselves. As they model the life of Jesus, they will in turn attract others to faith in Jesus. Young people will grow when they become reproducers themselves. The best way to strengthen our own faith is to help produce faith in someone else. Not only be a builder of faith by teaching the students in a convincing manner—by modeling Jesus' example yourself—but also strengthen your faith by enlisting young adults in the work of convincing and convicting others. When this kind of instruction is given, this college-age group will be an ever-growing one. Remem-

Young people not only need to see Bible truths being lived out by others, but they also need to live that truth for themselves.

ber, you are training them for world leadership. Give them plenty of opportunities to express themselves. Let them air their own views and submit their own questions.

The College Department

In many churches, this must be a college-age group rather than a college group. If they have a department of their own—and of course they should have if there are enough to do it—the organization should follow almost the same pattern as has been described for the High School Department.

On Sundays, be sure to let the students conduct the class session. This is a valuable training period for the leaders. First, there is the physical preparation of the room itself. Does it look attractive? Does it create a suitable atmosphere for teaching? Possibly, the class vice president could be responsible for this. If necessary, have class ushers take care of passing out songbooks and Bibles and handing out church bulletins as students come in, greeting everyone and creating a warm, friendly atmosphere.

The membership chairperson takes care of attendance records and notes any visitors. As soon as the class assembles, the president takes his or her place and presents a program for the morning session. The first half hour might consist of prayer, music, announcements, introduction of visitors, the Scripture reading, an offering, and any special addition to the program. The president must always watch the time, for Sunday morning class time is meant mainly for teaching of the Word. If all of these components have been well carried out, then the teacher will be able to begin to teach in an atmosphere that is already warm and expectant.

During the months when school is in session, when military personnel are away on assignment or when those with jobs must be absent, these young people should be kept in touch with until they return. Literature can be sent so that the absentees can keep up with what is going on in the group and in the church. When college students graduate or when military personnel return home, their achievements and accomplishments should be recognized. The church should show its interest in the academic pursuits and careers of these young adults. A bit of financial aid to help them in their training or career pursuits would provide a tie to the home church.

The College Teacher

It has been said that young people do not respond to programs but to personalities. This means that the first problem of the college-age group is to find a teacher who will attract young adults to the program and to whom the young adults will respond. They need to be challenged constantly to invest their every talent in the work of the Lord and to spend their time in the highest endeavors, both in thought, word and deed. They need to be taught to be their brother's keeper. The teacher must inspire and challenge this important group.

Teach with Love and Loyalty

There are only two ways of controlling this age group. One is by force and the other by love. Many dictators have tried the former. Christ's method was the latter. There is no way of forcing this group into the church. The teacher must draw them in by the cords of love and loyalty. The teacher must have a passion for human beings that must only be exceeded by his or her passion for Christ. The teacher's intenseness and sincerity will greatly influence these young adults. This does not mean a somber piousness. It means a holiness that reflects and honors the Lord Jesus Christ and draws others to His feet in adoration.

The teacher must draw them in by the cords of love and loyalty. The teacher must have a passion for human beings that must only be exceeded by his or her passion for Christ.

Teach with Truth

The teacher must have a passion for truth. When a teacher loves young people and adores the Lord, he or she will have an added passion to know the truth and to present it. The teacher should never indulge in speculation. When we are dealing with matters of life and death, the Lord Jesus Christ and eternal salvation, we can never be uncertain or obscure. Our teaching must be as clear as crystal and the kind that satisfies the wondering hearts of these students. We are not engaged in merely teaching subject matter but in teaching people.

Teach in Relationship

It is best when the teacher of young adults has a close relationship with his or her students. The Sunday School teacher is not the only teacher these individuals have. They are thrown into contact with many others who might also have a great influence on them: professors in college, mentors on the job, high-ranking military officers. These other people who they might look up to may be real intellectuals with winning personalities, but they also may treat the Bible lightly and make the student think that only morons believe the facts of the Book. This puts the student seeking knowledge in a position of conflicting loyalties to church, Sunday School teacher, pastor and parents and the teachings of this new voice that he or she has learned to admire. The teacher of the college-age group must constantly be aware of the everyday lives of the students so that any conflicts can quickly be resolved and proper loyalties reestablished.

It is best when the teacher of young adults has a close relationship with his or her students.

Teach with Outside Help (If Necessary)

The average young person has limited knowledge of the Bible, so the teacher should not be too surprised if this turns out to be the case with the students in the College Department. This, of course, must be taken care of and rectified in short order. But in the same class will be those who have come up through the Sunday School and have a real grasp of the Scriptures. It is often hard to teach them all at the same time. This means the teacher must seek outside help. Someone well versed in God's Word, someone who can encourage the students, mentoring them in the Scriptures, should be found and prevailed upon to meet privately with students who need help.

PART 3

Adult Sunday School

Period of Development	Sunday School Group Name	Ages
Adult	Business and Professional	25+
	Young Couples	25+
	Adults	35+

9

Adults

(AGES 25+)

Although adults are usually the church Sunday School teachers and church officers, this group is not usually thought of when it comes to Sunday School. But adults, roughly everyone over the age of 25, are an important part of the Sunday School. Many Sunday Schools believe that they have dispensed their duty when they have one Bible class for this whole group. Such a class generally interests only a few of the older men and women in the congregation, who seem perfectly willing to study out of a standard quarterly magazine.

Times, however, have changed. A growing emphasis on the importance of and need for adult education and/or retraining has led to a rise in attendance at local colleges; and evening classes are offered in many areas.

Christian education has lagged behind. It has always emphasized the importance of training children and youth, but suddenly, Christian educators began to realize that young people need trained adults to lead them. The education of these leaders most definitely must be a part of the Christian training program in the Sunday School. The adults are the foundation of the Sunday School and its teaching ministry. Every institution must produce its own leadership if it is to continue to exist. A properly organized Adult Department can supply the demand for men and women with a real heart of the mission of Christ and His Church.

Someone has well said that the affairs of democracy are in the hands of adults, and the success or failure of democracy depends directly upon the degree of intelligence and mastery exhibited by the people in whose hands its destiny rests. The influence that exerts the most power in our present society is the home, and adults definitely shape the plan and determine the purpose of the home. We should be very careful that the adult program is tied in with the church in every way. Adult work should be church centered and directed.

We must be careful, though, that an adult group does not become a law unto itself in its plans and gifts. If the class is too large, it may become too independent. It is to be preferred that several different classes be available for adults, and if any one class becomes too large, it should be divided into smaller groupings. And every group should contribute directly to the church in some way. At the very least, every adult class should be a Bible class. This must be the foundation of every Sunday School class.

Usually over 50 percent of any church is comprised of adults, yet probably close to 90 percent do not attend Sunday School. It seems as though the church has failed to develop a program that adults find interesting and vital.

The Bible, however, has a lot of answers, but it is a closed book to many. Men and women must be taught the Word. They must know Jesus and they must know how to win their neighbors and business associates to Christ.

Many homes today have difficult problems, but how far has the Church gone in solving these problems? Few adults turn to the church for counseling and guidance to resolve marital or family problems. Because the church has had little to offer in meeting adult needs, millions of adults *pass by* its doors without paying the slightest attention to it. Many people *pass through* its doors without paying much attention either. People do not think that the Church has answers. The Bible, however, has a lot of answers, but it is a closed book to many. Men and women must be taught the Word. They must know Jesus and they must know how to win their neighbors and business associates to Christ.

I know for a fact that a program based on the vital needs of adult men and women can be developed, and the program can attract hundreds of adults of all ages and from all walks of life. It has been done. In fact, the number of adults in the program equaled the number of students in the Sunday School for younger people.

Business and Professional

Young men or women who leave school and are not yet married must have a place for fellowship. In every young person that has a business or professional career, there is an innate hunger for fellowship. This group cannot fit in with the married people of the same age. Their interests are wide and varied. A church must not only recognize the needs of these adults but must be able to demonstrate that it is interested in meeting those needs and is ready and able to do so.

Youthful but Mature at the Same Time

These young adults are generally finished growing physically but are still growing emotionally, socially and spiritually. To a certain extent, the youthfulness of college age is still present, but real maturity is beginning. Very often, this is a period to which the very young look forward with keen interest and elderly look backward with great longing. Most people enter these years with keen enjoyment, looking forward to a regular paycheck and living in their own place. Not everyone realizes the hard work that is done during these years, with both men and women trying out their theories in practical living. How they think, how they problem-solve, is becoming permanent. Adults are in danger of settling down in a moving world and just staying there. Let us inspire in them the spirit of a prophet in looking beyond the immediate goals of food and shelter to the real ultimate goal of life. At this age young adults have passed through many of their intellectual doubts and flounderings and are willing to face the truth squarely. Help them deal with the social, doctrinal and practical themes of the Scripture.

Never Too Old to Play

Adults are never too old to play. We cannot ignore this great urge. Play gives a new zest to living and introduces a balance that adulthood needs. The Church has given a pew to adults but very little else. Plan recreational activities for this group. Hold the activities in the gym, the fellowship hall or a room of the church. If they cannot find the place for expression here, they will frequent bars and other places of amusement for their relaxation. Given the opportunity, they will amaze you by the ways they can entertain themselves. They grow tired of boxed amusements—puzzles and board games can become boring. This is not only true of business and professional age but every age!

Looking for a Life Partner

We must constantly keep in mind that members of this group of young adults are still looking for a life partner. They have become much more critical and weigh the matter of marriage very carefully. We must give people this age opportunities to meet people of the opposite sex who share their interests and spiritual maturity.

Enjoy Doing Things Together

The weekday program with this group should be varied. Groups of all kinds should be organized so that people can get together to share similar interests. These young people have much time on their hands. Most likely, every evening is free, and you may be sure that they are going to discover places to go. No one need be burdened with elaborate planning, and to be sure, a banquet or formal party ought to be held occasionally; but a provision for this group to often just do things together is what they need.

Need Worthwhile Projects

If you do not give young adults some projects to be interested in, they will become very selfish. Interest them in worthwhile things. Little assignments will never capture their interest or enthusiasm. They might be interested in deciding on ways to raise money to purchase provisions for a missionary, whereas they might spurn simply collecting canned goods for a local shelter.

Young Couples

Paralleling the business and professional group in age is the young-couples group, it is obvious that their interests are very different. The young businessperson is not interested in what a baby needs to be fed or how best to handle finances in a family, yet these are all-absorbing subjects for young couples. Young couples are making many adjustments, and the Church must help them solve some of their problems. I know from experience that when a young-couples class is taught by a teacher who gives real consideration to the members of such a class, many other young people will want to join the group. Young couples are interested in what the Word of God has to say about the home, the rearing of children, and their responsibility to the community, their country and their church.

Service Opportunities

This group is very service minded. They are more than willing to help make the rooms for the younger children in Sunday School attractive because they expect their own children to one day attend class in those rooms. Couples love to do things together, and anything that allows them to do this interests them. This includes helping the other if one of them teaches a Sunday School class.

Social Activities

Young couples will soon discover that it is not good for them to constantly stay at home, so they will look for a club to join or some social activity that allows them to attend together with others of their same age. Far better to have social activities in the church than to have the couples go off to join some club in the community. Because young couples usually do not have a lot of money to spend on a social life, the entertainment that the church offers can be a great boon for them.

Marital Concerns

Young couples have real problems on the sea of matrimony, and they will be very willing to voice their problems or difficulties when they know that the person leading the group is someone in whom they have confidence. They are very conscious of their inexperience with the marriage relationship. Have discussions where couples can raise questions and help each other with answers. If possible, have someone qualified to deal with such questions come to speak to your group. You might also consider having a couple mature in faith and years talk to your group about their experiences and how they dealt with problems and concerns through the years. You will find a great fellowship will be engendered on such occasions.

To save its life, the Church must save its home life. There is everything in the world to draw the husband and wife apart. The Church must see that Jesus, not the world, wins them.

> To save its life, the Church must save its home life. There is everything in the world to draw the husband and wife apart. The Church must see that Jesus, not the world, wins them.

Church Life

Too often young couples become so interested in each other and their social life that they bypass the church. Young couples that are invited only to social gatherings in the Young-Couples Department seldom attend anything else but the parties and functions, while the members who come to pray come to stay. Watch this carefully. Young men who would never come to church will go with their wives to meet a group of people in the community who are of the same age and have similar interests.

When there is an attractive place in the Sunday School for the children of these young couples, the fathers and mothers will bring them. This is the time to catch them. Once they're caught, you will see that they will have a growing concern about the quality of the Sunday School and its teaching, because they will have discovered what religious instruction can do for their children. It is incredible to think that we can build a Sunday School for children without interesting parents.

Class Makeup

It is definitely best to have a separate class for young couples. They will not be interested if you put them with adults who are much older than they are. Their lives are poles apart.

The officers of this class should be a husband and wife. This makes them feel an equal responsibility and an equal interest.

Mentoring Leadership

There is no age that is more important in its relationship to leading and mentoring younger generations of the church. These young adults should not devote all their time, talents and money to clubs and frivolous activities when there are boys and girls in the community and in the church who could use their help. They themselves must not neglect the Church of the Lord Jesus Christ, nor should they let the younger generations neglect the Church. They must learn and teach that the Church is the only institution that can bring hope for the younger generation and the many problems it has. Make every possible effort to train young couples to be teachers, mentors and friends of adolescents. They are old enough to be wise leaders and young enough to be desirable friends. This is the age that junior highers and teens idealize. Young couples have in their hands as Christians the only solution to the problems of the younger (and every) generation: the truth of the gospel of the Lord Jesus Christ. Help them realize that as members of Christ's Church, they have a responsibility to lead and mentor the younger generation.

Adults

What do we do with the adults beyond the age we have just discussed? Of course many of the things that we have said about other ages apply also to mature adults. But from 35 on, there seems to be no definite borderlines that separate different groups. And although adult men and women usually enjoy meeting during the week at clubs for their gender, it is still a good idea to have a Sunday School class for people of middle age. The organization of the adult Bible class need have very little variation from the organization of the younger groups.

All Have a Common Denominator

Men and women in this middle bracket of years are reaching their prime. For many, their earning capacity is great, their social standing has been established, and their children are beginning to make a mark in the world. On the other hand, there are those who do not have many resources and on whom life has been hard. But all find common denominators in Christ and His Word. How can the Church hold the interest of this dynamic group? The leader must offer a wide and varied program to command their attention. When the teacher presents the great needs of the world and brings to the attention of these adults what Christ has provided to meet these needs, you will find that both men and women are interested. Because of this, the adult Sunday School class can be the hatching ground for many ideas for missionary acts of service. During the Second World War, men and women of this age held meetings every Sunday for large groups of young servicemen. They provided a taste and touch of home and ended with a great challenge for the men to accept and serve the Lord Jesus Christ. At the time, the president of one of the large trust companies was the mover behind this tremendous program.

All Must Be Trained

There must be constant training during the adult years because it is people of this age who are the great movers and shakers in the Church. Practically all of the official body of the Church comes from this age group. People this age were the ones who set up campgrounds where thousands of young people can find a vital relationship with the Lord Jesus Christ. Mission programs and building projects running into hundreds of thousands have been sponsored and carried out under the leadership of people of this age. In fact the great mission of the Church will only move out as these men and women are gripped by a challenge from our wonderful Lord.

All Can Be Challenged

It is true that men of this age as well as the women often have definite interests of their own. Women are generally interested in the missionary and women's auxiliaries of the church, while most men are interested in the governance and business side of the church. In the past, the lives of many women centered around the home and the rearing of children, but now there are many women in the workplace as well. In the past the lives of most men centered around their place of employment, but there are now many men who run the household while their wives earn a wage. The "traditional" roles of men and women are no longer so traditional. Nevertheless, if husbands and wives are given common challenges in the Church through the Word of God, their homes and personal lives will experience spiritual growth. Too often the woman exceeds her husband in spiritual growth, and she finds herself very limited in her influence in her home if her husband is not with her. If the man excels, he too is handicapped. This is the reason why coed Bible classes are of tremendous importance and value. Both spouses receive the same instruction and inspiration and can talk things over together.

PART 4

Building Your Sunday School

Organization
Worship
Curriculum
Long-Range Planning

10

Organization

Much time and space has been spent in telling you about the children, youth and adults that the Sunday School must serve. This is a staggering assignment, isn't it? What do you do now to organize a Sunday School that will have a place for each age and meet the needs of each group?

This chapter will deal with the organization of a Sunday School that can do this very thing. If you are running a Sunday School of 65 or 200 or 500 or 1,000, the plans are basically the same. If you are building a five-room cottage or a twenty-room mansion, there are certain things that are necessary to both in order to make it possible to house a family. There must be a foundation and a roof, floors and windows, a place to cook, eat and sleep. And so it is with building a Sunday School to accommodate its members from the cradle to the grave.

The organization of a Sunday School should be like the works of a watch: ever going but out of sight; ever running, yet seldom seen.

We must remember that organization is a system. The lack of organization is confusion. The difference between a mob and a trained army is simply organization. Organization secures results in the best and quickest way with the least expenditure of time and effort. The organization of a Sunday School should be like the works of a watch: ever going but out of sight; ever running, yet seldom seen. People like to have a part in a working, growing organization.

Too long it has been thought that Sunday School is an organization just for children. Junior high students were usually deemed too hard to handle and so not included. High-schoolers were felt to be not interested, and young couples, too busy. And so it went. However, we are now going to talk about a Sunday School that takes care of *all* the ages of life, just as we have described in the previous chapters of this book.

Keep Your Goals in Mind

As you organize what you have dreamed and planned for your Sunday School, always keep your goals in mind. This question will give direction to your planning and work. No matter what the size of your Sunday School, there are certain things that all Sunday Schools share: All Sunday Schools have the same constituency—boys and girls, men and women. All have the same objective—winning all to Christ as Savior and to having all dedicate their lives to service. All are maintained by voluntary financial support. All are taught by laypeople who invest their time and talents for Christ.

**All have the same objective—
winning all to Christ as Savior and to having
all dedicate their lives to service.**

The main goals of a Sunday School are not reached by chance. Sunday Schools, like some businesses, can be run so poorly that they pay a very small interest on a large investment of time and talents. This is discouraging to everyone. When a Sunday School is well organized, however, plans can be carried out, goals can be met and enthusiasm can be maintained.

Hold Your Standard High

Once a program standard is attained, you have to maintain it. So many Sunday Schools have worked out a good program, but because of the lack of workers, of time or of interest, the schools have slipped back into being mediocre. Average is the worst enemy of the best. The former is fairly easy; the latter is very hard. Most Sunday School leaders have a short span of endurance. The sad fact is that one poor session in Sunday School, in choir or in a club offsets all the good programs you have worked so hard to put into place. If a student comes to one session and is not pleased, he or she will say, "Oh, I went to that Sunday School. I don't like it." You may reply, "When was that? We have a fine class. You must have been there that Sunday the teacher didn't come [or some other of a dozen other reasons]. Come on back." "No, I didn't like it." He or she only remembers the one bad time.

When I first arrived in California, I used to travel about 20 miles to a particular delightful restaurant when I wanted to impress my visiting friends. I would comment on the perfection of every dish. The soup was piping hot; the salad was icy cold; the pie was just out of the oven. But one day the pie was served a day old. I never went back again—not because it was too far or too expensive, but because *once* I was served pie with a soggy crust. You might say, "That isn't fair, when every other time for years it was so delicious." But you see I had lost confidence. That one failure made me wonder if at another time, something else would not be so good. It's hard to live down one failure. Don't have one in your Sunday School.

Public schools train for this life only. We have the responsibility of training for the life to come. Public school students learn about Caesar and his exploits but nothing about Christ, the greatest figure in history. Public school teachers spend most of their time training bodies and brains and let the soul go. All of our young people need God, yet the Bible is the most poorly taught book in the world. Students have learned how to control a soccer ball on a field, but can we teach them how to control their worldly appetites?

Organize to Teach (and Reach)

Because a Sunday School is organized to teach (and reach), your first task is to discover teachers. Don't say you cannot get teachers, because that means you cannot have a Sunday School. Remember, one adult and one child can make a class. Who can gather three or four around and effectively teach and reach our young?

Excellent teaching is the paramount need of every Sunday School. This means that you must put good teaching material in the hands of every teacher, a curriculum that will help the teacher know what he or she should teach the given class, and information about how to best teach the age group of the class. Good teaching material does both of these things. The only hopeless teachers are the ones who feel no need for improvement or who are unwilling to change even though convinced of the need. Our God-given commission calls for teaching at its best. Nothing less than this will satisfy Christ's command.

To Introduce Christ as Savior and Lord

Does your Sunday School introduce Christ as Savior to boys and girls and to men and women? How many have confessed Christ and joined the church this last year? The Sunday School offers such a great opportunity for soul winning because it is organized and graded from the Nursery to the Adult Department to *reach out and bring in people*. Christ's last commission must be obeyed: "Go ye into all the world"—make disciples by teaching and then make disciples teachers so that they can go out in ever-enlarging circles (Matthew 16:15). Success in teaching the Bible—harvesting the fruit of our labor—is like success in any other undertaking: It must be purchased at the price of effort. Remember, when you win one child to Christ, you may in the future win a continent.

The Sunday School offers such a great opportunity for soul winning because it is organized and graded from the Nursery to the Adult Department *to reach out and bring in people*.

For Worship

Every day is a day of reverence, but young people today have little regard for holy things. We must train all people to worship God, both in their private devotions and in the public services that are at the center of the church life on Sundays. We must constantly remember that the human character is like a right-angled triangle. Young people cannot increase along the horizontal in their relationship to the world until they increase their experiences on the perpendicular toward God. Here is exactly the reason why for worship, grouping people by age in separate services may be a good idea. Then there likely will be growth in spiritual discernment. Don't put Saul's armor on a little David. People need to worship God at their own level of understanding and in a manner in which they can best come into God's presence. If you can have only four worship service groups, have Elementary, Preteen, Junior High and Adult. (For more information on worship, see chapter 11.)

For Fellowship

Christian fellowship is essential in maintaining the Christian life. As mentioned earlier, Christ taught us this when He chose the 12 to "be with him" (Mark 3:14). Study the fellowship that was maintained in the Early Church and is described in the last part of Acts 2. Cultivate fellowship by the sharing of spiritual experiences, by playing together and meeting together to enjoy common interests. Plan social and recreational activities for every department in the Sunday School. This takes care of age interests. Remember, everyone likes to go where friends are, whether they be old or young. What provisions have you made for this?

Christian fellowship is essential in maintaining the Christian life.

For Service

Most young people want action. Channel this desire so that young people learn to serve in Christian projects. They want to do things that count. Make service an honor and a privilege. Teach the young the joy of service by providing a variety of projects for them to do.

You will find that young people will undertake tremendous things if someone helps them and gives them some direction. They will undertake missionary projects, organize clubs for younger children, be part of outreach teams and volunteer on work parties. Even little children can undertake projects through their classes as long as the projects are geared to match their abilities. Any good curriculum will include ideas for projects that can be accomplished by the age group for whom the curriculum has been written.

For Training

Although the Sunday School is organized for teaching the Word of God to all ages, its most important mission is to introduce boys and girls and men and women to the Lord Jesus Christ as their personal Savior—but this is not all. The Sunday School must train people of all ages for life. We must always emphasize the reason for living. "Why am I here?" and "What is the purpose of my life?" are the questions we must answer. Any teaching that falls short of this falls short of Christ's purpose.

Although the Sunday School is organized for teaching the Word of God to all ages, its most important mission is to introduce boys and girls and men and women to the Lord Jesus Christ as their personal Savior.

Christ's ministry on this earth was a training ministry. He worked with His chosen 12 for three years, sending them out on practical work projects. Many times they failed, but He was always patient. He was getting these men ready to bring the gospel of redemption to the world. Christ produced men and women that were in turn producers themselves. He taught them how to win other people, so in the first century the apostle Paul was able to say in Colossians 1:6 that the

Gospel had been preached to all men—an exaggeration, yes, but the spread of the gospel *was* amazing. Are our Sunday Schools organized to produce leadership? Do we even produce our own leadership? In our Sunday Schools, do we train men and women to take over the posts of teaching and all other phases of leadership that are so essential to maintain a school? There is a reason for the dearth of leaders in our Sunday School today. We have not trained them.

Someone has said that there is a riddle that all should answer: "When is a school not a school?" The answer is a sad one: "When it is a Sunday School." Let us organize the Sunday School in such a way that its students are taught to become active servants of our wonderful Lord and Savior Jesus Christ. May we see them going out in the power that Christ describes in Acts 1:8 to preach the gospel "unto the uttermost parts of the earth."

Let us organize the Sunday School in such a way that its students are taught to become active servants of our wonderful Lord and Savior Jesus Christ.

Organize to Attract

Group by Age

We must organize the Sunday School to teach one textbook, the Word of God, to a group people covering a great span of years. How can it be done? We have already stated that God's Word has a message for every age. There is "milk for babes," "bread for youth" and "meat for adults." Too often, though, we try to feed infants the steak of the Word and find it impossible for them to digest. Paul said that "babes in Christ" should be fed "with milk" (1 Corinthians 3:1-2). Perhaps it is a greater tragedy that we are still serving our spiritually mature adults the milk of the Word when they should be eating meat.

We must organize the Sunday School to
teach one textbook, the Word of God . . .
God's Word has a message for every age.

Because of this difference in diet, we must group our students by
age. This is the ideal toward which we must always work. Because
there is such a difference in the understanding of each age, grouping
by age is the way to achieve the best results from your teaching efforts—and the way to attract people of each age. Having a department
for each age group, however, may in the beginning be impossible for
small Sunday Schools. At first there may be just one class for each age
group. Then as the school grows, the class will be able to be divided
into separate departments.

If there is no department for the junior highers, there will be no
junior high children in Sunday School. If no department has been organized for the high-schoolers, that important group will be lacking.
Remember that we cannot group people together who have no common interests. Age differences are great barriers. The reason that so
many Sunday Schools do not have any junior high boys and girls in
their classes is because they have tried to put this highly misunderstood age group in with elementary students or with high schoolers.
They fit in neither place. If we do not provide a department specifically for them, we will lose them.

The best and most effective way of grouping children in Sunday
School is to group by the grade a child is in public school. This eliminates many problems. If a child enters your Sunday School and is in the
fourth grade, place the child with the fourth-grade students. Although
a parent may contend that the child is advanced for his or her age and
that the child's friends are in the fifth-grade Sunday School class, place
the child in the fourth-grade class. If you were to follow the parent's suggestion of putting a fourth-grade child in a fifth-grade class, you would
find that as long as the child attends the Sunday School, the child is out
of place. The next year it will be impossible to move him back.

Limit Class Size

The size of the class is important. Classes in the children's groups should ideally not have more than 8 students in each. If you have a strong teacher, a class of elementary students could have 10 or 12 students in it. Remember that if we are to accomplish our goals, we must treat our students as individuals, not as being all the same just because they are in the same group.

Remember that if we are to accomplish our goals, we must treat our students as individuals, not as being all the same just because they are in the same group.

Let us refer to Part 1 on the age group characteristics and look again at the organization that is necessary to carry on such a school. (Be sure to review the age-level characteristics that were given in earlier chapters for each age group and take these into consideration as you organize your Sunday School.)

Maintain the Organization in Order to Grow

It is one thing to organize an efficient Sunday School and quite another to maintain it. Everyone is interested in how they may increase their attendance numbers, because a live Sunday School must be a growing Sunday School. When someone remarked, "Why, Billy, how you're growing!" the four-year-old replied, "Of course I does, cause I'm alive." Is your Sunday School alive?

The ways to increase attendance in the Sunday School have been discussed earlier in this book, but here's a short list of what we should provide to increase our numbers:

1. Better leadership
2. Better teachers

3. Better curriculum
4. Better planning
5. Better program
6. Better equipment

Of course our numbers may increase simply because of an increase in the population of the community. But to attract new people to the Sunday School, we need better everything. And the list of what we need to provide is also a list of what we need to maintain if we want our numbers to increase further still.

Hold Individuals Once You Have Them

Study the reason for a declining class immediately. Every Sunday School class is organized for the individual, and in order for the class to grow, we must hold the individual after we have once gained his or her interest. The Sunday School does not grow by adding "bunches" of children. It is only as each child or adult is oriented into the program of your school that the Sunday School grows.

People should not doubt the statement that it is easier to get children than it is to hold them. You can get people of any age to come, if you put on a program that will interest and entertain them. They will come for a special event that attracts their interest, but the next Sunday, you won't see them. You must have a program that carries through from one Sunday to the next. There must be a careful follow-up of each individual person if you are to hold your boys and girls to Christ and the Church. This kind of building may be slow, but it is lasting.

Lock the Back Door

A good teacher must contact the home of each student. You will never get to know your students well unless you know what kind of homes they come from. Too many Sunday Schools spend a great deal of time in opening their front door and inviting young people in but then forget to close and lock the back door. Hence, they face the tragic problem of losing people as fast as they gain them.

One of the best ways to overcome this constant loss in the Sunday School is to have a definite program for getting in touch and keeping in touch with the students. There are two things that we must pay attention to if we would hold the people who come through our doors.

The first is to give them a cordial welcome. One of the most common criticisms that visitors make when they go to any church is the fact that nobody speaks to them. Never let this be said of your Sunday School. Be cordial to every visitor. Make everyone that comes be glad that they came. Every department—from the littlest child to the oldest adult—should have a definite plan for greeting new members.

The second important thing is a program of personal calling. If you want to have an effective calling program, you must have a very definite plan that you can carry out effectively. Christ sent out the 70 to gather the harvest (see Luke 10:1). And Christ's commission to every disciple was to *go* into all the world (see Matthew 28:19). How different has been our method. We lay out excellent plans and then expect the people to come to see what we have done. What is the best way to plan our calling? Each person must have a definitely assigned task. Like door-to-door salesmen of the past, every person must not be allowed to go just anywhere to sell the goods. They must have their own territory and hold to it.

Win with a Calling Team

The Team

Callers in your Sunday School should first call on the members of their class or department. Callers should cover the field systematically. One of the ways we covered a very large territory was to gather all the callers together for a simple lunch right after church on Sunday. This included all the officers and teachers of every department of the Sunday School and as many as we could interest in participating in this great task. It is easier to do things in a team, and this approach also allows for an early start. We also found that if a definite time is assigned, people will put other things aside and come together. If they have to go home for dinner, unexpected visitors or other hindrances may keep them from starting out.

After a word of challenge and prayer, the callers were supplied with cards on which were the names of the persons who were to be called upon (and their correct addresses) and any record about the people that might be of interest. The callers were also supplied with materials that were to be left in each home. Sometimes the supplies included copies of a paper that told what was going on in the church that may be of interest to each member of the family. This paper was left with the family along with the church bulletin of the day.

We let the callers know that their visiting in the home is of tremendous importance, even if no one is at home. If no one was home, the callers were given cards to leave at the home. When the family returned, they would discover that someone in the Sunday School had shown an interest in their household. Also if no one was home, a telephone call was made to the home as a very helpful follow-up. We had each teacher call on each member of his or her class, regardless of whether there are several other children from that family in the Sunday School or not. By the time six or seven callers arrived on a Sunday afternoon, the family would inevitably think that Sunday School is important.

At first the teachers may feel that this is a duplicate effort, but after one experience in our Sunday School, we never failed to do it. One family had a mother and a father and six children who attended our Sunday School. They were always there. When calling day came, each teacher felt that it was unnecessary to make a call on that home, but the family had made preparations for the coming visitors: Sandwiches and cake and things to drink had been made ready, but by five o'clock, no one had come. You can imagine the disappointment in that home.

When calling, do not neglect the regular attendees and anyone who has visited or in some way shown an interest. Calling can be very discouraging if you only go after no-shows. When people begin to close the door in your face or act bored at your coming, calling may cease to be a joy. On the other hand, when you go to a home and find real cordiality, your heart is warmed.

After the calls have been made, have your group come back to the church with the cards. If it is a cool evening, have refreshments available. Have everyone compare notes and bring in reports of those who have been missed or are sick or need help. Often we discovered families that were ready to be approached for the Lord Jesus Christ and ought to be in the fellowship of the church.

A Fruitful Ministry

This kind of calling is one of the most fruitful ministries of the church. Many people are not in church simply because no one has ever invited them. Honorable Wu Ting Fang, the former Chinese Ambassador of the United States, often praised Confucianism above Christianity. The last Sunday he was in the United States, he spoke in Rev. Huie Kim's church in New York. He accepted the invitation, saying, "When I was a boy in China I was much impressed by the lives of the missionaries. When I came to the United States, I determined to accept the first invitation to attend a Christian church." Then he paused and added, "This is the first invitation I have had."

How tragic to think that Leon Trotsky, one of the founders of communism in Russia, was born in New York City within the reach of hundreds of Christian churches, but no one ever invited him to hear the gospel. What would have happened if Gandhi had been reached for Christ when he was in England at college?

Just think about what a call will do, especially when the calling is not in the hands of just a few but in the hands of a whole class. Each member of the class will feel responsible for every other member. For many years at First Presbyterian Church of Hollywood, the College Department used Monday evening for their calling. They limited their time from seven till nine. Afterwards they gathered together to compare reports and have fellowship. Often they would invite one of the persons on whom they called to join them and go to the next place with them. This built real friendship and camaraderie. We also found that calling was likely to be unsuccessful if left to the teacher's convenience. Too many things can happen to keep one from carrying out the plan. The individual may do good work, but the fellowship and inspiration of working together have great benefits.

The Approach

Always have cards ready that give the correct information. The correct spelling of the name, the correct address, the record of attendance, whether the person is a Christian or not, whether the person is a member of the church or not. Put whatever data is necessary on the card to make reports complete. Have a card for each person in the family. Visitors to the church or the Sunday School classes must be constantly encouraged to return, and the older members must be convinced that they are still important. You will find that calling is one of the greatest solutions to the absentee problem. In the public school, anyone who is absent is always contacted by telephone. More biblical scholars are lost because the absentees are not followed up than for any other reason. If you carry on a careful follow-up program, you will notice a definite increase in the average attendance of your Sunday School. Some have claimed that there has been as much as a 25 percent increase. Someone else once well said that the Sunday School should plan crusades instead of contests.

If it is impossible for you to make a personal call, write a letter or send a card; but be aware that the returns are small in comparison with the personal visitation. It has been said that cards are 10 percent effective, letters 25 percent, phone calls 40 percent and personal calls 80 percent.

To illustrate what cards and letters have done when a call each time was impossible was demonstrated in our elementary department. The first Sunday after a child was absent, a postcard was sent home. On the second Sunday, if the child had not returned, a letter signed by the superintendent was on its way. On the third Sunday, an absentee secretary phoned the home. On the fourth Sunday, a double postcard was sent to the teacher, asking him or her to make a personal call and report back on the return card. On one Sunday out of a department of about 300, 34 were absent. After the first postcard, 27 responded; by the third Sunday, 7 were left that had to be followed up all the way through by a personal call.

Make your calls friendly and persuasive, and don't give up. Keep your real purpose in mind. Do not simply accept a report that reads "No answer" or "Called and no one home" or "Moved." This does not tell a thing. The caller might as well not have gone. Calls should be made until you do get an answer. Calls should be made until somebody is at home. Calls should be made until you find out the child has moved—and then find out the new address, because the child may still be within your community.

Anyone can be trained to call. Many people feel that they are not qualified to go calling. They wonder what they will do and say. Here are a few suggestions. If you are going into a home where you want to reach a prospect, first of all be sure you have all the information clearly in mind. Introduce yourself as coming from such and such a church. Ask if it is convenient for you to call at this time. After a few general remarks, get to the point of why you are there. Don't waste peoples' time with talk of irrelevant matters.

If you are talking with parents, tell them about the church, where it is, when the Sunday School convenes, and what it has to offer for their children. Every parent is easy to convince of the importance of spiritual training. Few will admit that they think the Church has no place in the life of children. Ask them where they have attended church and what is their religious background. Approach them as if you expected them to have had some affiliation with the Church somewhere.

Never argue or criticize. Be sure to discover the members that make up the family and whether any of them might be interested in coming to Sunday School. Be brief. We are living in a very busy time, and most people have every moment planned. Leave with a warm invitation to all the family to attend the Sunday School and the other church services.

A consistent program of calling on prospective names of those who might be reached for the Sunday School is one of the greatest means of building up your Sunday School constructively. These prospect lists can be kept filled by accessing every source possible. Encourage Sunday School members and church members to hand in names of those they think ought to be reached for the Lord Jesus Christ through your Sunday School.

Make Sure the Leadership Is Qualified

When we consider that Christ spent almost the entire three years of His public ministry in training just 12 men, we begin to realize the importance of leadership. I believe I can say without contradiction that the greatest task of the Sunday School is to train Christian leadership to meet the crisis hour into which the youth of today have been thrust.

There are qualities of leadership that must be kept in mind when choosing people to fill the position in the Sunday School, whether the position be the children's pastor, a teacher, a leader of teens or a teen being trained to be a leader of the very young.

Is a Christian

We assume that every leader must be a Christian consecrated to Christ and His service. This is obvious, but it needs mentioning.

Knows His or Her Purpose for Living

Knowing their purpose for living is the starting point for all leaders. The vast majority of the people in this world do not know what their purpose for living is. Paul said, "This one thing I do" (Philippians 3:13). His first prayer was "Lord, what wilt thou have me to do?" (Acts 9:6); and the greatest statement of all was, "For to me to live is Christ" (Philippians 1:21). Do you know what you expect to accomplish by your teaching?

Unwavering Decisions

One who wavers in his or her decision reveals a lack of self-assuredness, or self-confidence. Such a person cannot lead others. No one will follow such a person. A leader must be definite in all the plans he or she presents, whether it be for teaching or in the organization of the class. Let us remember the decision that had to be made in Philadelphia on July 4, 1776, when 56 men approved the wording of a document that they knew would declare freedom to all Americans or lead to the 56 being hung from the gallows. Joshua was a man of decision. He said, "Choose you this day whom ye will serve . . . as for me and my house, we will serve the LORD" (Joshua 24:15).

Unwavering Courage

No follower wishes to be directed by a leader who lacks courage. It takes courage to face the problems of a class—or any other group of people. There are many times when a leader may feel like giving up. But a good leader won't give up. The young Queen Esther became a leader when she dared to say with undaunted courage, "So will I go in unto the king, . . . and if I perish, I perish" (Esther 4:16). She left herself no way to retreat. She would win or perish.

Definitive Plans

We are engaged in an undertaking of major importance, both for time and eternity. To be sure of success, a leader must have plans that are sound and workable. In fact, a leader's achievement can be no greater than the soundness and definition of his or her plans.

A leader's achievement can be no greater than the soundness and definition of his or her plans.

Willingness to Do More than the Assigned Task

A leader does more than is required of his or her followers. A leader must be willing to render humble service. "He that is greatest among you, let him be as the younger; and he that is chief, as he that doth serve" (Luke 22:26). In other words, a good leader is one who is the servant of all and who asks how he or she can serve better. A leader must always go the second mile.

Pleasing Personality

No slovenly or careless person can become a successful leader. Leadership calls for respect, and egotism is fatal to success. Even Christ "grew . . . in favor with God and men" (Luke 2:52, *NIV*)!

Sympathetic and Understanding

There must be harmony between the leaders and the ones being led. Teachers, for example, must learn to pray not only *with* your class but also *for* your class.

Loyal and Cooperative

Inability to cooperate with others has lost more positions and big opportunities in life than all other reasons put together. Those who are not loyal to their trust and loyal to those above or beneath them cannot maintain leadership long. These are things no leader or follower will tolerate.

Enthusiastic

Without enthusiasm, a leader cannot be convincing. Enthusiasm is contagious. The person who is genuinely enthusiastic is welcome in any circle. An enthusiast never admits defeat, never quits. Remember that a quitter never wins and that a winner never quits.

Determine the Staff

Children's Pastor

The children's pastor should be an individual of generalship, gumption and grace; a leader, not a driver; a counselor, not a dictator. He or she should be able to inspire those working with him or her. The children's pastor should be a student who studies staff and school needs and reads every book that can be secured that will help him or her to become a better leader. The children's pastor should know what other schools are doing. The children's pastor not only must see the needs of the present but also make plans for the future.

The children's pastor should be a teacher, able to lead the best teachers and guide the school in its educational work.

Every children's pastor must conduct a regular staff meeting. To make the meeting a success, an agenda should be followed. To start a meeting and ask people what they want to discuss is deadly, while a well-planned meeting will attract the teachers and the rest of the staff. When this meeting is properly conducted, its value cannot be overestimated. The Sunday School is the most fertile field in the Church, and the teacher has the hardest task; therefore, the teacher needs to be trained and instructed in what is expected.

The staff meeting will take determination, work, perseverance, push and prayer to be a success, but it is worth more than it costs. Have regular staff meetings! No children's pastor who really knows the value of such meetings will go without them. Staff meetings will help everyone who has anything to do with the Sunday School. And they will help unify the work.

The children's pastor's duties also include being involved in teacher training, missionary projects, properly grading the Sunday School, the library, special days (Christmas, Easter, Children's Day, etc.), missionary rallies—in short, everything that touches the Sunday School. All of these should be discussed at the staff meeting. The soul of each student is a battleground, not a playground. The staff meetings should be briefing sessions, preparing the staff for the battle.

Secretary, or Administrative Assistant

Every Sunday School must have a general secretary, or administrative assistant. Much of the success of any organization depends upon the efficiency of this staff position. Records must be kept up; dead files are of no value. The constant maintenance of records demands patient and detailed service. A good secretary will mean a growing Sunday School. Leaks will be stopped. Letters will be sent out. Calls will be encouraged. The enrollment lists will not be just a list of names, but each name will represent a person that Christ died for and whom He needs. The secretary is also the best person to keep a record of what goes on at staff meetings.

Treasurer

A treasurer, too, is usually necessary. This does not mean a person who only counts the money every Sunday but one who will study the subject of stewardship in giving and suggest places and ways for making the best investment of the gifts of the Sunday School.

Missionary Chairman

Every Sunday School should have a missionary vision. If you want both young people and adults to be interested in missionary work, you must let them know the needs and possible avenues of service. It is the duty of every missionary chairman to bring materials before the group that will stimulate and maintain interest in projects that attract students to serve in one capacity or another.

Age-Level Coordinator

One person must always be responsible for a particular age group. As soon as a class is large enough to stand on its own, your organization must add an age-level coordinator for that class. Much work must be done by the age-level coordinator to study the age characteristics of the children in the class. New methods of teaching must constantly be sought. Home contacts must be maintained. The worship service suited to that age group is the age-level coordinator's responsibility. As the class grows and needs to be divided, you may find that now you have need of a department, which would consist of the classes of a particular age group. Growth is, of course, good; but growth also creates the problem of securing teachers and keeping a high standard of teaching. The latter must be the coordinator's constant concern. The coordinator is responsible for not only gaining new students but also holding them. Contests, letters home, telephone calls and calling on the home are also some of the responsibilities. The age-level coordinator will discover that what is left to chance will probably ultimately lead to failure, so the coordinator must never believe that something will turn up. The coordinator must make sure that everything and everyone is where they should be.

Age-Level Secretary and Age-Level Treasurer

As soon as there are several classes of one age level, it would be a good idea for that new department to have its own secretary. A good secretary will do more than you can imagine in building attendance and contacting homes, including sending out report cards. In the Junior Department especially, report cards giving the percentage of accomplishments for the month should be sent home, and absentees should be contacted. The help of a good secretary can be indispensable to the age-level coordinator. A treasurer for each department should be added as that position becomes necessary.

Education Committee

Every Sunday School should have an Education Committee appointed largely from the governing body of the church. This group of men and women ought to meet together regularly to study the needs of the Sunday School and to help formulate the policies for conducting its program. The committee can bring the needs of the Sunday School before the governing body of the church and make them aware of what is being done and/or needs to be done. They may supervise the calling, the stewardship, the missionary program and the curriculum. The standard of teaching and teacher training should also be their concern. They must constantly consider the physical needs of the Sunday School. A group like this will find enumerable opportunities to help build a successful Sunday School. Every church should have such a group.

11

Worship

Most of our young people today have been raised in an age of great scientific and technological advances. Because of this, they usually feel that they must approach all truth by the scientific method—they want proof and evidence. This is one of the things that has cultivated a rationalistic attitude in society in general, even toward spiritual things. We believe that the world is dying for a little bit of love. There is an irregularly shaped vacuum in the heart of every man, woman and child that can be filled only by God. It seems, though, that Christianity is not providing young people with the data and facts that would satisfy them. They are, therefore, instinctively turning away from worship and searching for reality in experience. They want this same reality in their religious experiences. Young people do not want religion today any more than they ever did—they want reality. Worship services must be meaningful and beautiful, if they are to attract the searching, reality-based young.

Through experiences of worship, young people *can* draw near to God. Here they can find the answer to their own needs and the needs of the world. We as Christians know that Christ is the answer. Notice that the college men and women who once sat back with arms folded, looking down their noses at the preacher as he or she delivered the message, today actually lean forward as if hoping that this same messenger from God might drop some jewels of truth that they can grasp. This great change in attitude has happened only relatively recently.

This all means that those of us who lead the worship part of any of the age levels of the Sunday School must never be guilty of careless preparation, mindless repetition or last-minute substitutes that will take away from the dignity of the service in which we are worshiping God. We want young people to be drawn near to God in a spirit of reverence and simple faith and great expectancy. After every worship experience, we want them to go away with a new understanding of God, a new desire to do His will and serve Him and, more than all else, a sense of His presence. This is our opportunity to make God real.

After every worship experience,
we want them to go away with a new
understanding of God, a new desire to do
His will and serve Him and, more than all
else, a sense of His presence. This is our
opportunity to make God real.

In all of our teaching, we are committed to the growth of our students. They must grow spiritually as well as intellectually and physically, just as Jesus grew. This is what we want our young people to do. Their lives should be filled with a consciousness of God and their responsibility to Him. Young learners must each have an adequate reason for living; they need to know why they are here. All of their learning is in the present, this very minute. When our students are in the presence of God, they are learning something about their heavenly Father revealed in the face and presence of Jesus Christ. Our teaching should uncover the needs of the learners, and help them to meet these needs. There is only one who knows all of our needs and supplies all of our needs. Let the children know the security of their position in the Lord Jesus Christ.

Worship should lead a young person to

· a knowledge of God,
· the understanding of God's plan, and
· the commitment of his or her life.

Worship, if it is real, should result in changes of

· thinking and
· conduct.

Worship will lead to real spiritual growth if the program is

- related to actual experiences of the group,
- planned to carry experience into the home,
- teaching the students to worship God alone, and
- planned to relate to the overall program of the church.

Worship should lead to service to share

- in the work of the church,
- in giving,
- in missions, and
- in stewardship of life.

Worship brings about experiences of fellowship

- with God and
- with other Christians.

Worship provides an opportunity for expression

- in talking to God and
- in voicing desires of the heart.

Worship will result in

- a growing conception of God,
- an unfolding of spiritual ideas,
- a direction to life, and
- a sense of reverence.

It is much easier for adult minds to prepare for and begin a worship experience than it is for the minds of boys and girls. For this reason, from the very beginning we have to take them by the hand and lead them into a sense of the reality of God's presence. "The LORD is in his holy temple: let all the earth keep silence before him" (Habakkuk 2:20).

What we must constantly consider is how to create a spirit of worship. Let us consider step by step the planning of a worship service.

A Proper Worship Environment

It is obvious that we must create an atmosphere of worship. You know how you feel when you enter a sanctuary where heads are bowed and soft strains of music meet your ears. We have all experienced this. When we talk of the worship service, we do not mean opening activities where attendance cards are passed out and announcements of all the functions of the school are made, with a few choruses interspersed here and there. We are talking now of a worship *program* that every age group should have.

In creating the proper atmosphere, then, let us look to the preparation of the room itself. If things are disorderly, confusion will reign. A simple worship center in any kind of room often is itself a call to worship. Eyes are immediately drawn to some object of beauty that is placed before them. While little children do not completely understand symbols, the central placement of the Bible or a beautiful picture will always attract their attention.

Worship Music

Music plays an important part in the life of children. Reproducible music with songs may be sent home so that parents may help children learn the words. Most children love this form of self-expression and find the rhythms and melodies of music fun to imitate. They usually learn songs easily and sing them lustily, and especially because of this, a powerful way to implant in children God's Word and its principles is to sing with them. Songs learned early in life retain significance and can plant truth deeply in children's lives. The songs in your curriculum communicate God's love and His work in children's lives in words they understand.

The thought of presenting music, however, can be scary for teachers who don't feel musically inclined. Some may feel that they sing off pitch, can't remember lyrics or can't sing as well as a professional recording artist. However, remember that you are singing in front of a room of children, not music critics. Younger children especially will not judge a less-than-perfect singer because they, too, are developing their own musical abilities and are less than perfect. And never tell a child to stop singing or to sing more quietly. When the noise level is too high, simply repeat the song in a whispery voice. "That was great! This time, let's sing the song in a whisper."

Children love music and movement, so don't hesitate to integrate these elements into worship. God sees the heart more than He hears the voice. Your singing teaches children that music is God's gift, that it brings joy and that it includes everyone. Even shy children can be encouraged to participate in group singing as you model your enthusiasm and the purpose of your singing: to give praise and worship to God.

Ways to Choose Songs

Songs should reinforce the Bible truth for the day and contain biblical concepts that are clear to all participants. Age-level curriculum provides songs developed specifically to teach students of different ages about God and to help them memorize Scripture in an age-appropriate way.

Songs should contain age-appropriate vocabulary. Some teachers may want to sing the old favorites. Too often, we adults have an emotional tie to a childhood song; however, our favorite childhood Sunday School songs may confuse some of the younger children. Consider first whether an old favorite will help children understand God's Word at their own level. Other teachers may feel most comfortable singing songs that they are used to singing in adult worship services. However, in most cases these songs use vocabulary and concepts that are abstract and symbolic in nature and, as a result, they are not understood by younger children.

Songs should be chosen by the leader, not the children. Children should not be asked "What do you want to sing?" It takes some time for a very young child to make you understand what song he or she wants to sing, and the songs any child may choose may not necessarily relate to the lesson of the day.

Ways to Use Music

A song can fill in time gaps, regain children's attention or give them a chance to move. These are all good reasons to sing. And all of these are also opportunities to worship.

To signal transition times—A transition "theme song" signals the group that it is time to move on to another activity. Depending on the age of your group, consider using songs during transitions as children arrive and depart, move to and from large-group times, and clean up supplies. When the children hear and/or sing the song, they can prepare themselves for the next activity. Choose a favorite upbeat children's song from the curriculum you use or an instrumental recording of a lively classical song to use as a transition signal.

As a mood changer—Using a variety of songs in group singing is a good way to offer a change of pace. Some songs are livelier and will encourage participation. Other slower-paced songs can help to settle students and prepare them for prayer or a Bible story.

To encourage movement—Children like activity and love fast, bouncy tunes. Use hand gestures or other motions (clapping hands, stomping feet, etc.) while singing to illustrate the lyrics. Many songs tell a story, express emotions or describe actions. Let the children act out the words or create motions as they sing. Many children are familiar with American Sign Language and will enjoy signing the words to a song. (Keep in mind, though, that some songs with motions attempt to express highly symbolic concepts that younger children often misunderstand. Just because a tune is catchy and the motions are fun does not mean children are learning the intended concept.)

To play instruments—Children can easily learn to play percussion instruments, such as drums, shakers, cymbals, triangles, chimes and bells. Older children may be skilled at piano or guitar. Find and use the talent in your group. However, avoid pressuring a child to be a regular accompanist. Using rhythm instruments, especially with younger children, helps develop the children's minds and coordination as well as being another way for children to participate:

- *Have a praise parade.* Play a selected song from a children's album while they march around the room, playing the instruments. Children may also simply play without a recording as they march.

- *Play a freeze game.* Play recorded music while children play instruments and walk in a circle. Stop the recorded music as a signal for the children to freeze in place. After the children freeze, have them trade instruments with others and then continue again at your signal.

- *Allow the children to explore.* At times, leave several instruments out with which the children may experiment. You may wish to play some children's music and have them use the instruments to practice keeping time to the music.

Children may find ways to use the instruments that we adults haven't imagined. If a child uses an instrument as a weapon, simply take it and show the child the correct way to use it. Then invite the child to repeat your actions. "Landon, would you please show me how to use the sticks like I showed you?" Most children will need no further instruction.

Children may also have difficulty sharing rhythm instruments. Be alert to reinforce their positive behavior. "David, I know you like the red shaker best. Thank you for giving Jake a turn with it, even when it's hard to do!"

As a ministry—Children can practice and sing songs during worship or for nursing-home residents, homebound church members or church events.

As part of an art project—Let children create their own songbooks of favorite songs by writing out the words, decorating the pages and attaching the pages with brads or ribbons. Children will also enjoy drawing pictures for some of the lyrics. Invite the children to contribute to the worship services by providing various materials for them to use in designing and creating banners that illustrate a phrase or two from a favorite song.

Ways to Present Music

Remember, you are not performing or providing entertainment. You are using a song to guide the children in learning. Your musical perfection is unimportant. However, your enthusiasm and interest are vital! Be willing to make mistakes. If you forget the tune, keep going with the words. Children will be delighted that you, too, are learning. Relax and enjoy the children's response to the songs. When you truly sing from a heart of love for the Lord, children are quick to catch your feeling of joy.

Sing a solo. Sometimes a teacher is intimidated when a group of small children stare glassy-eyed while he or she sings a solo. Remember, though, that children who have experienced music only as something to listen to will participate first by simply watching and listening. (The younger the child, the more listening and less singing he or she will do.)

Add motions. If a song doesn't include motions or clapping, add them. Clap on the beat or invent motions to go with it. When you do the motions, children can be involved as they imitate you, whether or not they are singing. One goal of music is to involve every child so that each one learns Scripture and biblical concepts in a fun and memorable way.

Recite the lyrics. If you are deeply uncomfortable singing a song, repeat the words of the song as a poem.

Invite a member of the choir to perform. Inviting someone who you know has a good voice to sing is, of course, an option. This gives you a break, and at the same time gives children a change of pace.

Listen to a recording. You may also play the music to help both you and the children enjoy the music.

Ways to Teach Music

A teacher need not be a musical expert to lead singing and teach new songs. The main key is preparation, not talent.

Know the song. When introducing new music, memorize the words and tune so that you can give attention to the children, not to looking at the sheet music. Practice singing at home to feel comfortable with the song.

Use prerecorded music. Children's music is available with your curriculum and/or from church supply stores and music stores. Learn a new song by playing the recording several times and then play the recording to introduce the song to the children. Sing along with the recording and invite your students to sing along with you until the song is learned. Some music is available in karaoke version—only the instrumental track. If prerecorded music can't be found, make a recording of a musical friend singing and/or playing the song, or invite your friend (or a choir member) to teach the song in person.

Use visual aids to help learn new lyrics. Write the words to a new song on a large poster, chalkboard, whiteboard or overhead transparency so that children can easily see them. Displaying the words helps children look up, so they can sing louder than if their faces are buried in song-books or looking down at song sheets. Another advantage of display-ing words is that children don't have anything to play with and can concentrate on the song. For young children still learning to read, use pictures instead of words when appropriate.

Talk with children about the songs you sing together. Ask questions: "What does this song help us learn about God?" "What does this song remind us to do?" "When would be a good time to remember and sing the words of this song?" Explain any unfamiliar words. For effective learning and reinforcement of your aims, use the songs that are provided with your curriculum and/or select songs that fit with the lesson's Bible truth. Do not choose songs simply because they sound nice or are useful as a time filler. To be understood by younger children, songs should not use abstract words that express little spe-cific action or feelings. Make sure it's clear what the words in the song are teaching.

Repeat the songs several times. When children—especially younger children—like something, they want to experience it over and over. They may want to sing a song they like several times in one session. Repetition also helps the children memorize the lyrics. When teach-ing a new song, sing it during several services in a row.

The Worship Service

Each of the components of a worship service is very important. Do not allow any of these necessary things to be an afterthought to a well-thought-out and well-planned worship service.

Preparation

Preparation by prayer for the worship service is most important. En-courage the formation of a teachers' prayer circle, and let children see the staff praying. The attitude of the teachers affects the attitudes of the students in a very definite way, and the pre-session activity on the part of the children plays a great part in how they approach the wor-ship service. If they enter in a loud and disorderly manner, it is hard to shift them immediately into a spirit of worship. All should ap-proach this time in a spirit of reverence.

Call to Worship

Call the children to worship with appropriate music. Let the music rather than the human voice give the signal for coming together. Use some beautiful Scripture song, such as "The Lord Is in His Holy Temple" (based on Habakkuk 2:20) or "Let Us Adore" (based on Psalm 19:1). All such songs bring the young people as worshipers into the presence of God. The students themselves may also be encouraged to memorize some beautiful bit of Scripture or stanza of a worship hymn to use as an appropriate opening. Or you may wish to vary the call to worship and adapt it to the theme for the day—prayer, missions, consecration, stewardship, and so forth.

Praise—"Praise ye the Lord" (Psalm 104:35)

Music releases tension and stimulates worshipful emotions. It is a means of awakening feelings of awe, reverence, joy and devotion, and a sense of the presence of God. It enhances the meaning and deepens the impression of our other teaching. Music must be carefully chosen—spend time on this. Great thought and care should be used. Too few leaders are serious about this important matter.

All songs should have real musical value and be written in the vocal range of the group. The words, too, must have meaning. Choose songs that deepen the meaning of the theme for the day. Some of the beautiful old hymns of the church are a good choice, but be sure that the different age groups will understand all of the words and concepts in the lyrics. We want the songs to provide a medium for expressing certain longings and aspirations, even in the hearts of young people. Some great songs call us to service. Always choose the song to fit the theme. Sometimes the words of a song may be read as a poem while the tune is played. This teaches young people that there is a real message in the words of the song.

Remember, Christ sang a song at the Last Supper (see Matthew 26:30; Mark 14:26). We do not know what the song was, but we may be sure that it became part of the very spirit of that holy place.

Paul said, "Let the word of Christ dwell in you richly in all wisdom; teaching and admonishing one another with psalms and hymns and spiritual songs" (Colossians 3:16). This is a part of teaching. Remember, songs have been sung through the ages to worship God.

The psalms are full of songs. Use as many instruments as is possible from time to time: piano, violin, xylophone—almost any instrument can be used, and sometimes even use a recording. Have the age-level groups go into the sanctuary and listen quietly while one or two beloved songs are played. In this way, the music of the church will begin to mean more to them. Bells and chimes will be delightful novelties. Have a good leader conduct the group and follow the rules that the great songwriter of the Christian faith, John Wesley, gave us:

1. Learn the tune.
2. Sing the words as they are printed.
3. Sing lustily and with a good courage.
4. All sing. "If it is a cross to you, take it up, and you will find a blessing."
5. Sing modestly. Strive to unite your voices together.
6. Sing in time. Do not run before nor stay behind.
7. Above all, sing spiritually. Have an eye to God in every word you sing. Aim at pleasing Him more than yourself or any other creature. Attend strictly to the sense of what you sing, and see that your heart is not carried away with the sound but offered to God continually.

Don't wear out a few songs. There is a great storehouse from which we should draw.

Prayer—"Lord, teach us to pray" (Luke 1:11)

We will all agree that prayer must be part of the worship service, for it is of utmost importance in a vital worship experience. Every individual should be taught to reverence this high and holy privilege of being able to come with boldness before the throne of grace. Insist on absolute silence. The only talking is to God. The prayer should express the experience of the age group(s) involved in the service. We do not want them to use a shibboleth that is far beyond them. Vary the prayer experience. Opportunities should be given to individuals from different age groups to take part. When an adult prays, he or she should remember to make the prayer short because the children's capacity for quiet and attention is very limited. Be very positive in thought and expression. Do not let the children associate a whine with talking to God. Make the language simple. Study the Lord's Prayer as a model.

Sometimes have the whole group pray in unison. Group experiences are powerful in the lives of young people. An illustration of this is the recitation of the Lord's Prayer. Too often it is repeated only casually and with little meaning when it ought to be said with great expression.

Do not always open with "Let us pray," but find a verse of Scripture or a stanza of a great worship song or a bit of a poem that might set everyone's heart in tune with God.

Older groups of young people may unite in periods of silence just to worship God. Do not open a service with silent prayer, but wait until the desire to commune with God has been stimulated by singing and the reading of Scripture. (For more information about using prayer with specific age groups, see previous age-level chapters.)

Scripture—"Thy word is a lamp unto my feet" (Psalm 119:105)

We take for granted that the Scripture is an essential part of the worship service, but too often the preparation for this important feature is entered into lightly. Scripture plays an important part during the prayer time and the singing of worship songs and the call to worship, but there should also be a period when the words of the Holy Word will bear directly on the theme of the morning. Decide on Scripture that is very meaningful for the group you are leading. This means that the passage must be carefully and prayerfully selected. Frequently use the Scripture that has been memorized by the group and let them repeat it together.

Careful preparation on the part of the one chosen to read is always essential, whether that person is the children's pastor, a teacher or a student. Suggest that the passage be read over a number of times, preferably aloud. It should be read with great expression so that all will understand it and all may enjoy it. Let the reader find a message in it for him- or herself. It must be the reader's before he or she can give it out. The reading of the Scripture must be done intelligently so that the sublime beauty and simplicity of the very Word will be brought out and the divine authority of its teaching emphasized. Have the Scripture read directly from the Bible, and make sure that the Bible is handled with reverence. We want the devotional message from the Word to meet the needs of the pupil. The Scripture is our eternal challenge.

You will find that the meaning of a great Scripture passage will be enhanced if an attractive reproduction of some great artwork that has to do with the content of the lesson is used in conjunction with the reading. You may use slides as well as the larger pictures, or a PowerPoint presentation or a DVD. Small reproductions, purchased or copied from the Internet, can be given to the students.

Giving—"It is more blessed to give than to receive" (Acts 20:35)

Some of the most important lessons in Christian stewardship are given during the offering of gifts. Never speak of bringing a collection of pennies and nickels and dimes; rather, refer to their "love gifts" of offering. Our object in emphasizing this part of the worship service is not to secure as much money as possible from students but to train them in feeling their responsibility for the support of the church and the spreading of the gospel. This will widen their sympathies and develop in them spirits of generosity and the desire to give because they love.

If you have a Sunday devoted to missions and/or missionaries, may the theme of missions inspire within hearts a desire to give both themselves and their money to the Lord. After seeing a film picturing the need of people suffering with Hansen's disease, one boy in Vacation Bible School came to the superintendent and told him that he wanted to have his camp money ($15) sent to the sufferers. By seeing their distress, the boy was moved to action. Do you inspire your students to be real investors in the kingdom of God? Knowledge creates interest.

Message

The message part of the worship service should not be given over to preaching a sermon or even giving a sermonette. The message must be brief, for the instruction period is the teaching period. Do not use the Sunday School lesson in the worship service. It is unfair to the teacher to have the cream of the story taken off beforehand. The lesson will be anticlimactic if the story has been well told in the worship service.

The message in the worship service should just be an emphasis on certain phases of the Christian life, missionary stories, temperance lessons, meaning and stories of worship songs or the discussion of the meaning of the Scripture that is to be memorized.

Vary the program. Use dramatic teaching here. One may use flannelgraphs to tell the story in the Scriptures or of one of the worship songs. Visual recordings might be presented to illustrate worship songs or to give a mission challenge. A simple play with a mission or stewardship theme or with a direct connection to activities in the curriculum will enhance the importance of the activities. An occasional object lesson talk could be used to break up any monotony that may set in. Any one of a number of other ways to fill 10 or 12 minutes can also be used to present a message that has meaning.

Fellowship Period

Almost every age group needs a few minutes in which to welcome new students and to celebrate birthdays or make special announcements directly to the students in that group. This of course is not directly a part of the worship service, but a fellowship period is always important.

Suggestions

- Begin right! Choose a theme. Know what your aim is.
- Have unity throughout. Let everything contribute to the theme.
- Build up to a climax. Let each component come in logical order and the climax strike the purpose with force.
- Carry out the service with dignity.
- Do not include irrelevant material.
- Have the worship experience fit the group experience.
- Involve the group in Scripture reading, prayers, responses and hymns.
- Let young people conduct their own services.
- Begin early to plan. Let young people suggest and collect materials.
- Rehearse until things run smoothly.

Evaluation

- Does the service satisfy the intellect?
- Does the service motivate the will?
- Does the service stir the emotions?
- Does the service regulate conduct?

Sources
Gospel Light, *Children's Ministry Smart Pages* (Ventura, CA: Gospel Light, 2004).
Gospel Light, *Preschool Smart Pages* (Ventura, CA: Gospel Light, 2010).

12

Curriculum

Has anyone ever asked you, "Why is it I have gone to Sunday School all my life and yet I know nothing about the Bible? I have been able to pass examinations in many other subjects; I have my degree, but I know that I would flunk if I had to take an exam in the Bible."

Let us consider for a moment the reasons for such ignorance of the world's greatest book. I believe that young people and adults have been confused by the "hop and skip" method that has too often been used to present the Word—jumping from Genesis to Jeremiah, from Saul the king to Saul the persecutor, from the acts of Abraham to the acts of the apostles. I believe that a plan to cover the Bible thoroughly and systematically will eliminate the hopeless confusion and unending repetition of the same stories that breed boredom and disgust.

Maybe your experience has been something like the small boy in the Junior Department who said, "Do I have to go to Sunday School anymore? It just gets dumber and dumber. All they do is to tell the same stories over and over again." Or has the trouble been that we have had no definite work assignments in our classes? We were never inspired to study. Our only instruction was "Children, we will look at Lesson 5 next Sunday," with no extra comment. How thrilling this all was! How stimulating to build study habits and interests!

Responsibility for Selection

Who is responsible for the selection of the curriculum of the Sunday School? Someone must always take the initiative. Although the teacher is the nearest to the students, it is not good to have the teacher make the choice, because the choice of curriculum will ultimately affect every class in the school. To be considered effective, the curriculum must meet the needs of all the students throughout the entire Sunday School. The children's pastor, possibly with input from the age-level coordinators, in connection with the Education Committee, should make the selection. As long as the teachers are the ones that are going to use it, it is well that they be called in to look over the materials to help in deciding what will be used. Never make the mistake of allowing each teacher or each age-level coordinator to select curriculum on his or her own; the whole group must be considered. This is so often the case in many Sunday Schools and means that there will be no continuity in the presentation of the lessons. Choose an overall curriculum that is best suited in its entirety to your Sunday School. In this way there will be the progression of study and growth.

 Choose an overall curriculum that is best suited in its entirety to your Sunday School. In this way there will be the progression of study and growth.

The Selection of a Curriculum

In choosing a curriculum, let us take certain facts into consideration. We know there is nothing wrong with our textbook, the Bible. It must be in the way we have presented the great facts and taught the Word. When we consider the reasons for the tragic lack of interest that exists in the study of the Scriptures, we will have to admit that we have committed a spiritual crime. We have made children say, "When I don't have to, I'll never go back to Sunday School. There's nothing there for me." Instead of a growing love for the Word of God and an acknowledgment that it gives the answers to the complex problems of life, we find so many high school and college students turning their backs on the Bible and treating it lightly.

We cannot say that the university professor is entirely to blame for all of this. The Sunday School is responsible to a great extent. Young people are not prepared "to give an answer to every man that asketh you a reason of the hope that is in you" (1 Peter 3:15). When a professor subtly repudiates the Bible by presenting what the student thinks is a logical reason for not believing it, the student bats an eye in confusion and thinks that for the first time he or she has seen the light of real truth. *We must face the fact that young people do not lose their faith in college—they had no faith to lose.* The aim of any curriculum should be to face these alarming facts and by the help of God to meet them.

Our question is, then, "What will we teach?" Over 20 years ago, I faced this question, and it led to the writing of a series of Sunday School lessons that built a Sunday School of over 5,000. When we ask this question, one ordinarily means what materials will we use. What curriculum will we study? The curriculum that we must consider is more than the printed material we are offered. It is the sum total of the real events that make up the student's life and from which he or she learns. This includes all types of experiences. In fact, it includes everything that affects the individual in any way. Because of the lack of both space and time, our discussion here will be limited primarily to the written materials.

Standards of a Good Curriculum

1. It Is Based on the Word of God

Because we believe that the Bible gives us the rule and practice of our lives, we must accept it as an authority. *It is God's Word.* We put great emphasis on the Word of God in the limited time that we have for teaching because *we recognize its power.* Paul makes a statement of this kind in Romans 1:16-17. *No other words can transform a life so rapidly or lead a person out of darkness into the marvelous light.* Other things are important, but this is the most important.

We put great emphasis on the Word of God in the limited time that we have for teaching because *we recognize its power.*

2. It Points Students to Christ and the Necessity of a Commitment to Him

Christ said, "I am the way, the truth, and the life" (John 14:6). When we teach Him, we teach everything. We will never be satisfied until we see young hearts and lives committed, *not to His teachings, but to Him*.

 We will never be satisfied until we see young hearts and lives committed, *not to His teachings, but to Him*.

3. It Emphasizes the Importance of the Church

On the day of Pentecost, the Body of believers was gathered together by the Holy Spirit. It has continued to grow until this day. Jesus said, "The gates of hell shall not prevail against it" (Matthew 16:18). Teaching apart and independent of the Church is likely to run off at a tangent. Be careful of this.

4. It Is Related Theologically to the Teaching of the Church in Which It Is Taught

Each denomination has a few of its own theological ideas and interpretations that make it a bit different from every other denomination, but most of our great denominations agree on the fundamental doctrines on which the great Protestant churches of the world have been established.

5. It Will Be Related to the Home

Unless what we teach has real practical applications, most of our ministry in the Sunday School will be lost. The home is the ground in which the child will grow. Therefore, it must be reached for Christ.

6. It Is Educationally Sound

Let us determine whether the age of the child and his or her capacity to learn have been carefully considered. This is absolutely necessary. The laws of learning should be observed. The needs and interests of each age group ought to be taken into consideration. A variety of good methods must be constantly introduced to stimulate interest and relieve boredom. There ought to be a chronological sequence in building material. See that the materials are simple and capable of enrichment. Look at the print. Not only is the type good, but is it the size that public school systems have suggested for each age group? This varies considerably from the first grade on. At this time, the student's materials are for each child to read. See that this is true as you look over your material.

A good curriculum will not try to teach more than can be taught effectively in the allotted time. Let a few truths be presented with a pristine purity that demands attention. It is good to let the students state the one thing they have learned that day in relation to their own lives.

7. It Offers Stimulating Help for the Teacher

Stimulating help for the teacher does not mean props for the lazy teacher. It does not mean that the teacher can read the manual on Saturday night and be ready to teach the lesson or, even worse, read directly from the manual on Sunday morning, even though the story is told in the language of the students. We believe that a good curriculum will teach the teachers and help them in the great ministry of creative teaching.

Teacher books should be replete with methods of teaching, the psychology of the age level, the classroom procedure and source materials that will illuminate the lesson material. We believe it is a good idea to have the story for the children in the teacher's book written in the language of the children of that age level, because few are aware of the vocabulary limitations of little children and the comprehension of older children. We know that teachers will search for material and ways and means of teaching, but many are limited by not having easily accessible libraries and places or funds to purchase the proper equipment.

8. It Is Well Balanced

The curriculum should not go over and over the same phase of teaching or the same portion of the Word or deal with only one phase of the Christian life. It should not stop with evangelism but introduce each boy or girl to Christ as Savior; then it should continue in this great ministry of evangelism by training each child to be, in turn, a teacher. Every student must be someone who can not only speak the great truths of Scripture but also live them out in his or her everyday life.

9. It Must Be Graded

Good curriculum must be graded. I base this statement on the information given in the previous chapters of this book concerning the varying and growing needs of each age group. We will discuss the different kinds of graded lessons in the next section of this chapter.

10. It Must Inspire Student Participation

Students must see that what they are learning can be applied to life situations. The lesson must not only be taught but also caught. Students must see the relationship between the teaching and their own lives or it will mean little to them. Be careful to see whether your curriculum is suited to the needs and capacity of the students. Consider the format carefully. The very appearance of the materials must be appealing. No matter how excellent the material may be, unless it is attractively set up students will reject it.

 The lesson must not only be taught but also caught. Students must see the relationship between the teaching and their own lives or it will mean little to them.

Types of Curriculum

There are several types of curriculum materials, but we will limit our discussion to the uniform, group graded (departmentally graded) and closely graded. (Of course, nowadays there is large group, small group and classroom curriculum. And these are uniform, group graded or closely graded, though these terms are probably not used much anymore. But when I wrote curriculum, those were the terms that were popular.)

Uniform

The uniform type of curriculum consists of lessons covering certain portions of the Bible. You will find both topical and chronological studies. The whole school studies the same lesson topics in all grades and classes from the nursery through adults.

Uniform lessons have been widely used. Because the same lesson is presented to every age group, the necessity of detailed organization and meticulous planning has been eliminated in the smaller Sunday School, and it also has the advantage of every member of every family learning together.

One of the disadvantages of uniform curriculum is the fact that trying to adapt the theological teaching of the Word to all age groups is not always successful. We all believe that the Bible is the only textbook, but the adapting of all the Word of God to every child of every age has to be questioned. Too often the child is adapted to the lesson rather than the lesson to the child. It is very doubtful that the teaching of all the truths of the Bible would be profitable or understandable to the young child. Another disadvantage is that in uniform lessons, reportedly only 35 percent of the Scriptures are covered.

Group Graded

In the group-graded plan, everyone in each department studies the same lesson. Whether the department is composed of one class or many classes, the lessons are all identical. For example, every elementary child, whether he or she is in first, second, third or fourth grade, learns the same lesson.

Group-graded lessons offer more Bible material for actual study from the nursery child to the Youth Department than uniform lessons. Even so, it is difficult to cover the whole Bible with this sort of presentation. If the man of God is to be "thoroughly furnished unto all good works," there must be more time given for the study of the Word in Sunday School curriculum (2 Timothy 3:17).

Closely Graded

Closely graded lessons are written in the language and with the experiences of the individual child in mind, not overlooking the fact that every child changes radically from year to year. Each year marks tremendous advances in children's interests and in their ability to understand, and the closely graded materials take advantage of every step in this progress. A closely graded curriculum has been carefully worked out and is in use in the public school system today. As a child advances in mastery of facts, the methods and subject matter are carefully suited to his or her age. Closely graded must become common in the Sunday School!

The closely graded lesson plan has a definite educational and pedagogical advantage over the group-graded lesson plan in that it is adapted to the needs of each age, which is so important. It is obvious that third-graders would be bored by what would be presented to first-graders. First-graders who do not know how to read would flounder in material that would challenge third-graders. Young children should be provided with work, content and preparation that meet their levels of understanding, interest and need. It is easy for us to see that the material and spiritual needs vary widely in children in a three-year span. This fact in itself should outweigh all other arguments. A third-grade teacher in a public school would consider it an impossibility to use the reader for that grade and expect the first-graders who are just learning to read to comprehend its content. Yet some Sunday Schools try to do just this very thing. Sunday School is the only place in the world where children of different age groups are clumped together for educational purposes.

Many small Sunday Schools feel that they cannot divide their classes in such a way as to present closely graded lessons. Be that as it may, many *are* doing it. If you have to start with group-graded materials, do it; but work toward the ultimate goal of a Sunday School that is graded like the public schools. Knowing the difficulty of some situations, group-graded lessons have been prepared as a stepping-stone to the closely graded lessons. But you may be sure that Sunday School educators have worked out the problems and have presented the results of years of research as to the best way to teach the children of different ages—and it is all closely graded instruction.

Think of your own Sunday School days when as a child of nine or ten, you were taught such lessons as "The Prophet Amos Denounces Self-Indulgence." Would you have been able to comprehend such a lesson? The teaching principles underlying closely graded materials are identical with those of our Lord, for He always had in mind as He taught the ability of His listeners to understand.

Reasons for Using a Curriculum

Many will ask, "Why should teachers have a curriculum to follow? Why not depend entirely upon the teacher's own resources when he or she is presenting the truths of the Bible?" It is difficult for every teacher to discover all the truths that the Spirit of God would have a particular group of students learn. The written curriculum should aid the teacher in the exposition and explanation of the Scripture itself and in applying it to the age group being taught.

In order that the greatest amount of material and subject matter is covered in any child's experience in Sunday School, it is dangerous to allow each teacher to choose for himself or herself what is to be taught. We would be apt to find too much overlapping and repetition. It would be impossible for any one teacher to know just what each of his or her students may have been taught in previous years. Also, many teachers have pet subjects and/or interpretations when it comes to teaching. There are many glorious facets of truth that must be presented so that every young person will be "thoroughly furnished unto all good works" (2 Timothy 3:17).

Good curriculums are written by those not only acquainted with the Bible but also with the characteristics and needs of the different age groups. It is just as necessary for the farmer to know the soil as it is for the farmer to know the seed if a good crop is expected. So the teacher must know the child's heart in order to be effective. It is important to remember that you are teaching children, not materials. Study a curriculum that moves along in instruction from the littlest child to the adult and does not repeatedly go over the same stories and materials. The overall objectives of a curriculum have to be carefully considered, and each student must be led from one experience into another, from one year to the next.

Objectives in Teaching

The most important thing to consider in regard to teaching is the need of the learner. This need must be fulfilled whether the student is 2 or 5, 12 or 20, or 30 or 50. Each age group has a particular need peculiar to age, sex, intellectual capacity, spiritual understanding and the environment. Let us consider then, the objectives of teaching.

To Bring Every Individual to a Knowledge of a Living Savior

We believe that the Bible, God's Holy Word, portrays such a Savior and states the great guiding principles that produce such a life. A good curriculum, then, should be Christ-centered and child-concerned, and the Bible should be our only textbook. Children's life experiences must be based upon the foundation of God's infallible Word. We must give them facts so that they will know how to build their lives correctly.

Imagine a boy eight years old on the other side of a brook, calling to his father to come to help him. He does not know how to cross the brook. His father does not answer. The boy begins to scream. Realizing that he must find his own way across the stream, the boy looks about himself. Muttering, he takes a pile of stones and builds a bridge. When he reaches his father, he asks, "Did you know the stones were there, Daddy?" Of course he did. He had seen to that.

Children's life experiences must be based upon the foundation of God's infallible Word.

Do we give stones to our children so that they can cross the turbulent stream of life? We must give them a pile of stones—facts they can use to build according to their needs. We must resist the urge to do all the building for them. Let them have the thrill and experience of knowing that God's Word leads them to Christ and security and is a guide for their lives.

To Go Beyond Just a Communication of Facts

We are not here merely to explain the meaning of Scripture. Only as the Word of God bears on the living experiences of the students is its ministry effective. Christianity is not a code of ethics or morals. It is not committing a lot of Scripture to memory but committing a life to Christ. Often one evaluates the effectiveness of a certain written curriculum by the number of dates and facts that a student can recite as a result of study. Let us be interested in the facts that create faith, and the study that brings salvation. A complete curriculum invades every area of life. This is what we must consider.

Let us be interested in the facts that create faith, and the study that brings salvation. A complete curriculum invades every area of life.

To Be Correct for Each Age Level

We all have a responsibility to know the characteristics of the age group we are going to teach. How can we meet the great needs in the hearts and lives of average high-schoolers unless we know them? How are we to meet their needs for security, for recognition, for adventure, and for the many other traits that make up their personalities? Our teaching must reach them right where they are.

Christ met His disciples at the point where they were: He said, "I have yet many things to say unto you, but ye cannot bear them now" (John 16:12). Even after three years of intimate association, He knew that there were areas of truth and revelation that the disciples could not comprehend as yet. Before Peter could be the great preacher at Pentecost, his personal life had to be purged. He had to have new experiences with the Lord, his Master, and to understand the power and guidance of the Holy Spirit. In a good curriculum, we will begin exactly where the child is and move along line upon line, precept upon precept, building the teaching of tomorrow upon the experiences and knowledge of today.

In a good curriculum, we will begin exactly where the child is and move along line upon line, precept upon precept, building the teaching of tomorrow upon the experiences and knowledge of today.

To Make God's Presence Known

What must our students know about God that will really affect their whole lives? They must first be taught their relationship to God the Father and be aware of His presence. They must understand the sovereignty of that same God. Then they must be taught how to know the will of God and the purpose for their lives. At an early age, children must come to an appreciation of Christ, God's only begotten Son, and the fact that He is God. They must become acquainted with Jesus in such a way that they will not hesitate to leave all and follow Him. We want to bring our students to a full commitment of their lives to a living, loving Savior. They will in turn be witnesses of that same Lord.

To Instill the Great Principles that Christ Has Set Down for the Christian Life

Paul said, "I live; yet not I, but Christ liveth in me" (Galatians 2:20) and "Christ in you, the hope of glory" (Colossians 1:27). The behavior of Christians must be determined by the standards that Christ has set up. Students must know God's power in the hour of temptation. They must be brought into a thorough understanding of the greatest law in the world, the law of love, which breeds tolerance but not compromise. They must learn, as Paul did, to evaluate the real things of life. They must learn that the Christian life is the hardest yet the most thrilling life to live. Let students know that there is nothing to compare with it.

To Introduce the Resources of Strength for Living as a Christian

The curriculum must present to students the resources of Christian living. The first is the Word of God. Let them have a knowledge of its authority and power. They must be trained in the techniques of a devotional life, for with the Word must come the great privilege of prayer. We must not fail to let them know the importance of Christian fellowship as is revealed in the book of Acts.

To Teach the Full Meaning of the Sacraments
Too often the Communion service is a mere ritual. Here is the place to teach the importance of symbolism. This is visual teaching at its best.

To Establish an Appreciation of the Ministry of the Holy Spirit
Few Christians today know the power and comfort of this unseen Helper. Students must be taught about this great gift (see Luke 11:13).

To Cultivate an Understanding of and a Commitment to the Church
The Church is the one institution that Christ came to establish and build. Jesus said, "I will build my church" (Matthew 16:18). Few understand the meaning of this great fellowship. Paul is careful to tell us about the visible Church and its leadership. We are to lay before our students their glorious responsibility to it.

Habits in church attendance, participation in worship, and respect for the building itself should be cultivated in the heart of every child. Have each child understand that the Church is our great heritage, for wherever the church spire rises in the community, the culture of that community is changed, the status of the individual is raised, hospitals are built, the aged are cared for, the orphans and prisoners are ministered to. Education in all its phases follows quickly. All should understand the good that the Church has done through the centuries.

To Encourage Participation in Missions or the Church's Outreach
Today the world has been brought into every home; even the littlest children know the names of countries like Korea and China and Iran. They are no longer strange territories. No curriculum should ever leave out this greatest of all studies next to the one of the person of Christ Himself. We are training young people for world leadership in answer to Christ's command that they should "Go ye into all the world, and preach the gospel to every creature" (Mark 16:15).

Content of Bible Teaching

Preschool

We can start out with the little two- and three-year-olds and tell them stories from the Bible about God and the wonder of the world around them. We want these children to know stories about the baby Jesus sent from God. They like to hear about Jesus' love and friendship. Meaningful play activities, beautiful songs about the same subject matter and pictures that tell the same story are very important parts of this curriculum. We want the experiences these children have in Sunday School to be so happy that even these little two- and three-year-olds will look forward with joy to the happy time they have in God's house.

Prekindergarten/Kindergarten

Teach four- and five-year-olds that all the stories that are presented to them are Bible stories. They are real true stories. This is a precious handful of years. Let us plant well.

If you don't want weeds of doubt, don't plant the seeds. Anything sown in these years grows abundantly later. Choose stories that will satisfy these little creatures of wonder and curiosity and credulity. Their senses are the windows to their souls. They must taste, smell and handle the Word of truth. In fact, they often see better with their fingers than with their eyes.

Children should receive instruction from the Word in the form of the beautiful stories that God has placed there. In God's Word, we will find enough to satisfy these young and sensitive hearts: stories of Jesus and His friends, Easter and Christmas, our heavenly Father's gifts, the loving Helper and our heavenly Father's plans will give us ample material. Prekindergarten and kindergarten children need meaningful play activities and plenty of time to talk about what they are learning.

Elementary

In creating interest in the stories of the Bible, we must take advantage of the fact that "activity" is the keyword of *younger elementary* children—first- and second-graders. Although elementary children are not chronologically minded, it would be good to show them the development of Bible stories in some sort of sequence. Stories from the Old and New Testaments should deal with things that are interesting to the children. First-grade children are our great opportunity. They can be taught to read God's Word from the beginning. They are thrilled to read Bible stories as soon as they enter the class.

By the end of fourth grade, children have come to understand a wealth of Bible stories both in the Old and New Testaments. Christ in our life and the importance of His Church can be stressed. There should be stories of Jesus and His words and deeds and stories about Jesus' helpers. The sweet stories of men like Joseph and David, and the thrilling stories of the kings and the prophets will intrigue them. The curriculum must include memory work, visual aids, a certain amount of artwork activity, and guidance in applying biblical principles to everyday life. The home should be encouraged to play an important part in the children's learning experiences.

In *older elementary* students—those in third and fourth grades—we find the hero worshiper and the lover of adventure. Children's activities have now been turned into driving energy. We must capture their interests and adventurous spirit, turning them to the great storybook of the Bible, the Old Testament, and telling them all the great stories from these fascinating pages. These children must be taught the Bible in chronological order. They are beginning to reason things out for themselves and appreciate the more-logical approach. Presenting the heroes of the Old Testament, we believe, follows Christ's statement in Luke 24:27 and 44: "And beginning at Moses and all the prophets, he expounded unto them in all the scriptures the things concerning himself. All things must be fulfilled, which were written in the law of Moses, and in the prophets, and in the psalms, concerning me."

The age-level characteristics and abilities must be considered in making Bible study intriguing for elementary students. Their lessons should be treasures of Bible knowledge, leading to a real understanding of what it means to know Jesus Christ and to "be doers of the Word" (James 1:22). The curriculum must contain age-appropriate memory work, because this age is the golden opportunity when the power of retention is at its peak. Children have learned to read for themselves. Questions can be answered intelligently. The stories that should be used to challenge this hero-worshiping age group should be those of the Patriarchs, Joseph and Moses, the conquests and adventures in the Promised Land, the kings and the prophets—always remembering that every story in the Old Testament points forward to the greatest of all heroes, their Lord and Savior, Jesus Christ. Lessons from the Old Testament point to Christ the Light of the World, the lamb of God, the Passover lamb, the manna come down from heaven. This age group presents a strong evangelistic challenge. They are quickly approaching the peak age of conversion (before age 14); therefore, every piece of curriculum should lead up to this most important step in a child's life.

Preteen

Preteens want to talk about important topics, so be sure to include regular, meaningful times of verbal interaction for the students. Use Bible stories that show how people in the Bible lived. Guide preteens to use the Bible, and help them to see how Bible truths apply to their own lives through firsthand exploration of Bible truths—have them discuss among themselves how they think the main character in the Bible story felt when trying to follow God, and times when preteens their age feel the same way. Then allow them the time they need to discuss their discoveries with their peers—what they would do in a situation like this to show that they want to follow God. The discussion that leads them through the cognitive comparison of the known to the unknown by using the application of the Bible truth will be significant in helping them enjoy class, identify the Bible principle and follow through on life-changing application.

Remember, preteens are changing how they think about God and faith from concrete concepts to abstract ones. They have a lot of questions that must be explored and answered. Guide preteens to use the Bible. The preteen's faith may look new, as in never before existing, but in reality it is simply different. Help each preteen personalize his or her new understanding of the faith from the point of view of an abstract thinker. Preteens have learned lots of biblical content and spiritual truths on a concrete level, but now they must rethink and re-own all of the concepts they have previously embraced. The preteen must understand him- or herself and God on a more abstract level. This process does not negate the reality of childhood faith any more than multiple subsequent reaffirmations of faith in teen and adult years negate the reality of teen faith. They are progressive, not mutually exclusive.

Capitalize on the preteen's spiritual openness and interest in a higher, relational power. This may well be a God-given longing for connection with Him. The new ability to think abstractly allows the preteen to renew his or her search to understand the unfathomable God!

Early adolescents need to see the Christian life as vital and exciting. All we do in the name of the Lord should be attractive to others, but it should be especially attractive if we want to win early adolescents. Preteens who are bored with church are in spiritual danger. Although we never want to forsake the gospel and the foundations of faith for fun and games, we need to remember that fun and games have a lot to do with faith for preteens.

Junior High

Junior high students are breaking away from the traditions of their pasts and as yet have found no anchor for their minds or souls; therefore, we must be very careful in the kind of material that is offered to challenge the growing intellect of these seventh-, eighth- and ninth-graders. They have knowledge but little experience, and things can bore them considerably.

During this breaking away from childhood patterns, they must be intelligently and tactfully guided. They are beginning to doubt the reality of the things that they had accepted without question during childhood. Because of their study of science and their introduction to many new fields of learning, they often question the authority of the Word of God, the feasibility of prayer and even the sovereignty of God. Be very careful that the content of the lesson material to be taught is accurate and well chosen. Intellectually, this age group is interested in grasping new facts and learning new things. Let them be taught how to study the Bible through daily assignments and interesting and challenging homework.

Whatever you do, never insult their intelligence. Help junior highers find meaning in their own lives by studying the life of their wonderful hero Jesus Christ, who will challenge them with the things that

He said and did. They should be taught the fact of the deity of the Lord Jesus Christ, which is so contested today. A study of the book of John would provide the necessary data for a series of lessons to cover that subject. They should begin to understand the sovereignty of God in His dealing with His creatures and His plans in this great world of ours. Students of this age should be challenged by instruction in the founding of the Church and its first great missionary outreach as described in the book of Acts.

High School

The curriculum for high school students must prepare each of them to be able to tell why they believe in Jesus Christ and what Christ has done in their lives. This is the time for building their faith and securely entrenching it in the Word of God. High school students must be fortified for the intellectual questions of doubt that will be presented to them when they leave school. The teaching they receive now must give them a sure foundation for their futures.

If we are to build a faith that will stand the insidious attacks of the adversary, we must dig deep and lay the foundation stones securely. High school students have left their childhood days behind. They know the stories of the Word and their moral and spiritual teaching, and the fundamental facts of the Christian faith have been simply presented. They now must be introduced to the more comprehensive truths of the Scriptures.

Present the Bible as a whole. Instead of studying the life of Christ, present to high-schoolers the miracles, parables and outstanding teachings of the Lord Jesus Christ. Give them specific studies in Christian doctrines and evidence. Go to science, archaeology and history to find illustrations that prove that the Bible is true, and also to make the Scripture live. The horizons of this age group are widening rap-

This is the time for building their faith and securely entrenching it in the Word of God.

idly. They are capable of grasping these greater and more intensive Bible truths. Present problems and assignments that will develop intelligent Bible study habits. Let every Bible truth be related to the challenge of daily living.

College

College-age young adults need to have their belief that the Bible is the truth firmed up. They are living in a world that casts doubt on faith in God and that tries to entice young people to store up "treasures on earth" instead of "treasures in heaven" (Matthew 6:19-20). These young adults are concerned about their future lives, and they need to understand that God has a purpose for each of them. They need to be guided to find that purpose and know that "where your treasure is, there will your heart be also" (Matthew 6:21). Their hearts must be with Jesus Christ.

Young adults need to make the Bible truths their own. They need to discuss how those truths apply to their everyday lives and how to live the faith they profess. They need a curriculum that allows for discussion of topics of personal and social concerns, such as how to uphold Christian principles as they navigate dating and how they can make a difference in the world. Curriculum for these future leaders should also include suggestions for outreach activities so that they get practical leadership experiences.

Adults

Adults must have a curriculum that gives them food for their spiritual maturity. They want to gain new spiritual insights into Christian living and service. Their relationship to the Church and the teachings regarding it in the New Testament should be carefully studied. The epistles afford excellent textbooks for this age group. Give adults good questions and outlines and other materials to stimulate a thorough study of the Word.

Writing Your Own Curriculum

Because it may seem like a struggle to find a workable curriculum, some churches have chosen to write their own curriculum. Before such a task is undertaken, however, consider the pros and cons of writing your own material.

The Advantages

- You'll be in complete control of what you are teaching students.
- You can include lessons to cover your church's or denomination's doctrine and traditions.
- You are the best one to understand the special needs of your specific students and your lessons will reflect this.
- Your culture is slightly different from anyone else's and you can address this in your writing.
- There is a certain creative energy in designing your own materials that will be reflected by those involved in the process.
- You won't have to pay someone for the materials.

The Disadvantages

- Writing your own curriculum is a lot of work. Some larger churches have actually hired full-time or part-time curriculum writers to accomplish this task. It is almost always easier to adapt a published curriculum rather than write a curriculum from scratch.
- Even the most creative individual eventually runs out of ideas. (Producing one creative, well-written lesson is a lot of work. Producing the thirteenth or the fifty-second lesson seems almost impossible at times.)
- The costs of photocopying and distributing lessons may match or exceed the cost of buying published curriculum.
- The time it takes for a person (or team) to write curriculum (even if the person is an unpaid volunteer) does come out of some other area in which this gifted individual (or these several team members) might have been serving in your church. (This person might be the right person to pull together a variety of ideas from published resource books to liven up the published curriculum you select.)
- You will not have the benefit of field-testing that most publishers use to see if a lesson will actually work before it gets distributed.

- Unless you are a professionally trained educator, you may not realize how much you need to know to produce a good lesson that others can follow easily and that meets the needs of a variety of learning styles and interests.
- It would be difficult to match the colorful artwork and support materials that publishers are able to offer to make their resources so appealing.

Evaluation of Curriculum

We have been considering together the characteristics and requisites of a good curriculum. Now is the time to evaluate your own Sunday School curriculum and discover whether it is good or, we would rather say, the best that you can get for your students. If you answer the following questions or, better, use them for group discussion in evaluating your material, you will get a clear understanding of just where you are as far as your own school is concerned. Remember, you can never judge a curriculum by one class or one age-level's materials. A good curriculum covers a progressive line of instructions from the nursery through adults.

Is the Whole Bible Presented?
- Is the Bible the only textbook and authority?
- Are the lessons true to the Bible?
- Is Scripture memorization outlined and stressed?
- Is a thorough mastery of the whole Bible attained?
- Are lifetime Bible study habits developed?

Is It Christ Centered?
- Is Christ presented in every lesson?
- Is the meaning of salvation made plain?
- Is the triumphant life in Christ taught?
- Does the selection of materials lay a firm foundation for Christlike living?
- Does it build step by step?

Is It Child Concerned?

- Is it educationally correct?
- Is it carefully planned and developed?
- Does it do away with confusion?
- Does it do away with unending repetition?
- Are the best educational methods employed in their application to the fundamental teaching of God's Word?
- Is there variation in presentation, methods, activities and procedure?
- Are suitable visual aids suggested?
- Do the lessons provide active student participation?
- Do the student pages challenge the students to study?
- Do the lessons fit the length of the class period?
- Is the material closely graded?
- Are the objectives stated so that the teacher understands what to accomplish in each lesson?
- Can the average teacher use the course successfully?
- Do the plans and procedures lead to dynamic teaching?

Source
Gordon and Becki West, *Preteen Ministry Smart Pages* (Ventura, CA: Gospel Light, 2005).

13

Long-Range Planning

In running your Sunday School, you must constantly think, *What do I want my school to be in one year, in five years, or even in ten years?* This we will call long-range planning. No business in this world is carried on successfully without knowing what the business should be a year from now. Even the teacher who plans from Sunday to Sunday will soon discover that teaching this way is a terrific burden. By Friday night the teacher will think, *Horrors, another Sunday! The week seemed to just fly by. I just can't face that class again. What will I do? I'll just have to resign. I don't have time to do the job well.* On the other hand, the teacher who plans a whole unit of teaching and knows that in three Sundays some fine films on the life of Paul or the wonders of the universe will be presented, or is ready with a great missionary challenge at the end of the quarter, begins to plan and look forward to every Sunday. The same is true of the children's pastor or the age-level coordinator. There is nothing that will unify and strengthen the program of a Sunday School like the experience of planning ahead.

There is nothing that will unify and strengthen the program of a Sunday School like the experience of planning ahead.

Planning ahead prevents situations like reaching a Sunday or two before Christmas and finding out that it is impossible to plan for a program that will honor the birth of Christ. You will not come back in the fall after vacation and meet the impossible situation of an enrollment list much depleted because families have been away for the summer and teachers have not yet come back to their posts. This lack of preparation makes leadership a nightmare. The joy of service is lost.

When you take part in long-range planning, you will have to set down and define the objectives of your Sunday School and determine which areas of the Sunday School program will meet your goals, what projects will be undertaken, what missionary projects will be considered, what is the school budget and when is the best time to introduce it, when should communicants classes be held to get young people ready for church membership—among many other subjects to be considered. Every church should have at least a one-year plan laid out before them. There is one place where this is typically done in the church and that is the budget. Carefully, the board figures out how much money they expect to raise, where the money will come from and how and when they are going to spend it. This kind of budget planning should be part of the long-range planning of the Sunday School as well.

Once the long-range plan is in place, let every worker in the Sunday School know that there is a calendar of events that has been planned ahead. Then they will be able to determine where they will fit in. There will be set days for staff meetings, missionary projects, camps and conferences, staff retreats, celebrations of special days, special periods of evangelism, regularly scheduled meetings of the calling team, and so on.

The most important thing to be planned ahead is the curriculum. What is each teacher going to teach in the coming year? This kind of planning avoids a repetition year after year of the same program that so many churches have had in the past. It steers people on a course out of the endless confusion into which the church without plans finds itself thrown. When there is careful planning, people will discover that they have more time than they think to carry out larger and improved projects, programs and activities of all sorts.

Let us consider a year in the Sunday School and see just how we can plan ahead. Many churches now begin their planning by following the calendar year, and we will generally follow that plan, going through season by season. If we start out with January 1 and look forward through the coming year, there is a certain thrill of a new beginning. One desires to make a fresh start. Like Paul, we forget those things that are behind and we reach forward to those things that are before us. This should be a time of unifying the leadership, remembering that "one can chase a thousand, and two put ten thousand to flight." Then, too, it may be a time for new teachers to take their place or for the senior teachers to have a day of recognition. If the group has worked long together, let this be a time of renewing relationships. Here is the opportunity to lay before every volunteer of the Sunday School and of every department a year's plan. See that every volunteer of your Sunday School has the year's plan in his or her possession.

Winter

Winter goes from January through March. Easter is often included in this group of months or comes at the first Sunday or so in April. This is an excellent time for a long, continuous building of a program. There are few interruptions from January through June, in fact. This is an excellent time to emphasize different areas of stewardship.

Pursue Stewardship

Stewardship of life—See that your teaching and training lead up to decisions for Christ and dedication of life at Easter time. The new sense of the living Christ makes this season an important one in regard to bringing people in and keeping them. Many Sundays should be spent in preparation for this.

Stewardship of money—Talk over with the Sunday School staff the investments that they are making for the church and missions. Emphasize their faithfulness in giving. Special days might be set aside to consider the various phases of missionary work, and the gifts for that cause may be considered. Let the staff know the importance of the stewardship of money as well as of life.

Stewardship of prayer—Have someone in charge in each class or department to take care of the devotional life of the students. This is imperative. We are likely to fail in our spiritual program at this particular point. People need to be constantly encouraged to study and pray. Specific assignments of Bible study and yearbooks of prayer often make this part of your program effective.

Stewardship of service—Carefully define your service program. See to it that classes and departments undertake something that they can accomplish during these winter months when outdoor activities are limited. This is the very finest time of all the year to really begin the study of and execution of projects for missionary service. Winter evenings can be made very fruitful in different kinds of service.

Be on the constant lookout for missionaries home on furlough. After they have given their messages to the church and/or Sunday School classes, establish a relationship between them and the department before they return to the field. Every age level should have special missionary days at designated times throughout the year. At some Sunday Schools, missionary days are held as often as once a month. If you leave this to chance, you will discover that your interest in missions will wane considerably.

Display pictures of the missionaries from your church or area.

You will discover that a tremendous interest in missions can be sparked by taking a trip to one of your home mission stations. Of course these must be carefully thought out and executed. Mission stations must be informed and a program arranged there before you make your final plans for such an undertaking. A trip to our home mission station among Native Americans was one of the highlights of our Sunday School.

Discover new ways and means of increasing your missionary giving. Do not ask children just to give to missions, but let them know about the projects that their age group has undertaken. Use skits that deal with missionaries to make the lives of the missionaries real.

Increase Attendance and Membership

These first months of the year are excellent months to build attendance and membership. The time of year that has many events and activities—including the important holidays of Thanksgiving and Christmas—is past. Now there is a period of relative quiet. If you are going to have attendance contests or calling campaigns of any kind, this is the time.

This is also a good time to stress the friendship and social life of the Sunday School students and staff. Everyone needs to socialize. God has made us social creatures. Christian fellowship is our greatest attraction in building attendance and spiritual power. Now is the time for seasonal outings and parties: snow parties, a Valentine's Day party, activities to acknowledge the birthdays of Lincoln and Washington, a St. Patrick's Day celebration, and many other special events held to foster fellowship and grow attendance.

Spring

April through June is the period during which Children's Day and most school graduations occur. Easter has passed and now we look forward to the close of public school for children and vacation time for all. This is an excellent time for retreats, for staff as well as young people. This follows up on the new spiritual impetus that Easter always gives to a group. Let's encourage its growth by a time apart.

For many of us, this time is filled with making ready for graduation. We understand that some Sunday Schools have graduation in the fall, but if you are following the public school system, you will have a spring graduation. Even if you do not hold graduation ceremonies for Sunday School during this period, you will probably still want to in some way acknowledge the public-school graduations that some of your students will be celebrating.

Parties for the graduates of public schools are not inappropriate at this time. Let us recognize what our young people are doing in their educational work. A class day for your seniors graduating from high school, or a Sunday service given over to them will make a great impression on their parents as well as the students.

Now is the time for careful planning for the summer months. All the details must be worked out in advance if you expect a successful working program. Teachers will be taking their vacations, and coordinators are likely to be away for a few Sundays. Do not let the classes and departments slip back at this time. In most places, visitors will come to your community and they ought to be invited to attend the Sunday School. Encourage all of the students to tell you where they will be going during the summer and what they will be doing. This will allow you to keep in touch with them while they are absent. It should be added that not only must you make plans for the summer months, but also you should be considering what you are going to do in the fall, or you will find your work beginning at that time with no preparation in hand. It is hard to get people together for planning in the summer, so it is best to do it now.

Summer

July through September is a period for camps, conferences, and Vacation Bible School for all ages. This means busy days at the church, but they are happy and profitable days. Any leaders who start the summer season without preparation will know the meaning of "summer slump." Your summer can be alive with activity or dead with nothing to do. If you are in a locale that attracts many visitors during the summer, plan to have your Sunday School interest them. Let them know they are very welcome to visit and attend the school. Don't let anyone miss the opportunity to attend church because you did not invite them. This is the time for reports from "the front," from those who have gone away on vacation. Encourage teachers to visit other classes in other churches during their vacation times. This will prove to be an eye-opening and refreshing experience for many of them.

Fall

The period from October through December includes Thanksgiving and Christmas. Evaluate your program in light of the past year and decide what you wish to do next year. By now you know that if the year is not planned ahead, much will be left undone or will be at best done poorly. This is the season of paramount importance. Plan a time to set new goals and lift your sights.

Get-Togethers and Holidays

Schedule fall get-togethers. Everything should be done to establish new interest in every program. It is homecoming time.

Decide what your group should do about Thanksgiving. This is the time of "Thanks-living" as well as "Thanks-giving." Let everyone be encouraged to do something about it. The church should be teeming with service projects. The children themselves should be filling baskets and carrying food to shut-ins and children who have less than they. This may be the beginning of many service projects carried out through the year.

Plan early for Christmas. Early in October begin collecting gifts to distribute to missionaries and needy people in the community and around the world. Of course this is the time of Christmas festivity.

Plan any social events well in advance, but whatever you do, remember that Christmas is Christ's birthday. Emphasize the spiritual significance of Christmas. This should be a period of heart searching and rededication of life. Make this period very personal for everyone. Find ways to emphasize the fact that what Christ wants more than anything else is the gift of themselves to Him. Every church and Sunday School should have a Christmas program. Don't pass this by. Send home with the students a list and description of all of the Christmas worship programs you plan. You may reach parents who take little time to think about the significance of this season.

Budget

Those of you who have the fiscal year of your church start January 1 must plan for the Sunday School budget during these months. It is amazing and gratifying what your young people will do if they are called on to take part in the planning of the budget for the year. Consult your church board about this important subject.

Calendars

To help carry out the suggestions just given, give each teacher (and every other staff member) a blank calendar. Teachers should sit down the first week of the New Year and make plans for the coming months. They will be astonished at the enormous task that lies before them. But filling in the details for the year will lead to success for everyone involved. In January, the staff can fill in the dates of when many things are planned to occur, be the events in January or October or December. Having the staff fill in calendars this way will not really add to the workload of the staff, and it will allow staff to become familiar with the year ahead. When someone knows the overall program, they can keep it in mind and think about it all during the year.

General Considerations

When you are doing your long-range planning, there are many considerations that should come to mind and influence your thinking.

Some people are afraid that planned programs will become too repetitive, the same year after year, but a planned program does not mean that no changes can be made. Often in looking at the calendar in advance, one sees variations and changes that can be made that will help to enhance the overall program considerably.

In making your overall plan, determine the functions and goals of every age level. First is Bible teaching. We must not allow anything else to interfere or take precedence over this.

If you intend to employ workers, then look at your program and see what you are doing to train good leadership. The Sunday School must include training for leadership, so see if your classes are getting the future leaders of your church ready to take the posts. Remember that if you do not do this, your church will die.

The Sunday School must teach all to be stewards. It takes money and investment to keep the work of the church moving. Right training along these lines is our duty and privilege.

The Sunday School is an outreach agency. See if you have been selfish in your planning or whether during the 12 months you are going to take Christ *to* people.

The Sunday School is an outreach agency. See if you have been selfish in your planning or whether during the 12 months you are going to take Christ *to* people.

If your school has a soul-winning mission, see if you have a calling program in place. Then the staff will be ready to go out and bring people back to the church and Sunday School so that Christ may be introduced to as many children and parents as possible.

Do not forget the importance of stressing the social life of the staff and students. Are there activities in your plan that will help students find their friends in the church?

Have you planned service projects for different age groups? Both young people and adults would be quick to point out that if we do not use them, we will lose them.

Analyze your long-range planning and see if you are making Sunday School an integral part of the whole church in regard to its membership, its mission, its giving and its service.

Where do the teachers fit in all of this planning? The teachers should be well acquainted with all of the plans and know exactly where they fit in and what they are supposed to do at any time. If teachers do not carry out these plans, the whole thing will fall through. It should be noted that teachers may be more interested in the long-range planning of curriculum than in the long-range planning of seasons or years.

Teachers should know what they are to teach for the whole year that lies ahead of them. They must set up goals for what they wish to accomplish during the year, not only in covering the lesson material to be taught, but also in planning ahead what they will do to make the lesson and the unit of lessons attractive. One of the chief goals of teachers, of course, is to know what they expect to accomplish in the lives of their students. One would not expect to take a trip without first considering the destination and the best way to get there. This is all done before one starts on the journey. Teachers should do this same thing: Determine at the beginning of the year the goals and then choose the best means to achieve the goals. This will give direction and meaning to every Sunday. If teachers do not do this, they will find themselves going on detours and making very little headway as far as real accomplishments are concerned. Long-range planning means that you must have ultimate goals as well as immediate goals. There are things you must do this Sunday if, ultimately, you want to be certain that other things will be accomplished.

Again I say, *plan ahead.*

GOSPEL LIGHT

TEACH JESUS T[O]

Baby Beginnings

Ages newborn to 2

Baby Beginnings® Nursery Kit
978.08307.46743 • $129.99 ($140 value)

Kit includes: (Items also available separately)
- **Two Teacher Guides with CD-ROM**
  0 to 18 Months: 978.08307.44961 • $14.99
  18 to 36 Months: 978.08307.46699 • $14.99
- **I Love to Wiggle and Giggle! Easel Book**
  Babies will love all 144 on-the-spot
  play activities
  978.08307.46712 • $14.99
- **I Love to Look! Bible Story Picture Cards**
  Colorful cards picture the Bible story,
  plus provides a simple Bible verse and activity
  978.08307.46705 • $3.99
- **Baby Beginnings® Nursery Posters**
  978.08307.44978 • $29.99
- **I Love to Sing! Music CD**
  42 sing-along songs on reproducible CD
  607135.014928 • $19.99
- **Nursery Smart Pages with DVD**
  Guidance, tips and training video
  978.08307.44985 • $39.99

Preschool/PreK/K

Ages 2 to 5

Winter 2013

Preschool Quarterly Classroom Kit
Ages 2 & 3
978.08307.62934 • $99.99

**PreK/Kindergarten
Quarterly Classroom Kit**
Ages 4 & 5
978.08307.62965 • $99.99

Everything you need for 10 kids and one teacher

Each kit includes:
- 1 Teacher Guide
- 1 Visual Resources
- 1 Preschool Music #1 CD
- 10 TalkTime Activity Pages
- 10 Family FunTime Pages
- HomeLight FREE for a year

Elementary

Ages 6 to 10

Winter 2013
Quarterly Classroom Kit Grades 1
978.08307.63023 • $99.99 ($135 Value)

Quarterly Classroom Kit Grades 3
978.08307.63061 • $99.99 ($135 Value)

Everything you need for 10 kids and one teac

Each kit includes:
- 1 Teacher's Guide
- 1 Get Going! Worship CD
- 1 poster pack with 14 posters
- Homelight FREE for a year
- 2 packs of Student Kid Talk Cards
  (enough for 10 kids)
- 1 pack of Family Fridge Fun Magnets
  (enough for 10 families)
- 2 packs of Family Fridge Fun pads
  (enough for 10 families)

SUNDAY SCHOOL

EVERY GENERATION

Preteen	Jr. High/High School	Adult
Ages 10 to 12	Ages 13 to 18	Ages 18 +

Winter 2013

Quarterly Classroom Kit Grades 5 & 6

978.08307.63139 • $99.99 ($133 value)

Everything you need for 10 preteens and one teacher

Each kit includes:

1 Teacher Guide

1 Visual Edge Poster Pack

10 Get the Edge Take-Home Comics

1 Sonic Edge #1 Worship Music CD

10 Student Guides

HomeLight FREE for a year

(Items also available separately)

UNCOMMON JUNIOR HIGH
GROUP STUDY

The Life of Jesus
978.08307.46439 • $14.99

UNCOMMON HIGH SCHOOL
GROUP STUDY

The Life of Jesus
978.08307.47269 • $14.99

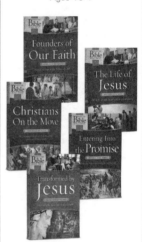

WHAT THE BIBLE IS ALL ABOUT
BIBLE STUDY SERIES

Founders of our Faith
978.08307.59484 • $9.99

The Life of Jesus
978.08307.59460 • $9.99

Christians on the Move
978.08307.61302 • $9.99

Entering into the Promise
978.08307.62200 • $9.99

Transformed by Jesus
978.08307.64099 • $9.99